BLACK AMERICA SERIES

DURHAM'S HAYTI

BLACK AMERICA SERIES

DURHAM'S HAYTI

Andre D. Vann and Beverly Washington Jones

ARCADIA PUBLISHING

ISBN 978-0-7385-6735-8

Published by Arcadia Publishing
Charleston, South Carolina

Printed in the United States of America

Library of Congress Catalog Card Number: applied for.

For all general information contact Arcadia Publishing at:
Telephone 843-853-2070
Fax 843-853-0044
E-Mail sales@arcadiapublishing.com
For customer service and orders:
Toll-Free 1-888-313-2665

Visit us on the Internet at www.arcadiapublishing.com

This work is dedicated to Hayti's pioneers in the profession.

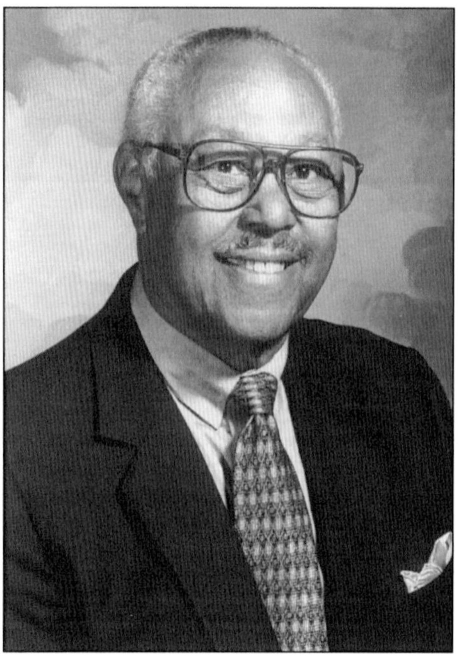

ALEX M. RIVERA, PHOTOJOURNALIST

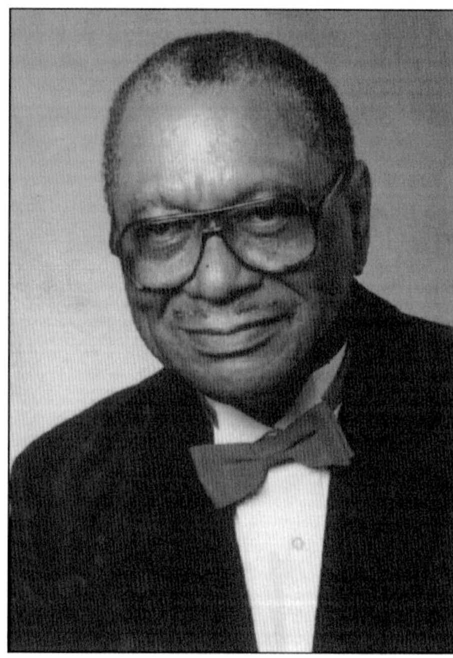

CHARLES STANBACK, PHOTOGRAPHER

Others include Claudie Coleman Burthey of Burthey's Photographic Lab, Carlton Graham of Graham Studios, and Nat Purefoy of Purefoy's Lab.

Contents

ACKNOWLEDGMENTS

Anyone who has ever published a book knows that it is a collaborative work and a joint venture. This book has benefited greatly from the cooperation, assistance, wisdom, and generosity of many persons. It is not possible to name all of the individuals who have contributed, in one way or another, to *Durham's Hayti*, but I would like to acknowledge several persons who have been instrumental in providing the vision, enthusiasm, and support that made it possible.

The idea for the book came from my brother in Alphadom, Herman "Skip" Mason, an accomplished author, minister, and professor who said such a work was needed on such a notable black community as Hayti. I would like to thank the staff at Arcadia Publishing, especially Sarah Maineri and Mark Berry, who have since 1997 been patient and generous in offering wonderful editorial assistance and support for this book. Others will be mentioned throughout the work for their assistance and support. Thanks go to Earl Ijames and Stephen Massengill for their valuable assistance at the North Carolina Division of Archives and History.

The authors are deeply grateful to an entire host of individuals who have gone beyond the call of duty to assist in the completion of this work. We have been supported by colleagues, former professors, friends, and family who have sustained us along this journey to create for the first time a pictorial history of Hayti.

Professor Beverly Washington Jones and I have attempted to produce a book that would not only remind an older generation about its past, but also tell younger generations about an older way of life through the medium of photography. To C. Ray Jones and Tammy M. Collier, thanks for the support.

I would like to thank many current and past residents of Hayti as well as countless individuals who allowed Dr. Jones and myself to tell their story and to tell it correctly. We would like to acknowledge several individuals who have freely given photographs and treasures from their personal collections: Maggie Bryant, Andolia Eaton, James A. Stewart, Ellis Allen, Theodora Speight Manley, Jessie Logan Pearson, Barbara Logan Cooke, Margaret Kennedy Goodwin, Gladys H. Rennick, Alex Rivera, Dr. Howard Fitts, Lavinia Parker, Josephine Dobbs Clement, Gazella P. Lipscomb, Ernestine Y. Evans, Vivian A. Edmonds, Charles and Constance Watts, John C. Scarborough III, Selena W. Wheeler, John Ainsley, Lenzie Barnes, Robert Dawson, Frances Dyer, Janet H. Lynch, Dorothy Parker, and Viola Pindle.

Special thanks go to the staffs at the Stanford L. Warren Branch Library; the Durham County Public Library; the James E. Shepard Memorial Library, North Carolina Central University; the North Carolina Division of Archives and History—Photography Division; the North Carolina Mutual Life Insurance Company Heritage Room; the Hayti Heritage Center; and the Southern Historical Collection, University of North Carolina, Chapel Hill.

Most importantly, this work is dedicated to pioneers in the profession in Hayti: Alex Rivera, Charles Stanback, Nat Purefoy, Carlton Graham, and Claude Burthey.

INTRODUCTION

Durham, like most Southern cities in the 1880s and 1900s, had rigidly segregated communities. The majority of African Americans resided in the southern and southeastern sections known as Hayti, pronounced as "hay-tie." In 1920, W.E.B. DuBois, a prominent African-American historian, referred to Durham, specifically the Hayti area, as the "Negro business mecca of the South." He wrote, "There is in this small city a group of five thousand or more colored people, whose social and economic development is perhaps more striking than that of any similar group in the nation." Booker T. Washington, the noted African-American leader and educator at Tuskegee Institute, agreed with DuBois that Durham provided an opportunity for African Americans to excel economically. But Washington also recognized the existence of friendly relations between African Americans and whites. He stated, "Of all the Southern cities that I have visited I found here the sanest attitude (among) white people toward the blacks."

With this interracial and economically progressive environment, Durham emerged as one of the centers of the African-American middle class in North Carolina and the South. Many members of this middle class resided in impressive, large residents in the Hayti district. The architecture of the houses was Victorian. They had spacious porches and large lawns. Also located in Hayti were churches, stores, a hospital, a library, a college, clubs, and fraternal lodges.

Three leaders of the African-American community helped to create and sustain the community's economic, social, and political structure—John Merrick, Aaron M. Moore, and Charles C. Spaulding. Their most noted joint achievement was the reorganization of the North Carolina Mutual and Provident Association, later known as the North Carolina Mutual Life Insurance Company (Mutual), in the late 1890s. Originally established to provide sickness and burial insurance (which African Americans could not get from white-owned companies then), it expanded within a half century into the largest black-owned business in the United States and subsequently the world.

Although Hayti was the residential and social center of African-American life, Parrish Street, in the very center of Durham's business district, became the hub of African-American business and commerce. Here, in 1911, Merrick and his associates built a brick building to house the offices of their rapidly expanding insurance company, which by then had associated itself with the Mechanics and Farmers Bank, another black-owned enterprise chartered in 1907. Within two years, Mutual purchased additional lots and added to its offices, forming an African-American business complex that included two clothing stores, a barbershop, a real estate company, a large drugstore, a tailoring shop, offices of the *Durham Negro Observer*, the Mechanics and Farmers Bank, and a hosiery mill.

More African-American businesses were founded, such as the Banker's Fire Insurance Company in 1920, the Durham Textile Mill in the 1920s, and Southern Fidelity Mutual Insurance Company in 1926, which aided in the financing of numerous additional black businesses. The part of Parrish Street that housed the Mutual and its neighbors became known as the "Black Wall Street."

As African Americans in Durham progressed materially, their culture, through its social institutions and music, created strong community bonds. The oldest African-American social institution in Durham, as in other cities, was the church. St. Joseph's African Methodist Episcopal (A.M.E.) Church, founded in 1869, and White Rock Baptist Church, organized in 1866, were among the earliest. Schools also shaped the community. In 1885, Durham County records reported 32 African-American schools with 1,133 pupils. Thirty white schools enrolled 1,082 pupils. In 1889, a grade school for African-American children opened in the city of Durham. It was named the Whitted School in honor of James Whitted, a noted educator from Durham.

James Edward Shepard, a pharmacist, founded the National Religious Training School and Chautauqua in 1910. This institution's original objective was to provide religious training for African-American ministers. In 1925, it became one of the first African-American tax-supported liberal arts colleges in the nation. It is now North Carolina Central University.

The sound of blues music dominated the streets of Hayti, where the Biltmore Hotel played host to entertainers such as Bessie Smith, Cab Calloway, and Count Basie. Musicians like Blind Boy Fuller and Gary Davis made much of their early money singing on the streets of Hayti. African Americans living in Durham enjoyed a strong and independent social, economic, and cultural life. But they could not escape from Jim Crow. Outside of their communities, blacks were still treated as inferiors.

All that began to change in 1935 when the Durham Committee on Negro Affairs was founded by Durham's leading businessmen, including Shepard and Spaulding. The purpose of the Durham Committee was the pursuit of social and economic justice for African Americans. Its strategies of boycotts, voter registration, and court battles helped to usher in the nonviolent Civil Rights Movement. Some Durham African Americans criticized the Durham Committee for being too conservative. As a result, in the mid-1950s and 1960s, they began joining local chapters of more radical groups like the National Association for the Advancement of Colored People (NAACP), the Congress of Racial Equality (CORE), the Southern Christian Leadership Conference (SCLC), and the Student NonViolent Coordinating Committee (SNCC). Still, the Durham Committee continued to follow a course that had proved productive in promoting interracial communication.

In spite of their nonviolent philosophy, actions by the Durham Committee and the more radical views of other groups led to racial incidents in Durham, as African Americans challenged the South's Jim Crow laws. In one incident, Doris Lyon refused to observe a Jim Crow practice and moved to a seat in the back of the bus in 1943. After she hit a detective when he forcibly moved her, she was arrested, found guilty of assault and battery, and fined.

Following the United States Supreme Court's Brown vs. Board of Education decision in 1954, the Durham school system used every possible method to slow the desegregation of its schools. African Americans looked to the courts for assistance. In the fall of 1959, the mothers of Jocelyn McKissick and Elaine Richardson successfully brought suit to have their daughters reassigned to Durham High School, a predominantly white school, after they had been denied admission by the school board.

Another aspect of the civil rights struggles was desegregation of public accommodation. On June 23, 1957, Douglas E. Moore, pastor of Ashbury Temple United Methodist Church, and seven students from ages 17 to 20 sat at a lunch counter at the Royal Ice Cream Parlor in Durham and waited for service. Moore and six students were arrested and fined $25 for trespassing.

The struggle for civil rights was at the same time taking place in other cities throughout North Carolina, even across the country. From the fight for equal access to buses, restaurants, movie theaters, and hotels to efforts to desegregate schools and other institutions, the nation watched the African-American quest for equality.

One

Early Pioneers and Leaders

Durham offers none of the color and creative life we find among Negroes in New York City. It is not a place where men write and dream; but a place where black men calculate and work.

—Noted black sociologist E. Franklin Frazier in 1925, during the Harlem Renaissance.

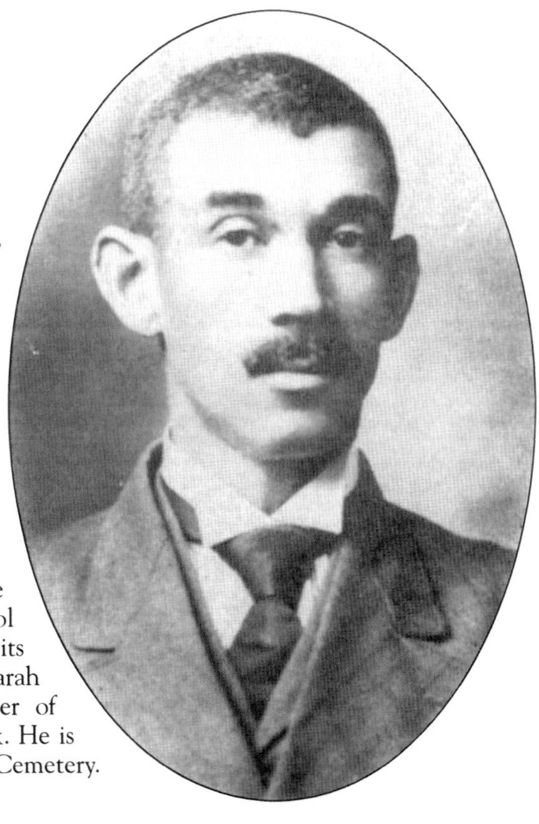

Dr. Aaron McDuffie Moore (1864–1923), a resident of 606 Fayetteville Street, was a pioneer, visionary, builder, and the true spirit of the Hayti community. Moore came to Durham in 1888 and was the city's first black physician. He was the founder of such institutions as the Lincoln Hospital, Mechanics and Farmers Bank, and the Bull City Drug Store and was co-founder of the North Carolina Mutual Life Insurance Company, of which he served as its president from 1919 until his death on April 29, 1923. In 1888 he graduated from the Leonard Medical School at Shaw University and later served on its board of trustees. He was married to Sarah Cottie Dancy Moore and was the father of Mattie L. McDougald and Lyda V. Merrick. He is interred in the Moore plot in Beechwood Cemetery. (Courtesy of Andre D. Vann.)

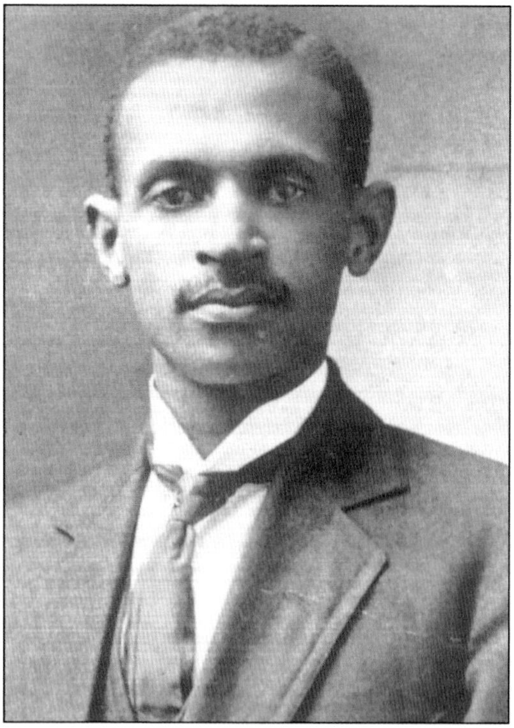

Dr. James Edward Shepard (1875–1947), a resident of 1902 Fayetteville Street, was a druggist, preacher, and founder of the National Religious Training School and Chautauqua and is seen here in this early-1900s photograph. Shepard was founder and president of what is now North Carolina Central University. Acquired by the State in 1925, it became North Carolina College for Negroes, the first state-supported liberal arts college for African Americans in the country. Shepard served as president from 1910 until his death in 1947. (Courtesy of North Carolina Division of Archives and History.)

Dr. Charles Haddon Shepard (1878–1935), a resident of 1601 Fayetteville Street, was born in Raleigh, North Carolina. He was the son of Reverend Augustus S. and Hattie C. Whitted Shepard and was the brother of Dr. James Shepard. Shepard was educated in the early schools of Raleigh and received his M.D. degree from Shaw University's Leonard Medical School. He later moved to Durham and practiced at Lincoln Hospital, where he also served as its second superintendent, from 1924 to 1934. He was a member of the Kappa Alpha Psi Fraternity, the NAACP, the National Medical Association, and the Old North State Medical, Dental, and Pharmaceutical Association. Politically, he was registered as an Independent and was a member of the White Rock Baptist Church, where he served on the Trustee Board. He married Mary H. Adams and had one daughter, Dorothy S. Manley. He died in 1935 and is interred in Beechwood Cemetery in the Shepard plot. (Courtesy of Andre D. Vann.)

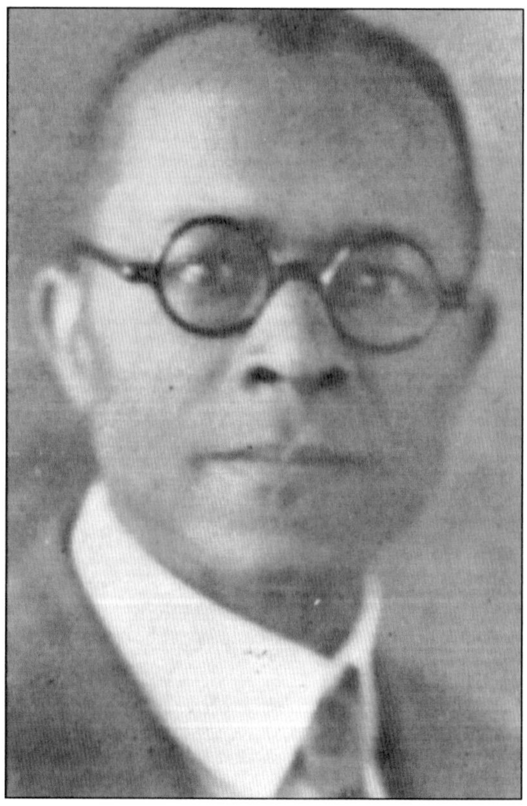

This is a 1930s photograph of Dr. Stanford Lee Warren (1863–1940), a resident of Brant Street, a noted physician, businessman, civic leader, and president of the Durham Colored Library from 1923 until his passing in 1940. Born in Caswell County, he moved to Durham at age two and attended the local public schools and graduated from Kittrell College and Shaw University's Leonard Medical School. Warren married Julia McCauley on December 28, 1904, and had one daughter, Selena Warren Wheeler. He held membership on the boards of Mechanics and Farmers Bank, Lincoln Hospital, St. Joseph's African Methodist Episcopal Church, and the Durham Alumni Chapter of Kappa Alpha Psi. He died on January 31, 1940, and was interred in Beechwood Cemetery. The Stanford L. Warren Public Library was named in his honor because of his donation of land for the present site. (Courtesy of Andre D. Vann.)

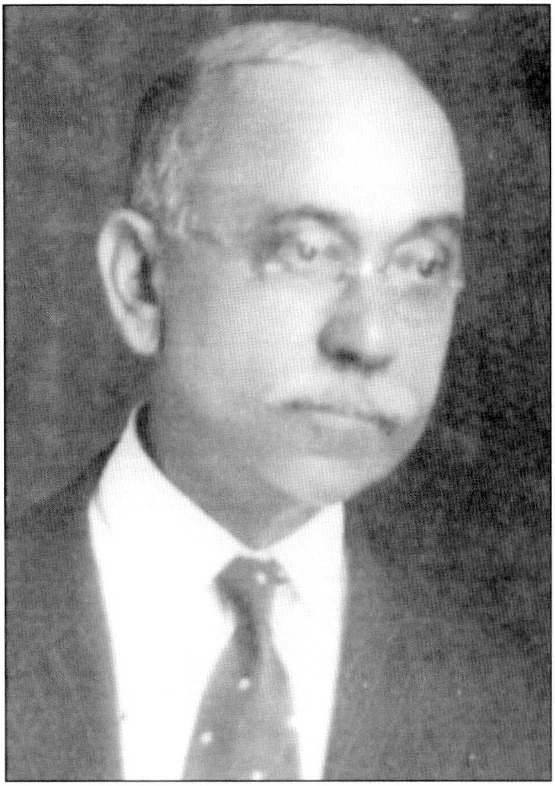

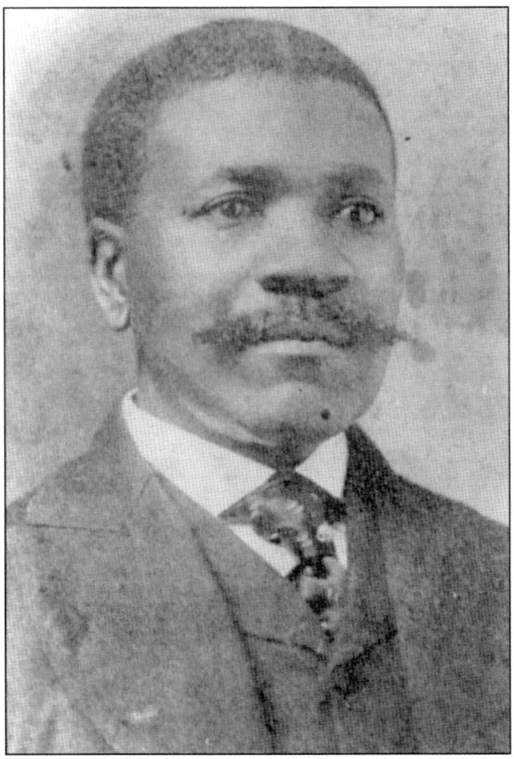

James Rufus Evans (1865–1943), a resident of 812 Glenn Street, was an 1880s graduate of Shaw University, an educator, and among the first black barbers in Durham. He was treasurer at North Carolina Mutual Life Insurance Company; the director and vice-president at Mechanics and Farmers Bank; the president and manager of Community Damp Wash Laundry, now Doby Cleaners; and a member of the Board of Trustees and Board of Deacons at the White Rock Baptist Church. Evans was married to Effie Sellers and was the father of nine: Elease, Ruby, Julia, Mary, and Ernestine and four sons that died in infancy. He died in 1943 and was interred in Beechwood Cemetery. (Courtesy of Ernestine E. Young / Andre D. Vann.)

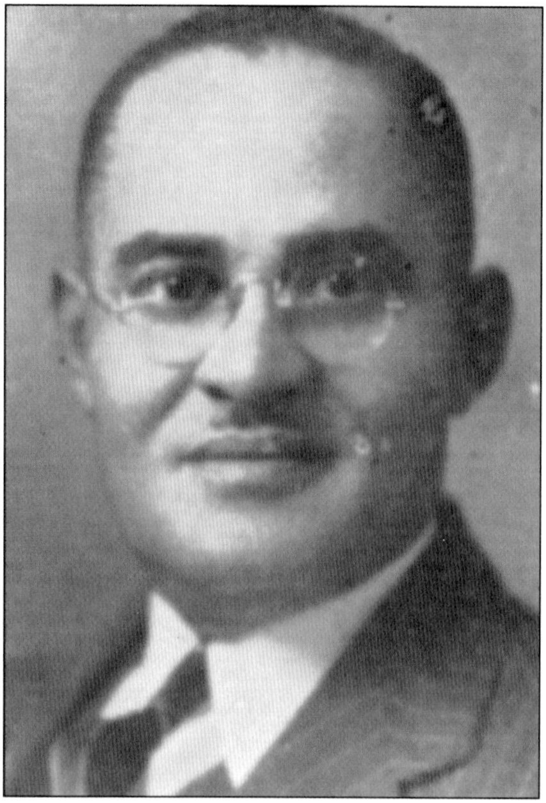

Attorney Hugh Thompson (1898–1974), one of the state's pioneer black activist lawyers, received his A.B. degree from Syracuse University in New York and joined the U.S. Army, where he fought during World War I. Later he graduated from Howard University's Law School with a LL.B. degree and was a classmate of Justice Thurgood Marshall. He came to Durham in 1924 and was of counsel to the North Carolina Mutual Life Insurance Company, Mutual Building and Loan Association, and Mechanics and Farmers Bank. Thompson was a member of Omega Psi Phi Fraternity, a former trustee of North Carolina Central University, and a member of St. Joseph's A.M.E. Church, NAACP, and the Elks. (Courtesy of Andre D. Vann.)

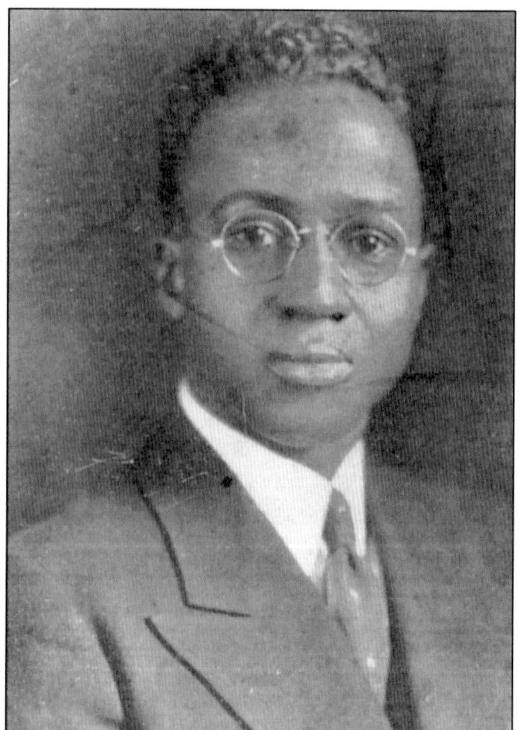

Reverend Dr. Miles Mark Fisher (1899–1970), shown in this 1940s photo, received a wide reputation as a clergyman, educator, author, and humanitarian. Fisher served as pastor of the White Rock Baptist Church from 1933 until 1965. He practiced a social gospel in the Hayti community that provided such services as recreation, employment information, adult education classes, summer softball league, a boxing team, and a Boy Scout troop, and also established a health clinic and began a nursery. Fisher also wrote *Negro Slave Songs in the United States*, which won the American Historical Association's prize for the outstanding historical volume in 1953, and was considered a foremost scholar on the Spiritual. (Courtesy of Andre D. Vann.)

This is a 1930s photo of the Goodloes, who were residents of 710 W. Glenn Street. Flonnie Arrington (1888–1980), left, and Allen Lucius Goodloe (1873–1939) were married in 1913 and were leaders in business, religious, and civic endeavors. Allen Goodloe was a former district manager of North Carolina Mutual Life Insurance Company's, Durham branch and was the father of Joseph Goodloe, the sixth president of the Mutual. Both father and son were staunch members of the White Rock Baptist Church. (Courtesy of Andre D. Vann.)

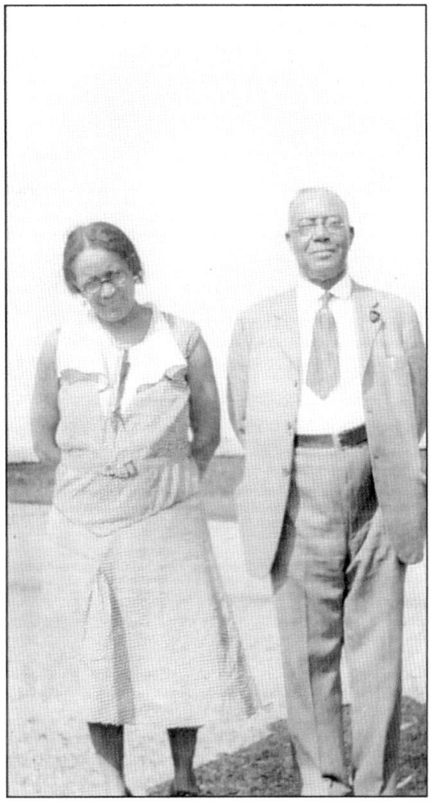

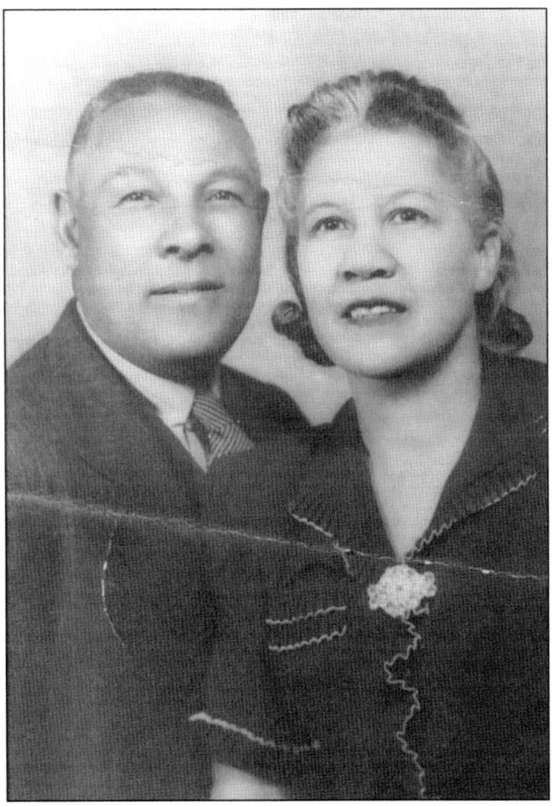

George W. (1889–1977) and Maude E. Lewis Logan (1892–1972) were both graduates of Hampton Institute in the Class of 1909. They both migrated to Durham in 1918 and became actively involved in operating the Wonderland movie theater before building the Regal Theater. The Regal was one of four movie theaters in Hayti between 1918 and 1950. It was located on Pettigrew Street next to the Biltmore Hotel. The Regal during the 1950s was frequented by Ella Fitzgerald, Fats Waller, Cab Calloway, Ethel Waters, Count Basie, and Bessie Smith. The Logans also operated the Donut Shop, which also was located on Pettigrew Street. (Courtesy of Jessie Pearson / Barbara Cooke / Andre D. Vann.)

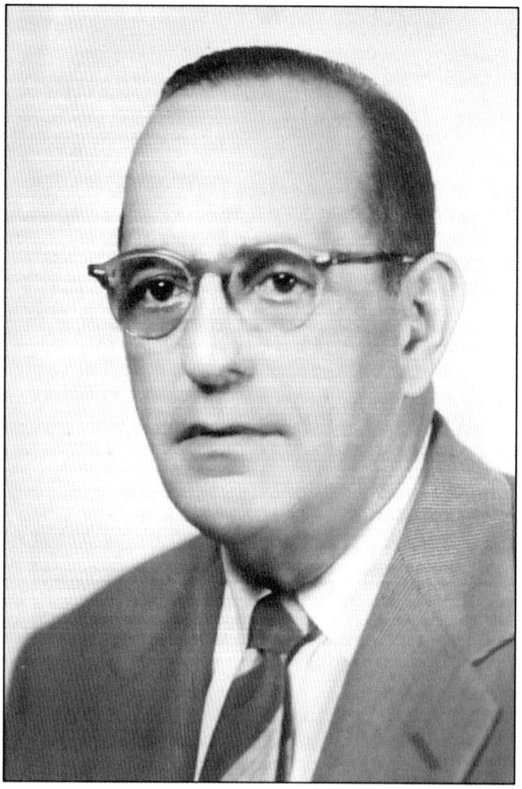

Rencher Nicholas Harris (1900–1965), a resident of Formosa Avenue, came to Durham in 1921 after graduation from Virginia Union University in Richmond, Virginia. In 1921, Harris joined Bankers Fire and Casualty Insurance Company as a special agent and served in leadership positions until his death. He was elected the first "Negro member of the Durham City Council" in 1953 and served until 1957. In 1958, Harris was appointed by the city council to the board of education, becoming the first black appointed. He also was a founder of the Durham Committee on Negro Affairs, a trustee of Lincoln Hospital, and a member of St. Titus Episcopal Church. He was married to Plassie Williams Harris and was a member of the Omega Psi Phi Fraternity. The R.N. Harris Elementary School is named in his honor in Durham. (Courtesy of Andre D. Vann.)

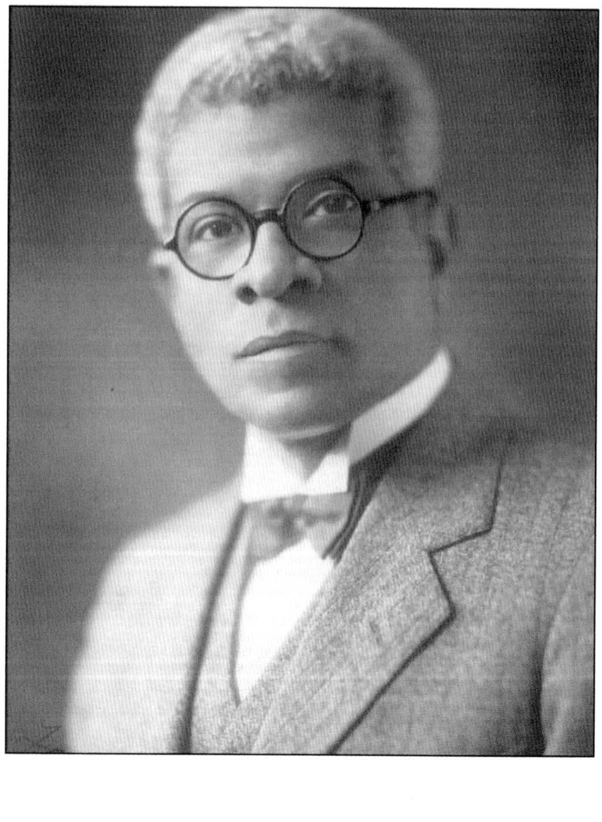

Charles Clinton Spaulding (1874–1952), a resident of 1006 Fayetteville Street and pictured here in 1925, was a founder of the North Carolina Mutual Life Insurance Company in 1899. He rose through the ranks and eventually became president in 1923, following the death of his uncle, Dr. A.M. Moore; Spaulding served as the second president of the company until his death on August 1, 1952. He also served as president of the Mechanics and Farmers Bank and Mutual Savings and Loan Association. The Charles Clinton Spaulding Elementary School on Roxboro Road is named in his honor. (Courtesy of Andre D. Vann.)

William Daniel Hill (1890–1945), a resident of 1202 Fayetteville Street, was a social, civic, business executive, and religious leader. He graduated from Virginia Union University and was a veteran of World War I. He spent his entire professional career at North Carolina Mutual, from 1917 until his death in 1945. Hill was a board member of the Mechanics and Farmers Bank and Bankers Fire Insurance Company and a member of the Volkamenia Literary Club, Algonquin Tennis Club, Omega Psi Phi Fraternity, and White Rock Baptist Church. The W.D. Hill Recreation Center on Fayetteville Street is named in his honor. (Courtesy of Howard Fitts / Andre D. Vann.)

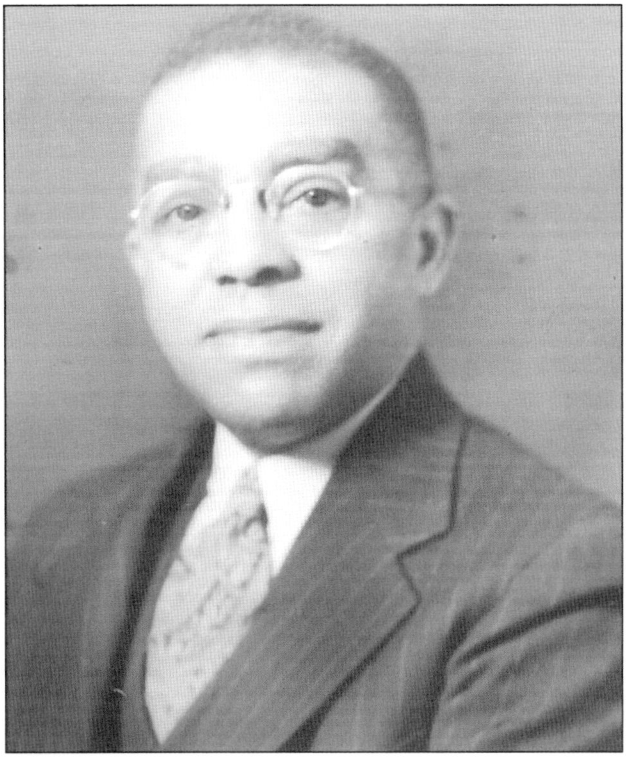

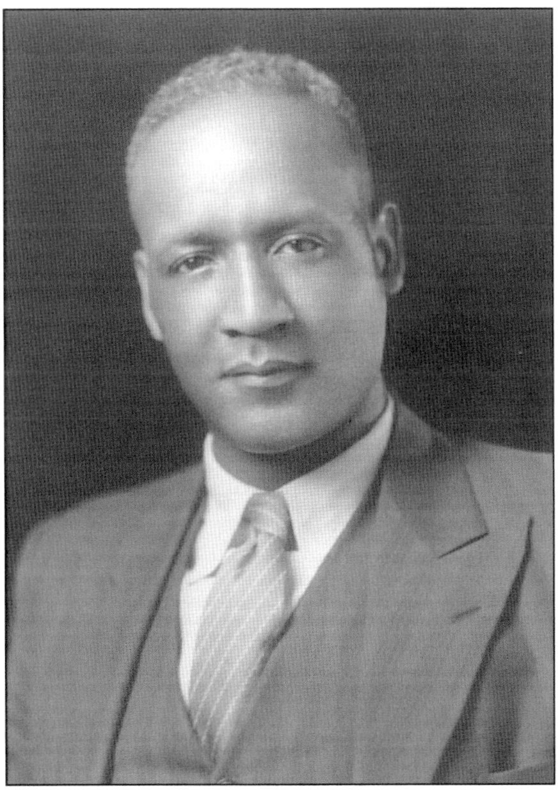

William Jesse Kennedy Jr. (1889–1985), a resident of 1008 Fayetteville Street, was educated at Americus Institute in Georgia and took extension courses at Columbia University. He was transferred to the home office in 1919 and served as office manager, assistant secretary-manager, and vice-president-secretary. He was a member of the board of directors from 1920 until his death in 1985. Kennedy was named the fourth president in 1952 and served until 1958. He wrote the *North Carolina Mutual Story* in 1970. He was married to Margaret Spaulding and was the father of three. White Rock Baptist Church consumed a great portion of his life, as he served as a trustee, treasurer, business manager, and Sunday school teacher. (Courtesy of Andre D. Vann.)

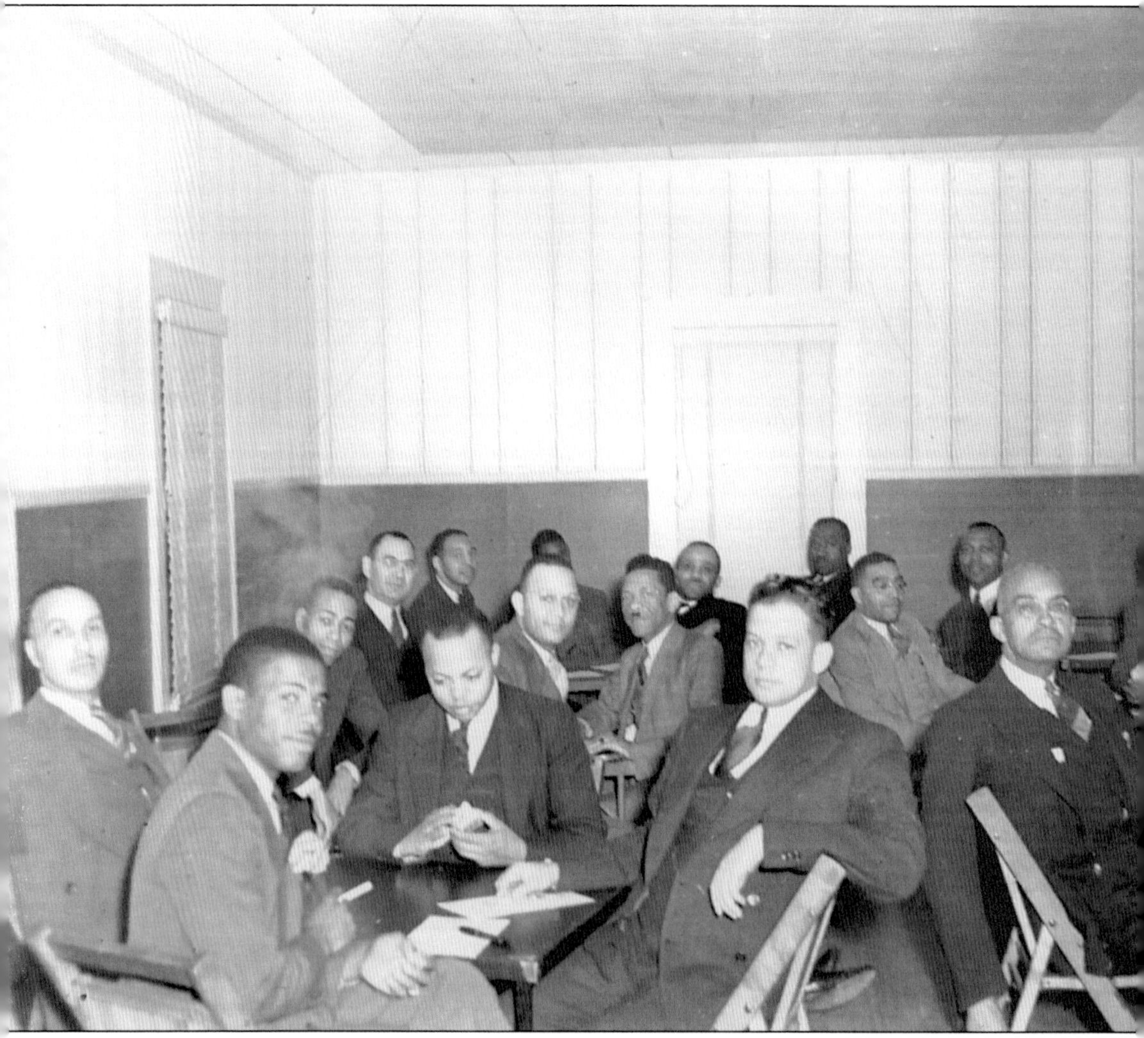

This is a 1940 photograph of members of Durham's black professional class that helped to dub Durham "The Capital of the Black Middle-Class," taken at the Algonquin Tennis Club. (Courtesy of Andre D. Vann.)

Two

Women of Hayti
Professionals and Entrepreneurs

My father passed a torch to me, which I have never let go out. We are blessed to serve.

—Lyda Merrick Moore (the daughter of Dr. Aaron M. Moore), editor and founder of *The Negro Braille Magazine* (now *The Merrick/Washington Magazine for the Blind*), the only work guided toward minorities who are sightless.

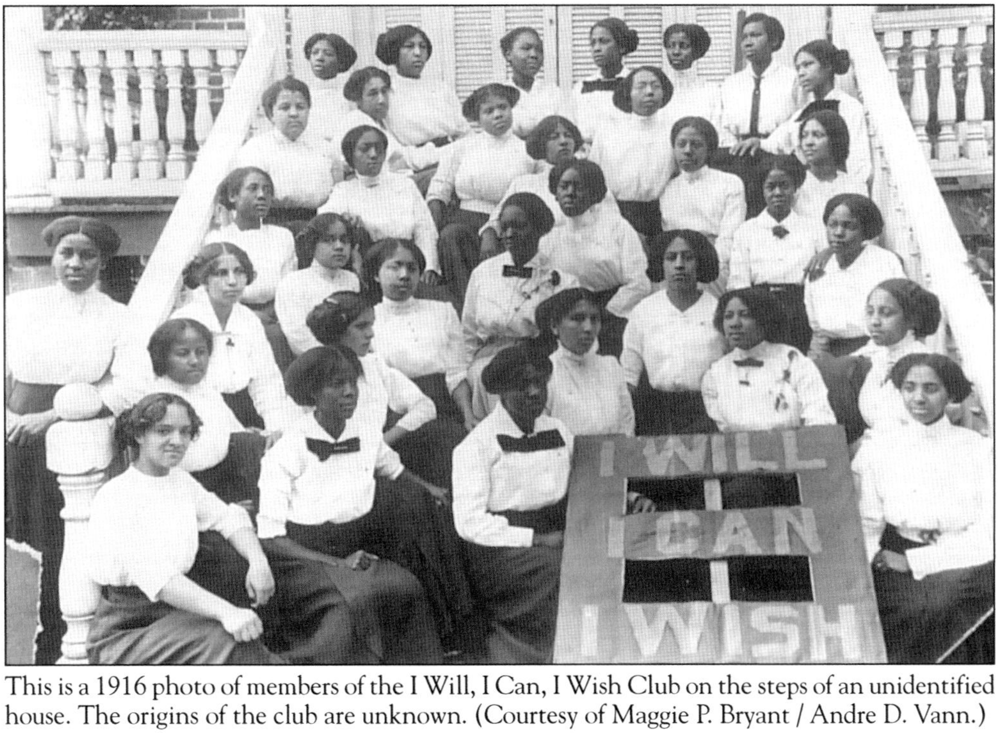

This is a 1916 photo of members of the I Will, I Can, I Wish Club on the steps of an unidentified house. The origins of the club are unknown. (Courtesy of Maggie P. Bryant / Andre D. Vann.)

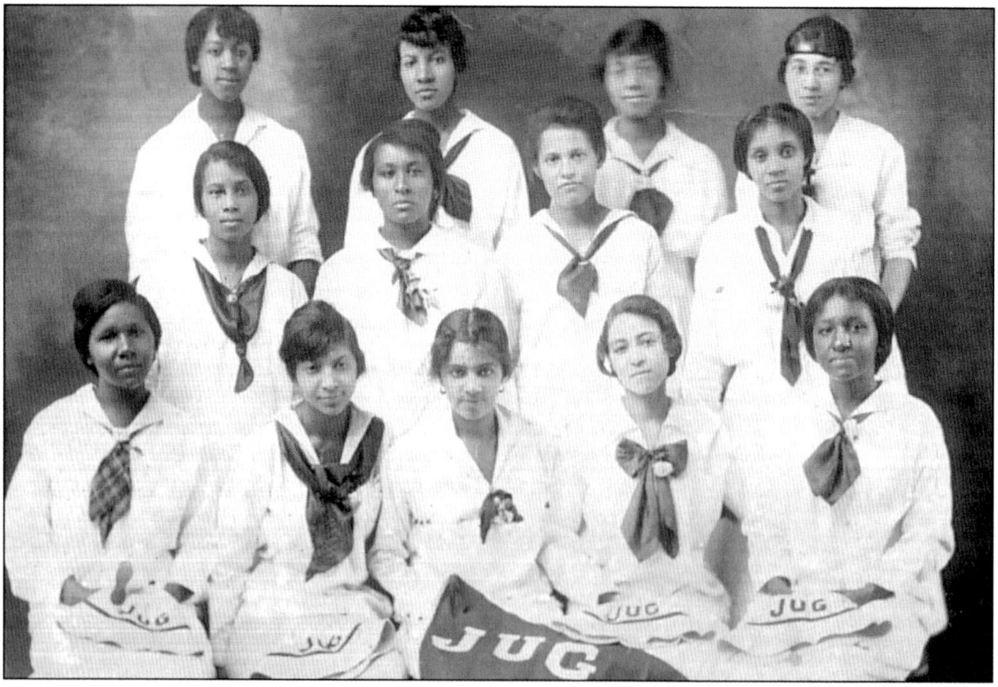

This is a 1911 photo of the JUG (Just for Us Girls), a group of single women that were educated, middle class, and community leaders. The club members are, from left to right, as follows: (first row, seated) Gazella Poole, Eula Ruffin, Martha Merrick, Sarah Amey, and Fannie Poole; (second row, standing) Minnie Whitted, Ora Sneed, Henrietta Christmas, and Beatrice Bynum; (third row) Theresa Shepard, Mittie Ray, Benena Shepard, and Mattie L. Moore. (Courtesy of Maggie P. Bryant / Andre D. Vann.)

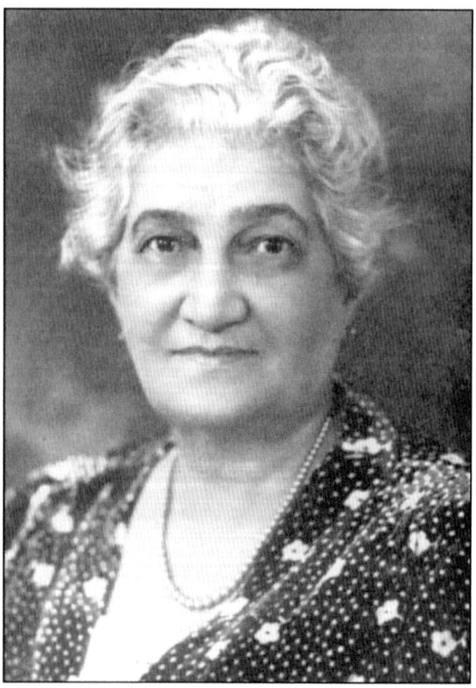

Annie Day Shepard (1879–1947) was born in Yanceyville, North Carolina, the daughter of Thomas and Mary Day of Virginia. She also was the granddaughter of the renowned furniture maker Thomas Day. Annie Day was married to Dr. James E. Shepard on November 7, 1895, and to this union were born Annie Day and Marjorie. She aided her husband in the founding of the National Religious Training School and Chautauqua (now NCCU). During the 1930s, Annie Day Shepard dedicated much of her time, money, and food to the students of the college—she also wrote the school's alma mater. The college named its women's dormitory, in 1930, Annie Day Shepard Hall. Annie Day Shepard was a leader in the North Carolina Federation of Negro Women's Clubs and was a member of the Daughters of Dorcas Club. Shepard died on February 8, 1947, and was interred in Beechwood Cemetery. (Courtesy of Andre D. Vann.)

Molly Markham worked fervently with her husband, Reverend Edian D. Markham, to found the St. Joseph's A.M.E. Church, Durham's second black congregation. (Courtesy of Andre D. Vann.)

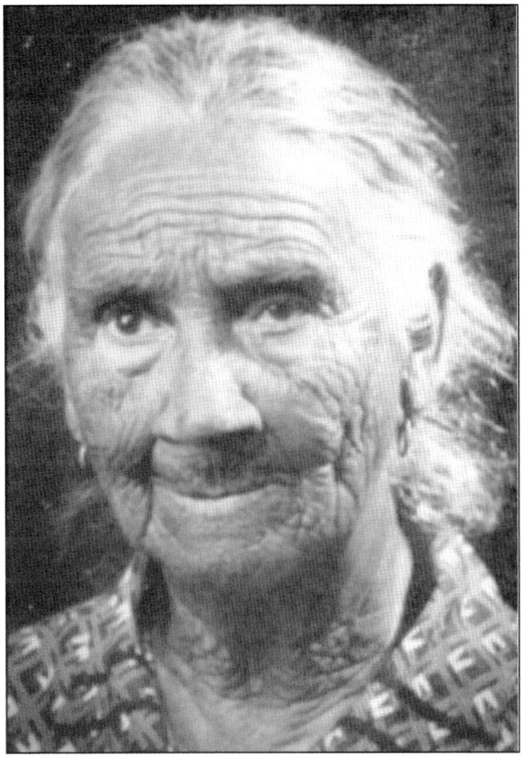

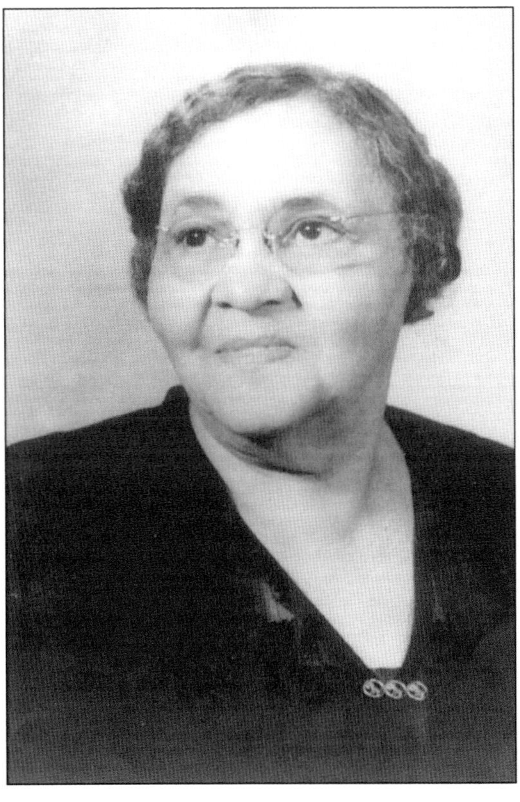

This is a 1946 photo of Ms. Pattie Hawkins Carter, R.N. (1881–1950), who came to Lincoln Hospital in 1911 to serve as assistant director under its founder. Besides working as head nurse, anesthetist, bookkeeper, and stewardess, she later served as the director of nurses until her retirement in 1938. Carter devoted her entire life to this institution and on numerous occasions refused to accept wage increases because the hospital needed the money. Receiving her early training in the Warren County Schools, she graduated from Shaw University and interned at St. Augustine's, St. Agnes Hospital in Raleigh, and the Lincoln School of Nursing in New York City. (Courtesy of Andre D. Vann.)

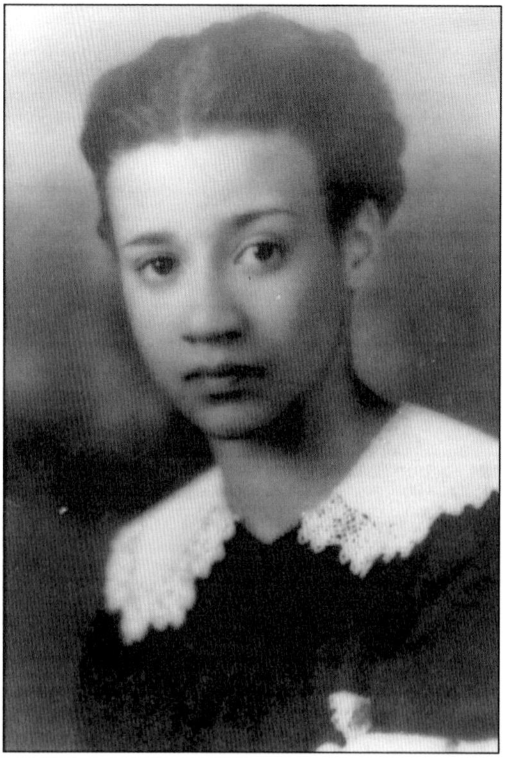

This is a 1940s photo of Margaret Kennedy Goodwin (born 1918), daughter of North Carolina Mutual executive William J. and Margaret Spaulding Kennedy. She received her high school training at Palmer Memorial Institute in Sedalia, North Carolina, and graduated from Talladega College in Alabama in 1938. In 1943 she joined Lincoln Hospital to head the X-ray department. In 1945 she received a year of special training at Philadelphia General Hospital and in 1947 became the first black X-ray technician in the country certified by the American Registry of Radiologic Technologists. Goodwin later became the first black member of the North Carolina Society of Radiologic Technicians and later served as its president from 1957 until 1958. She ran Lincoln's X-ray school from 1950 to 1968 and retired in 1983. She is an accomplished musician and is a member of the White Rock Baptist Church and the Delta Sigma Theta Sorority, Inc. (Courtesy of Margaret Goodwin / Andre D. Vann.)

Julia McCauley Warren (1877–1944) was a graduate of Howard University, where she received a teaching certificate. In 1900 she came to Durham to teach Domestic Science at the James A. Whitted School. In 1904, she married Dr. Stanford L. Warren, a noted physician and businessman in Durham. She later opened in 1919 Durham's first beauty salon, called the Warenetta Beauty Parlor, where she served both blacks and whites. She has the distinction of being Durham's first beautician and hair stylist. The establishment was located at Five Points in the Snow Building and later moved to her home on Brant Street. Warren also was a founder of the North Carolina Federation of Negro Women's Clubs, a member of the Volkamenia Literary Club, and a member of St. Joseph's A.M.E. Church. She is interred in Beechwood Cemetery. (Courtesy of Selena Wheeler / Andre D. Vann.)

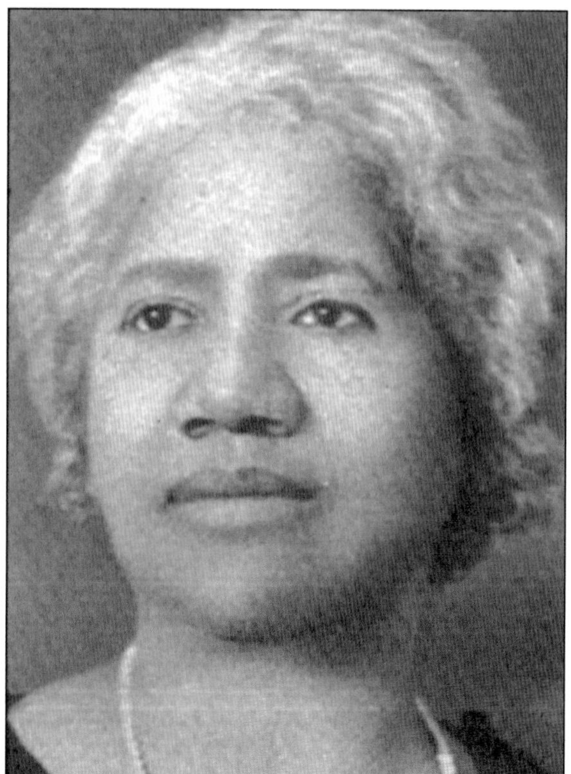

Minnie Sumner Pearson (1869–1940), a native of Charlotte, received her early training at Livingstone College in Salisbury. She taught for a few years and later married William Gaston Pearson on June 6, 1893. Coming to Durham to live, she taught in Durham County and later in the city school system. She was the chairwoman of the Ladies Board of Lincoln Hospital; a member of the Board of Stanford L. Warren Library, Harriet Tubman Branch YWCA, the 20th Century and Shubert-Shakespearian Literary Clubs, and St. Joseph's A.M.E. Church; the founder and president of the North Carolina Federation of Negro Women's Clubs; the state president of the Women's Home and Foreign Missionary Society of the Western North Carolina Conference of the African Methodist Episcopal Church. (Courtesy of Andre D. Vann.)

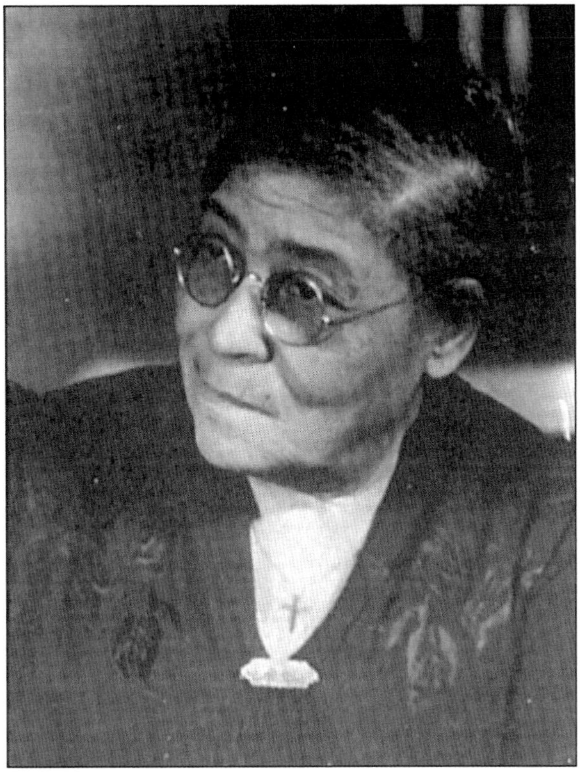

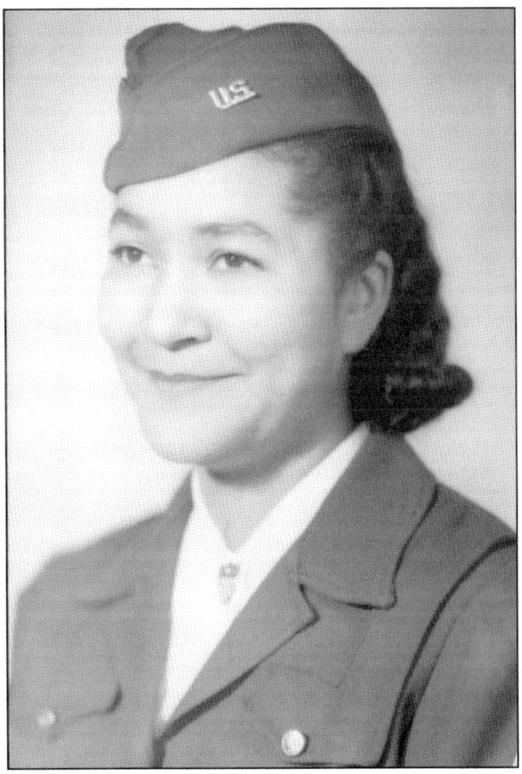

Nurse Emma Lee Randolph (?–1991) migrated to Durham in 1935 after graduation from the Tuskegee Institute in Alabama, where she received her early academic training and undergraduate training in nursing. In 1935 she accepted a job as an operating room supervisor at Lincoln Hospital. She also served as a relief nurse at North Carolina College (NCCU), where she also acted as a chaperon for the choir. During World War II, she served along with her husband, Dr. Robert Randolph, in the Army. She was past president of the North Carolina Federation of Garden Clubs, Merry Wives Bridge Club, Durham Chapter, Links, Inc., and the Chi Eta Phi Professional Nursing Sorority. (Courtesy of Frances Dyer / Andre D. Vann.)

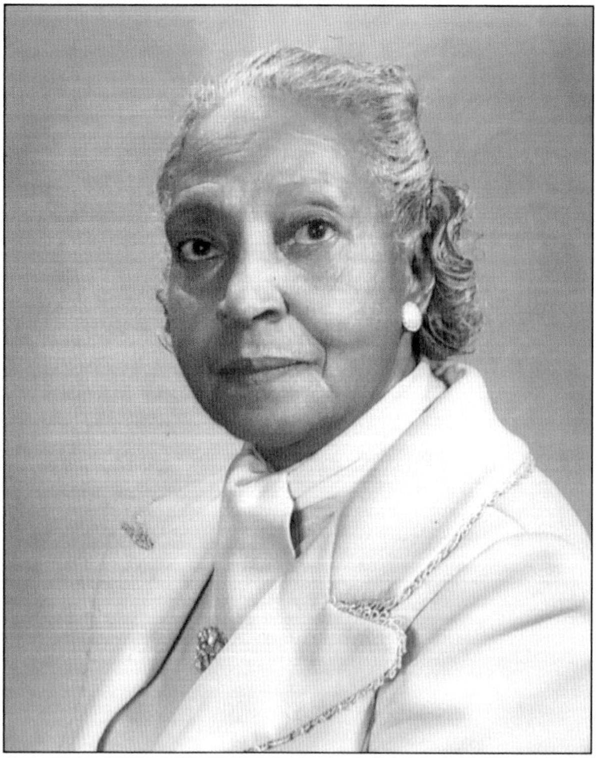

Dr. Johnnie Blunt McLester (1907–1999), educator, religious leader, and civic leader, came to Durham in the 1930s to work for the Harriet Tubman Branch of the YWCA on Umstead Street. She later married Reverend Dr. Charles McLester, and they became the founders of the Morehead Avenue Baptist Church. A graduate of Talladega College and Columbia University, she taught for 30 years as a teacher and counselor at Hillside High School, James A. Whitted Junior High School, and Shepard Middle School. McLester was a dynamic leader among black Baptist women and was an inspiration to her many students. (Courtesy of Andre D. Vann.)

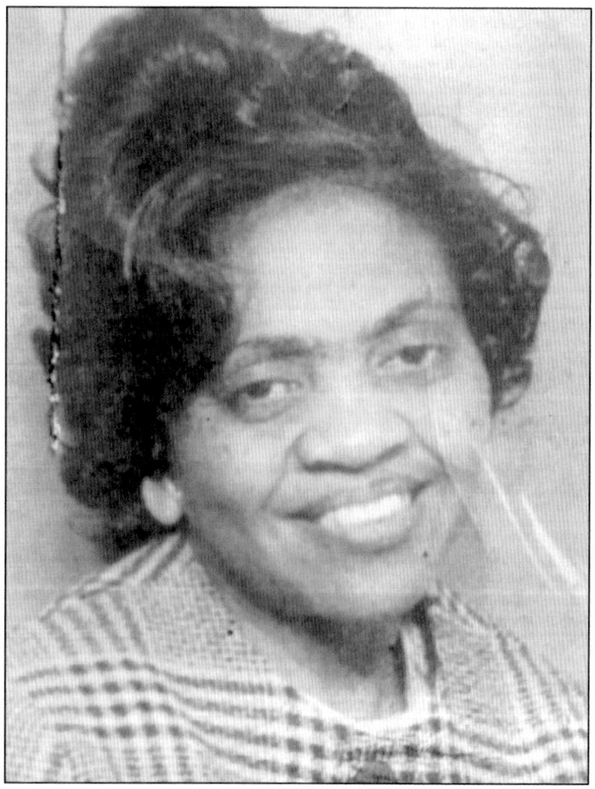

Ernestine Evans Young, daughter of James and Effie Sellers Evans, was born and reared in Hayti. She graduated from Hillside High School and North Carolina College and taught for a number of years. She has served as an oral historian of the community and is a faithful member of the Daughters of Dorcas Club and the White Rock Baptist Church. (Courtesy of Ernestine Young.)

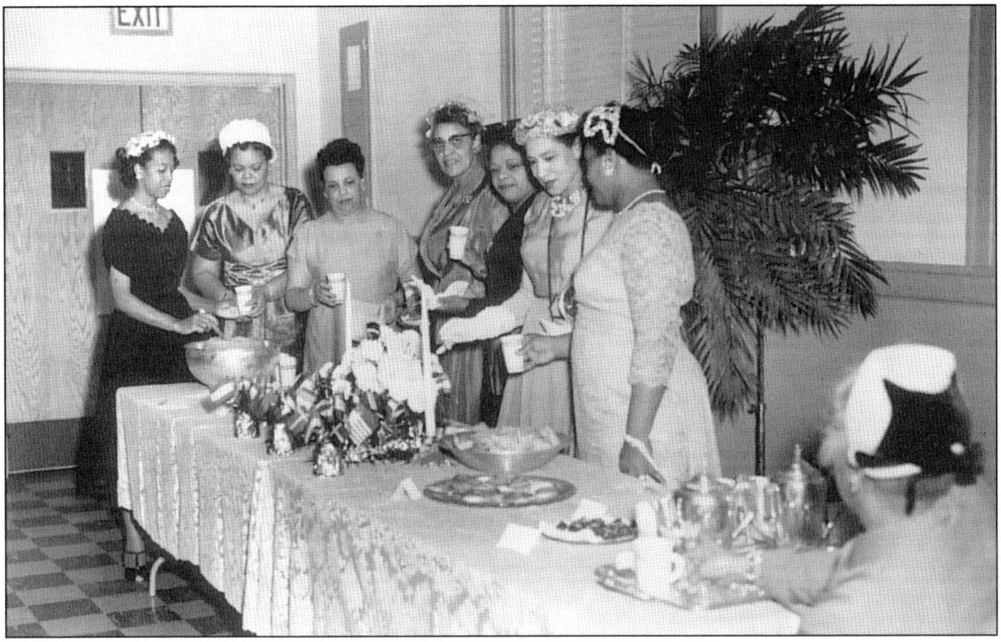

This is a 1959 photo of the National Council of Negro Women entertaining in the auditorium of the S.L. Warren Public Library. (Courtesy of S.L. Warren Branch Library.)

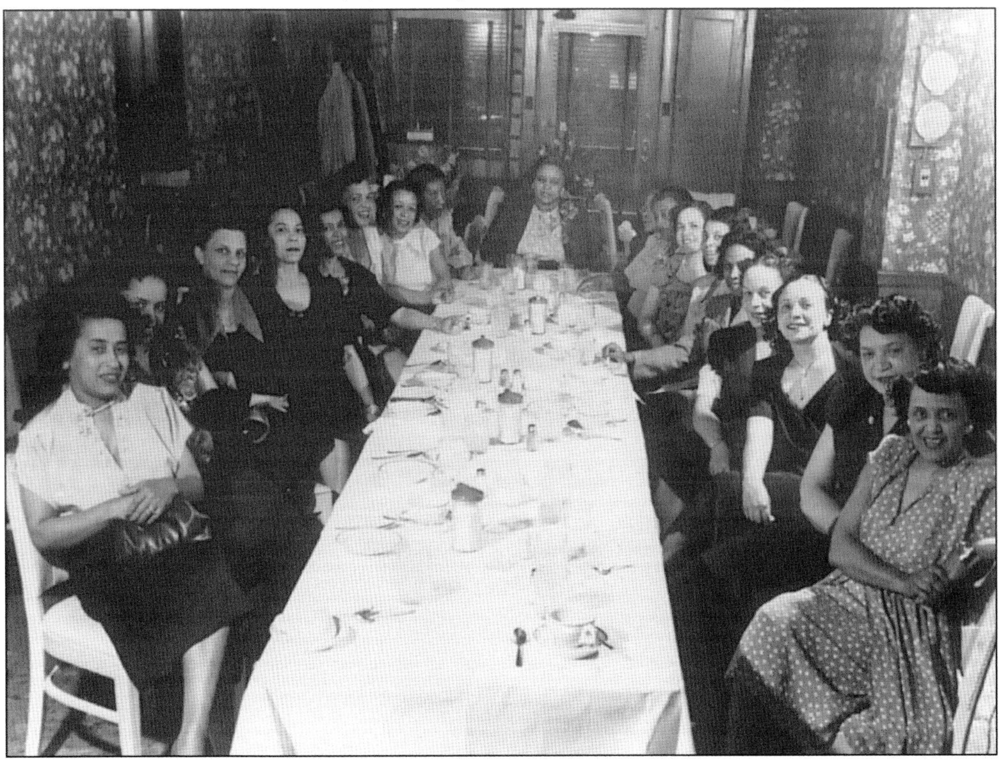

This is a *c.* 1947 photo of members of the Little Slam's Bridge Club in the Jade Room of the Donut Shop on Pettigrew Street. The hostess for this occasion was Hattie Bell Strong Scarborough (seated at the head of the table). (Courtesy of John Scarborough III / Andre D. Vann.)

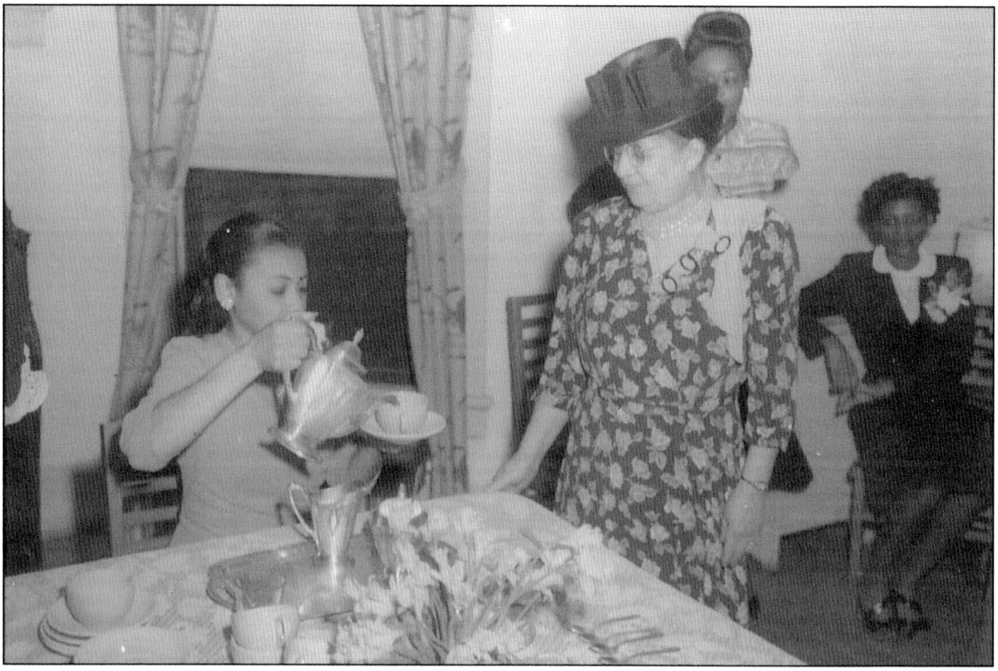

Durham businesswoman Janie Marie Spaulding, a resident of 509 Fayetteville Street and widow of Alonzo G. Spaulding, was one of Durham's earliest female real estate brokers. She is pictured here at a social gathering partaking of tea. (Courtesy of Andre D. Vann.)

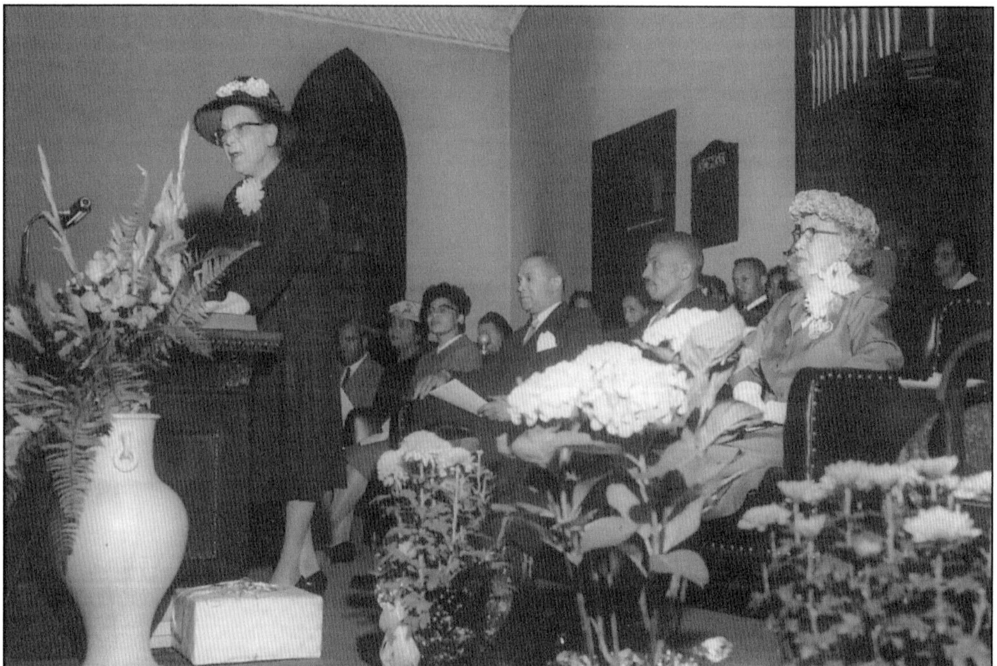

Maude E. Logan was honored with a testimonial by the Maude E. Logan District of White Rock Baptist Church on May 8, 1960. She is shown at the extreme right of the photo. (Courtesy of Andre D. Vann.)

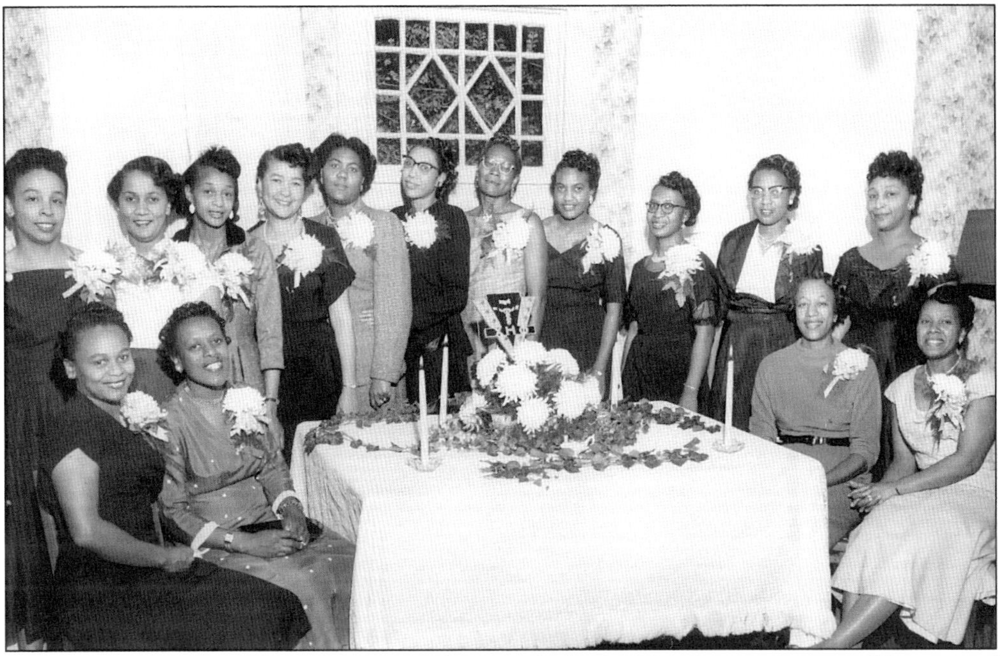

This is a 1950s photo of members of PI Chapter of Chi Eta Phi Nursing Sorority. (Courtesy of Andre D. Vann.)

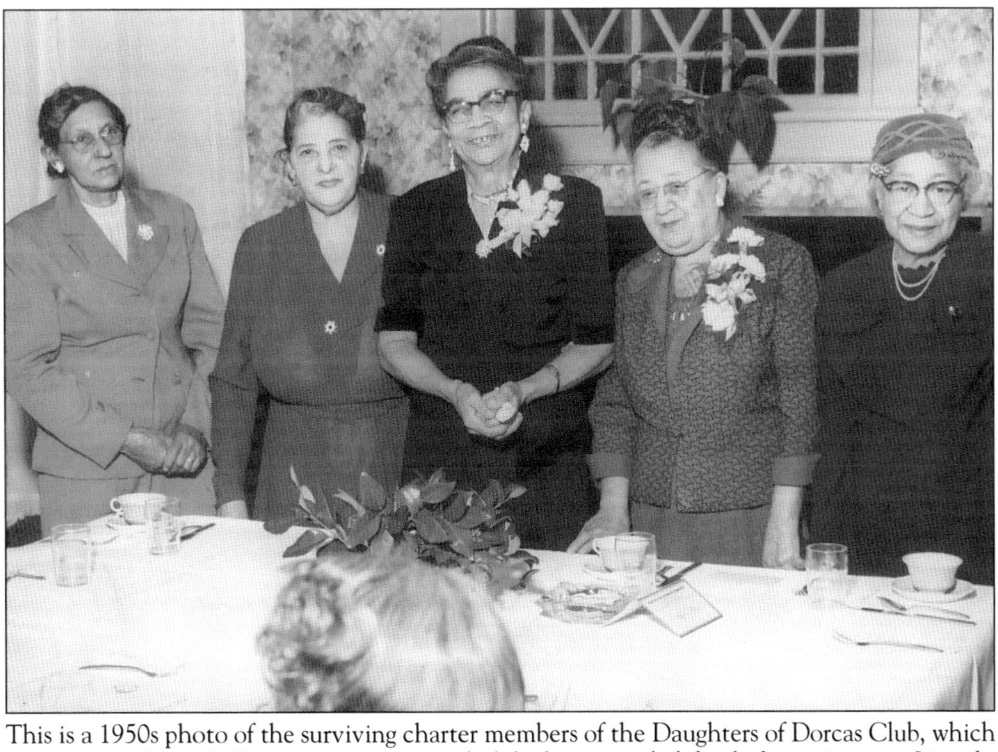

This is a 1950s photo of the surviving charter members of the Daughters of Dorcas Club, which was organized in 1917 as a service-oriented club that provided funds for patients at Lincoln Hospital in Hayti. They are, from left to right, as follows: Lillie Thompson, Sarah Felder, Maggie Lennon, Janie Spaulding, and Matilda Townsend. (Courtesy of Andre D. Vann.)

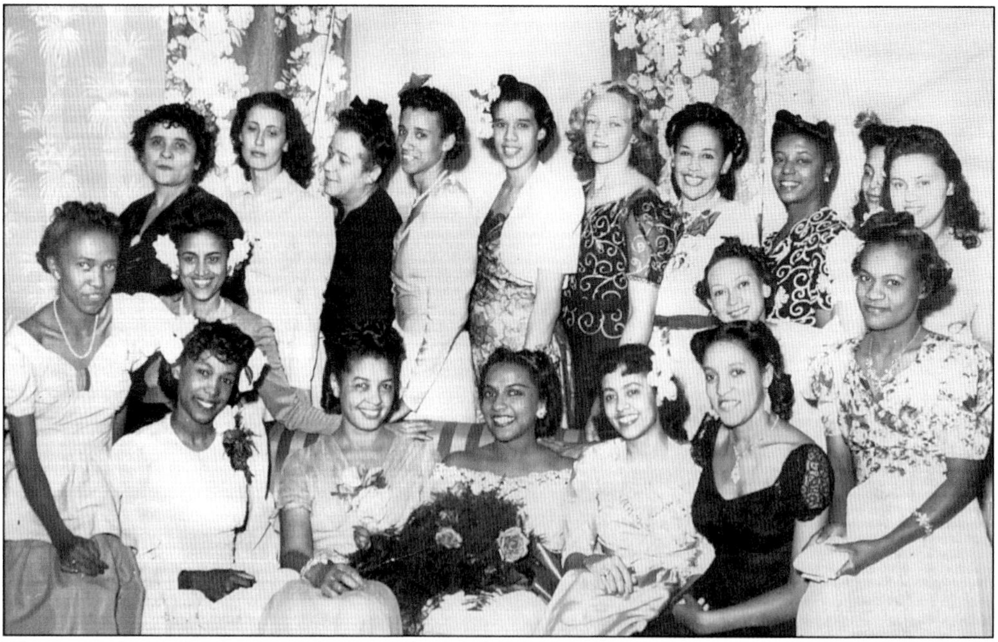

This is a 1940s photo of members of the Alpha Kappa Sigma Chapter of Delta Sigma Theta Sorority , Inc. The chapter hosted a presentation of Muriel Rahn in concert at the B.N. Duke Auditorium, and they made enough profit to pay for scholarships for worthy students. Muriel Rahn, seated in center with flowers, played Bess in the Broadway *Porgy and Bess* production. Constance Merrick Watts, president of the chapter, is seated front row and third from the right. (Courtesy of Andre D. Vann.)

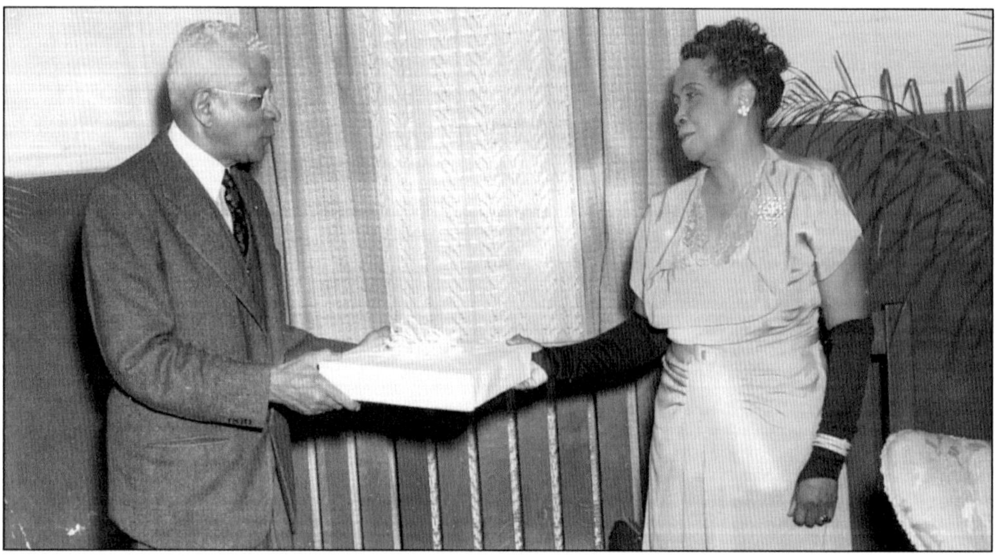

In 1949 Dr. Charles C. Spaulding, president of North Carolina Mutual Life Insurance Company, hosted a testimonial in honor of Susie Veta Norfleet. Norfleet was employed with the company on February 1, 1906, became the first stenographer employed by the company, and retired on September 1, 1949, as the first Home Office employee to retire under its modern pension plan. She was devoted to the cultural, social, and religious uplift of her adopted community. (Courtesy of Andre D. Vann.)

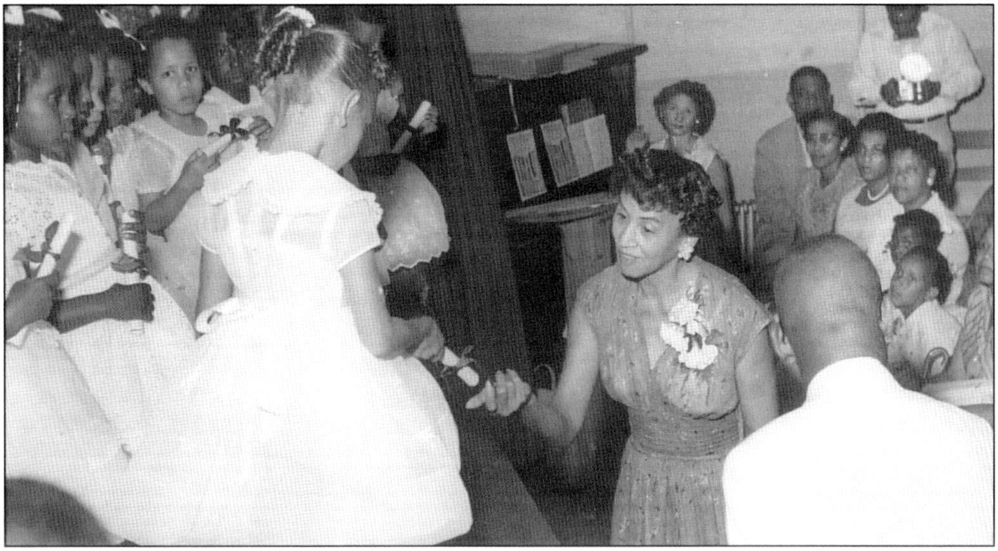

This 1950s photo shows Clydie Fullwood Scarborough (1899–1989), founder of the Daisy Scarborough Nursery, presenting graduation certificates of students during the graduation exercises. Aided by her husband, John C. Scarborough Sr., they founded the Daisy Scarborough Foundation to assist in the care of children. Under Clydie Scarborough's direction, the Scarborough Nursery cared for over 10,000 children, releasing 8,000 mothers to pursue jobs in the workforce. (Courtesy of Andre D. Vann.)

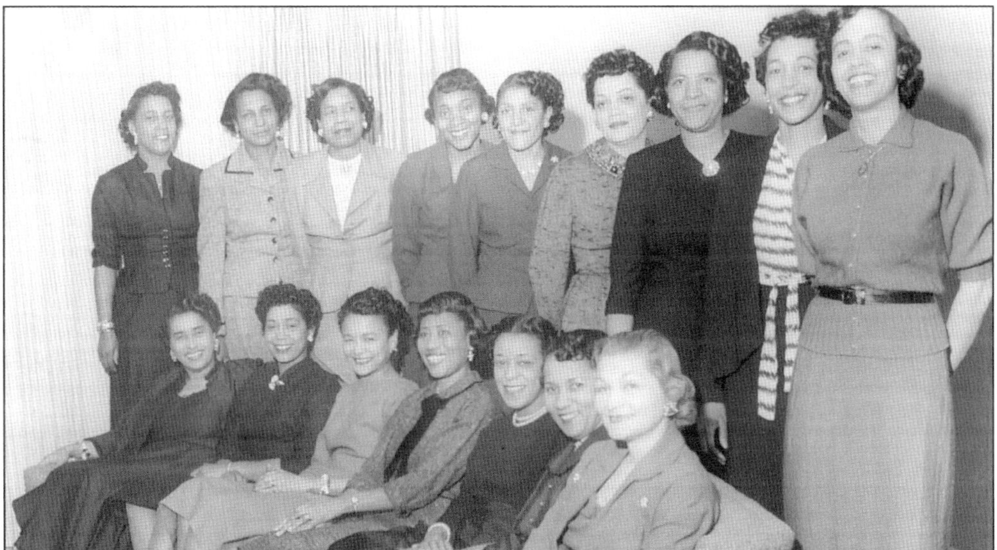

In 1956 a newly formed organization of wives of members of the Alpha Phi Alpha Fraternity, Inc. are shown in the new home of Dr. and Mrs. Charles D. Watts on Lawson Street. The group was formed to provide hospitality for members of the organization attending the Alpha Phi Alpha Southern Region Convention meeting in Durham on March 30–31, 1956. They are, from left to right, as follows: (seated) Fannie Robinson, Josephine Clement, Rosemary Funderburg, Alma Bennett, Helen Edwards, Adele Butts (president), and Edna Walker; (standing) Eugenia Younge, Norvia Coward, Oziebel Frasier, Lula C. Dawson, Jessie Kearney, Hazel Rivera, Alome Hudson, Alma Wade, and Constance Watts (hostess). (Courtesy of Andre D. Vann.)

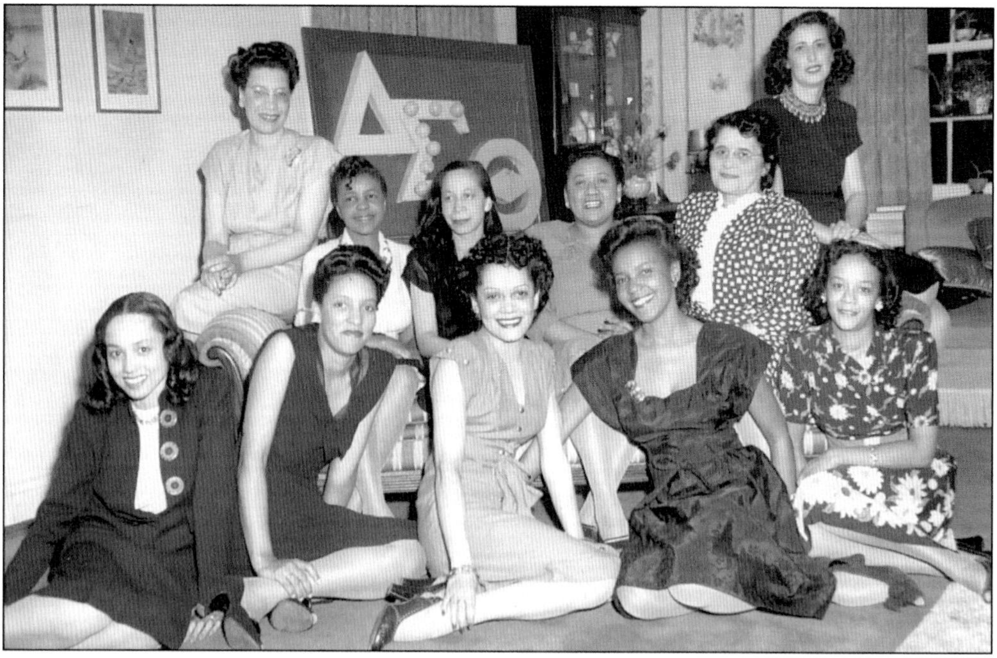

This is a 1950s photo of members of the Delta Sigma Theta Sorority, Inc. (Courtesy of Andre D. Vann.)

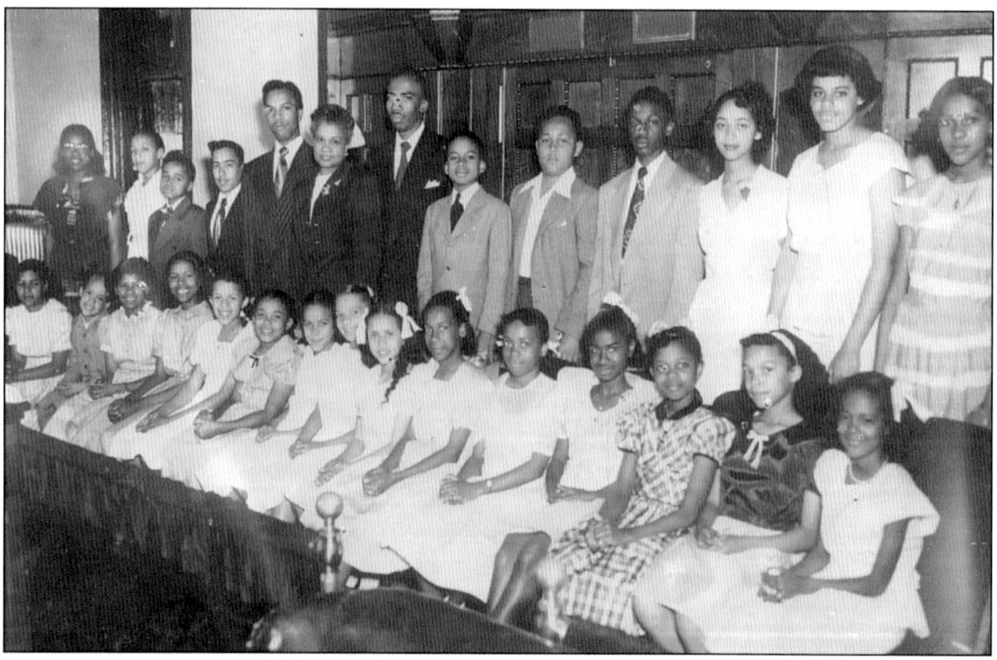

Margaret Spaulding Shearin (1901–1989), visible in the back row, sixth from the left, is pictured here with her students during the Chamberlin Studio Annual Piano recital. Shearin, the daughter of C.C. Spaulding, was a graduate of Scotia Seminary (1919) and attended Fisk University, where she studied music, piano, and composition. On October 5, 1925, Shearin founded the Chamberlin Studio and taught music continuously from 1925 until the early 1980s. (Courtesy of Andre D. Vann.)

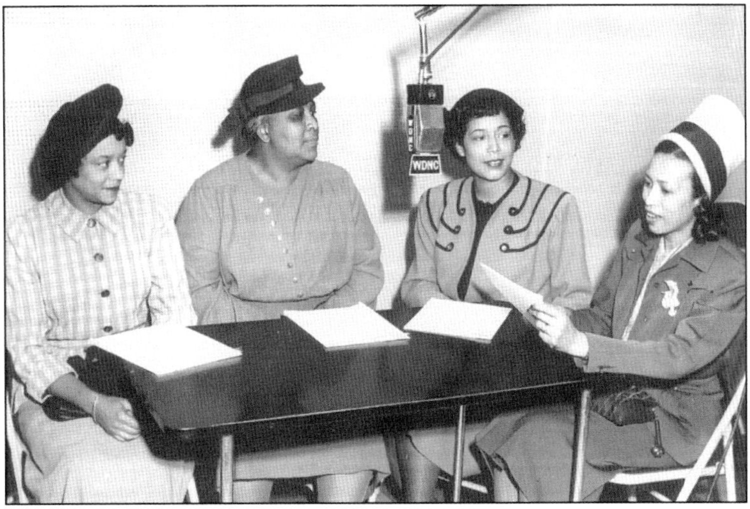

This is an early photo of women discussing issues on WDNC radio station. They are, from left to right, as follows: Dorothy Shepard Manley, Ora Sneed Lee, Josephine Dobbs Clement, and Ray Nichols Moore. (Courtesy of Beverly W. Jones.)

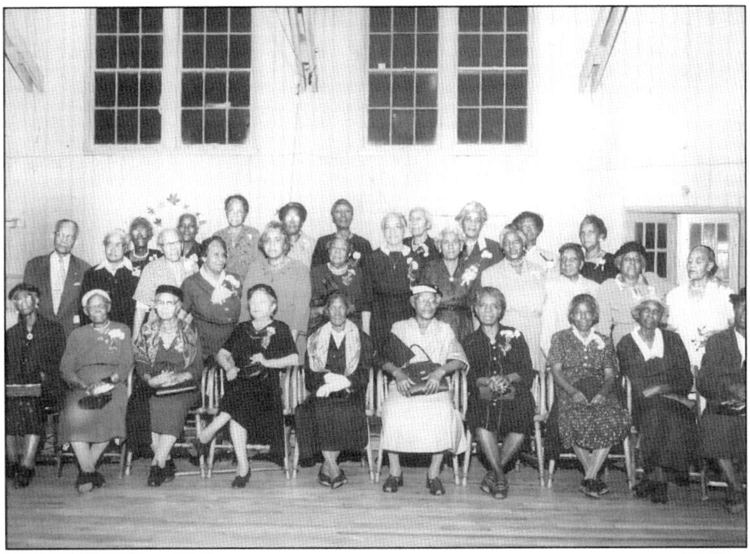

This is a 1950s photo of missionaries at the USO prior to the building of the present W.D. Hill Center on Fayetteville Street. (Courtesy of Andre D. Vann.)

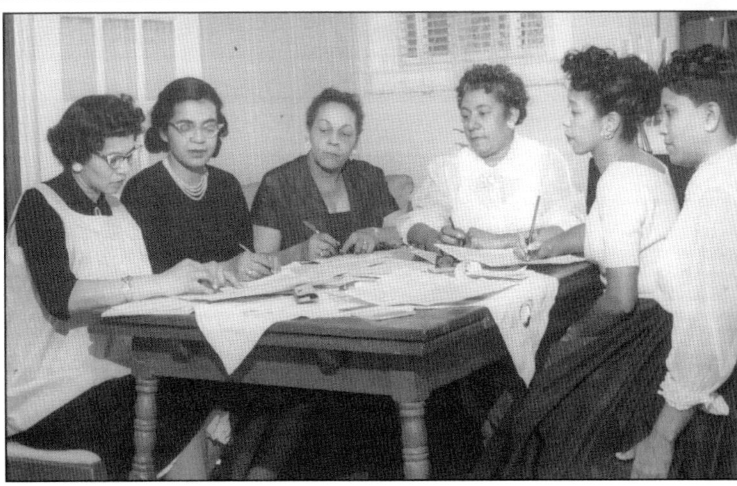

In this 1957 photo, Jack and Jill members prepare for the annual Mothers March on Polio. Jack and Jill provides educational, cultural, civic, and social programs for middle-class minority youth. (Courtesy of Andre D. Vann.)

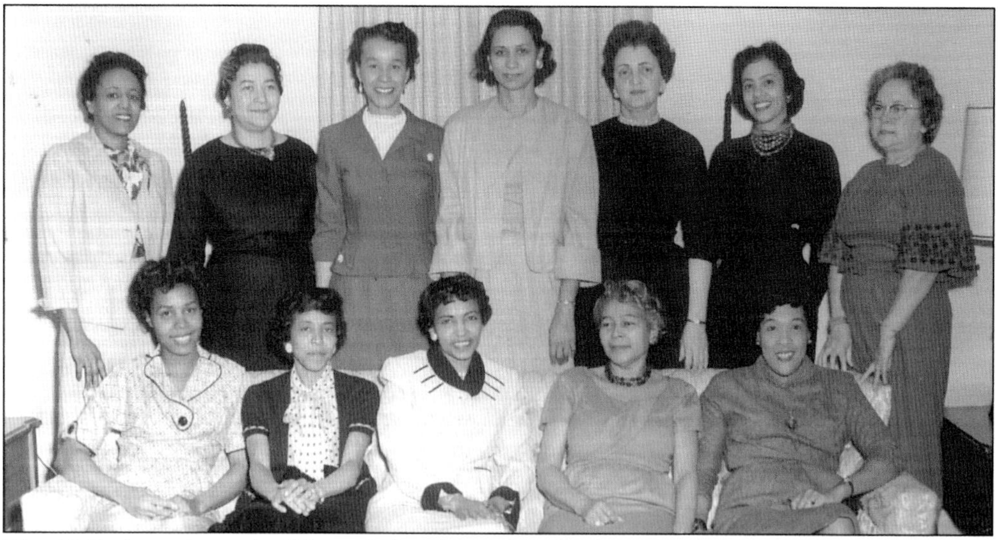

This 1962 photo shows the Women's Auxiliary of the Durham Academy of Medicine, Dentistry, and Pharmacy at the home of Dorthy Campbell. The women provided financial resources to various causes and volunteered in the Durham community. They are, from left to right, as follows: (seated) Dorthy Campbell, Thelma Bass, Ophelia Grandy, Al Thompson, and Barbara Cooke; (standing) Nelloise Watkins, Emma Randolph, Gloria Hubbard, Emma King, Stella Cleland, Constance Watts, and Julia Garret. (Courtesy of Andre D. Vann.)

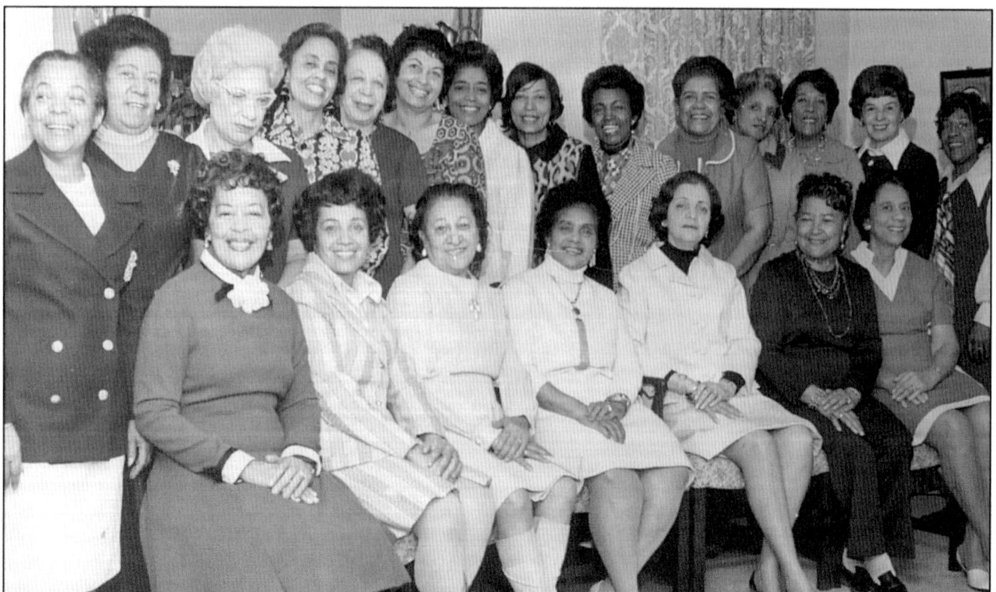

The Links, Inc. was formed in 1946 as a national, public service, non-partisan, volunteer organization with controlled membership. The Durham Chapter of the Links, Inc. was established on October 11, 1958. The founders included Josephine Clement, Barbara Cooke, Julia Dawson, Helen Edmonds, Rebecca Edmonds, Ophelia Grandy, Mollie Lee, Lola Riddick, Hazel Rivera, Fannie Robinson, Mae Spaulding, Otelia Stewart, Dessa Turner, Constance Watts, Selena Wheeler, and Frances Eagleson. This is a 1970 photo of the current members of the local chapter. (Courtesy of Andre D. Vann.)

Three

CHURCH: RELIGIOUS UPLIFT

In all my traveling I have never seen a finer Negro church than St. Joseph.

—Booker T. Washington referring to St. Joseph's A.M.E. Church
while visiting Durham's Hayti community in 1910.

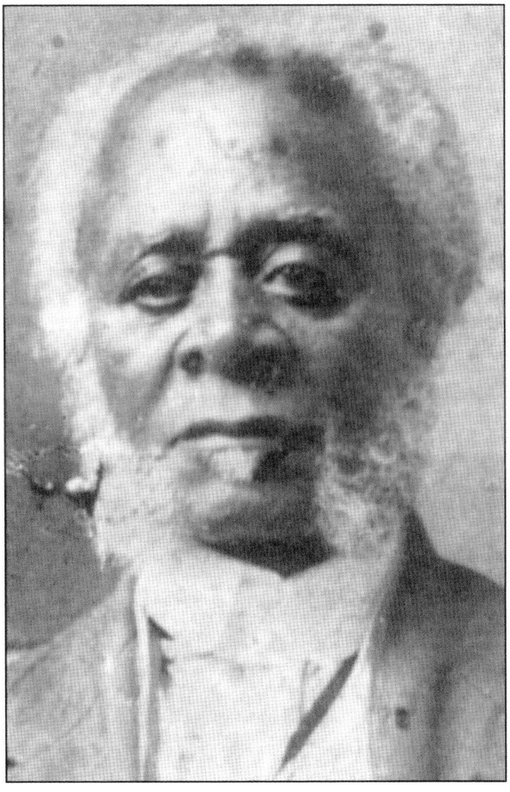

This is an early 1900s photo of Reverend Edian D. Markham (1824–1910), founder and first pastor of Bethel A.M.E. Church in the Hayti District. The church's name was later changed in 1891 to the St. Joseph's A.M.E. Markham, who was born in Elizabeth City to slave parents and was sold off to owners in Ohio, ran away from Ohio using the Underground Railroad into Canada, from there to New York, where he was called into the ministry to do missionary work. He came to Durham in 1868, purchased land, and built a log church, which was organized on August 20, 1869, with only six members and an abiding faith in the A.M.E. Church. He is interred in the Geer Street Cemetery. (Courtesy of Andre D. Vann.)

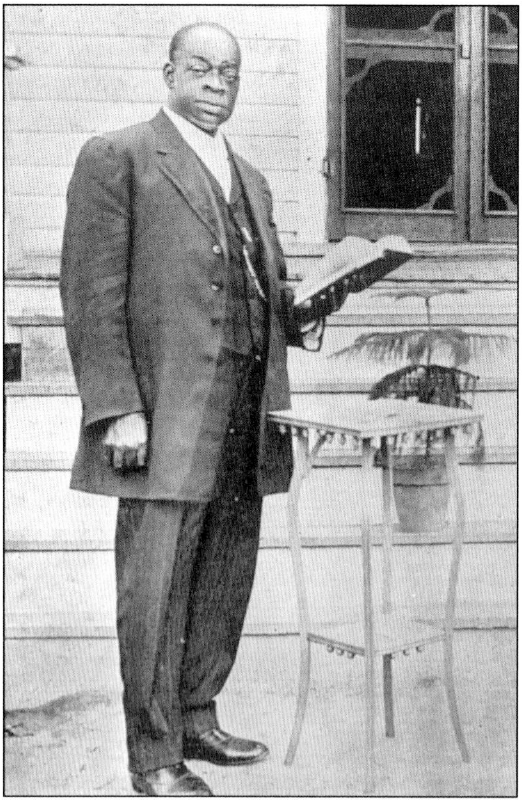

Reverend Dr. Augustus Shepard (1847–1911), a resident of 408 Cozart Avenue, was born in 1846 to slave parents Richard and Flora Shepard in Raleigh. In 1869, he enrolled in Shaw University in Raleigh, and in 1880 graduated from Shaw's Theological Department. Reverend Shepard was appointed general Sunday school missionary and colporteur for North Carolina by the American Baptist Publication Society of Philadelphia, Pennsylvania. He served as the first president of the North Carolina Baptist State Sunday School Convention and is noted as the founder of the Colored Orphan Asylum, in Oxford, North Carolina. Shepard served as pastor of White Rock Baptist Church from 1890 until his death in 1911. He was married to Harriet Shepard and was the father of 12 children that included Drs. James and Charles Shepard. He is interred in Beechwood Cemetery. (Courtesy of North Carolina Collection, University of North Carolina Library at Chapel Hill.)

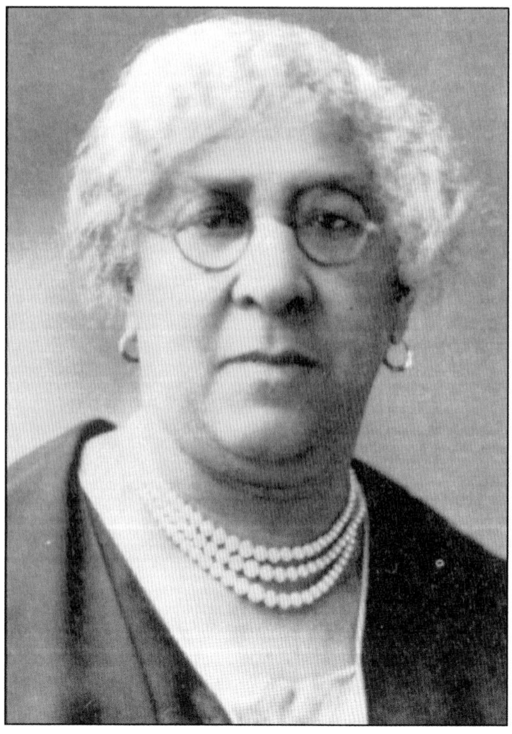

Seen here in 1940, Hattie Whitted Shepard (1858–1947) was born in Hillsborough, North Carolina, on April 12, 1858, one of the daughters of Austin Annie Whitted. She received her early training at Hampton Institute, Hampton, Virginia. She married the late Dr. Augustus Shepard and was the mother of 12 children. She aided her husband, who was pastor of the White Rock Baptist Church, where she organized the Missionary Circle and taught a Bible class. Shepard was the president of the Women's Home & Foreign Missionary Society of North Carolina from 1930 to 1933. She is interred in the Beechwood Cemetery. (Courtesy of Andre D. Vann.)

Shown here in 1920, Reverend Dr. Edward McKnight Brawley (1851–1923) served as pastor of White Rock Baptist Church from 1913 to 1919. He was an 1875 graduate of Bucknell University, where he was the first black student, and received his M.A. from the same university in 1878 and received an honorary Doctor of Divinity degree from State University in Louisville, Kentucky, in 1885. Brawley served as the president of Selma University (Alabama) and Morris College (South Carolina), which he helped to found. The last three years of his life were spent on the faculty of Shaw University (Raleigh), where he was a noted author and a professor of Old Testament history and evangelism. He was the father of noted scholar and author Dr. Benjamin Brawley. (Courtesy of Andre D. Vann.)

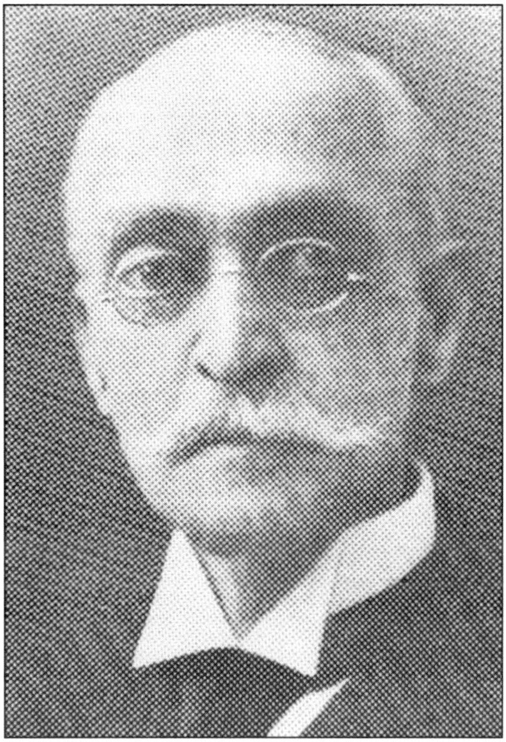

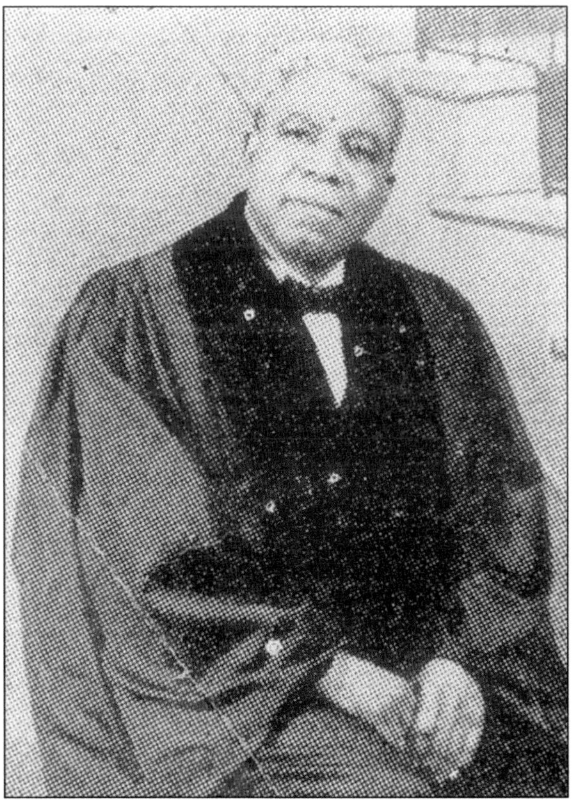

Bishop Henry Lee Fisher (1874–1947), in this 1940s photo, served as the senior bishop of the General Church; the president of the Southern Convocation, West Virginia District Convocation, Bermuda Island District, and Pacific Coast District Convocations; chairman of the General Executive Board of Missions; and president of the National Board of Foreign Missions. He attended Barber Scotia College (Concord, North Carolina) and was a graduate of Iowa Christian College (Oskaloosa, Iowa). Bishop Fisher was married and was the father of 14 children. He was considered a pioneer in the growth of the United Holy Church of America, Inc. The Fisher Memorial Holy Church of America is named in his honor in Durham. (Courtesy of Andre D. Vann.)

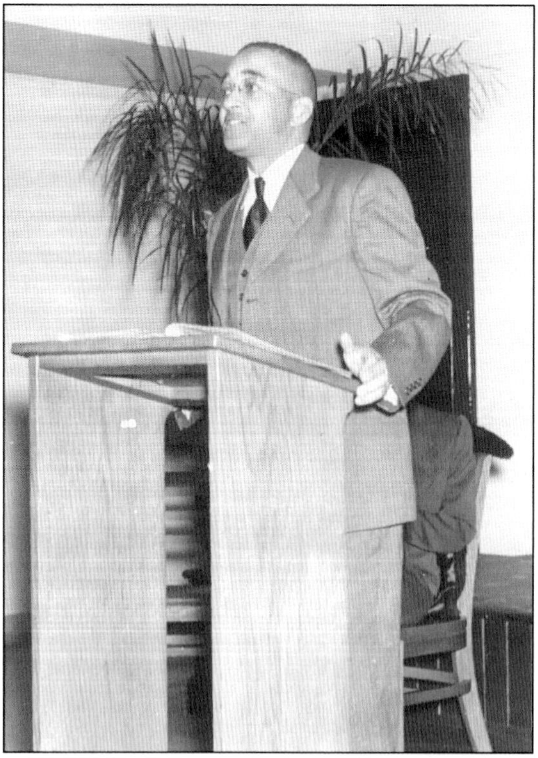

This is a 1950s photo of Reverend Harold Roland, pastor of Mount Gilead Baptist Church. He also wrote a weekly column entitled "Spiritual Insight" in the *Carolina Times*, a black weekly newspaper in Hayti. (Courtesy of Beverly Washington Jones.)

This is a 1940s photo of the Miles Mark Fisher (1899–1970) and Ada V. Foster Fisher (1909–1981) family taken at the White Rock Baptist Church parsonage at 1219 Fayetteville Street. Fisher was a pastor at White Rock from 1933 to 1965. They are, from left to right, as follows: (front row) Elijah J. III, Ada V. Fisher, Dr. Miles M. Fisher, and Alfred Fisher; (back row) Florida and Miles Mark IV. Fisher was a nationally recognized historian of the black church and an author, clergyman, and humanitarian who touched countless generations in Durham. (Courtesy of Andre D. Vann.)

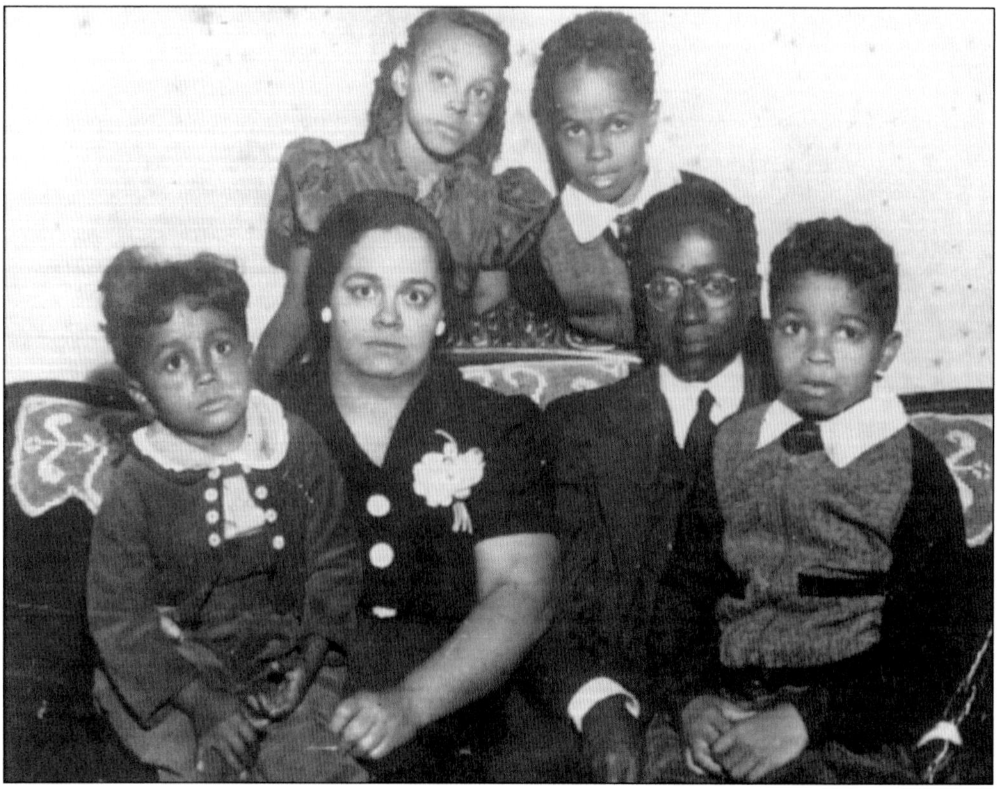

This photo captures a family shot of Reverend Dr. Emmett T. Browne and Dr. Rose Butler Browne and son Emmett T. Browne, Jr., who came to Durham in 1948. Reverend Browne served as pastor of Mount Vernon Baptist Church from 1948 until 1972, and Dr. Rose Browne taught and was chair of the department of education at North Carolina College at Durham from 1948 until 1963. In 1939 she became the first black woman to earn a doctorate in education from Harvard University and was the author of *Love My Children*, published in 1969 as her autobiography. (Courtesy of Andre D. Vann.)

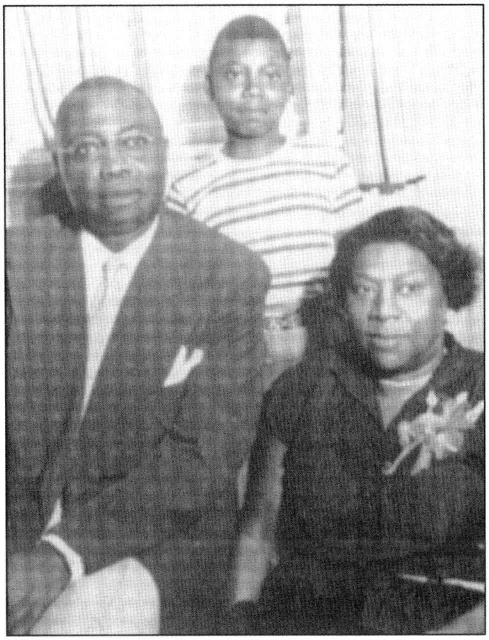

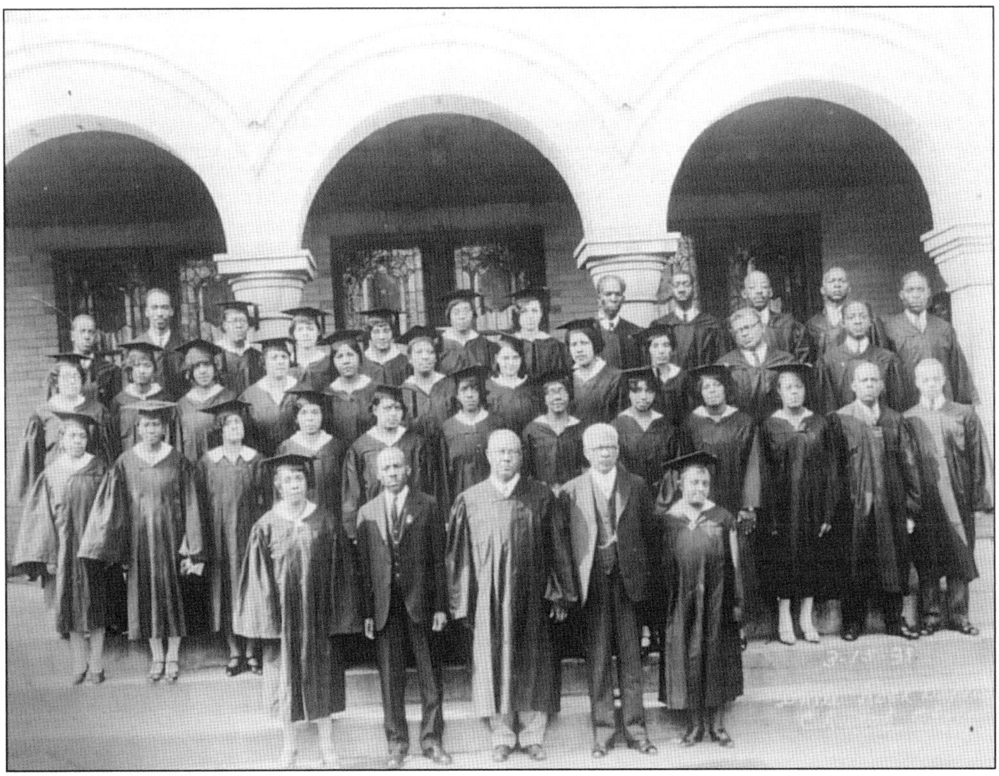

The White Rock Baptist Church Choir, featured in this 1931 photo, was taken in front of the main entrance to the church. In the front is, from left to right, the following: Susie V. Norfleet; Dr. William L. Ranson, pastor 1931–1932; Deacon Allen L. Goodloe; Deacon Charles C. Spaulding Sr.; and Hattie Livas. (Courtesy of Maggie Bryant / Andre D. Vann.)

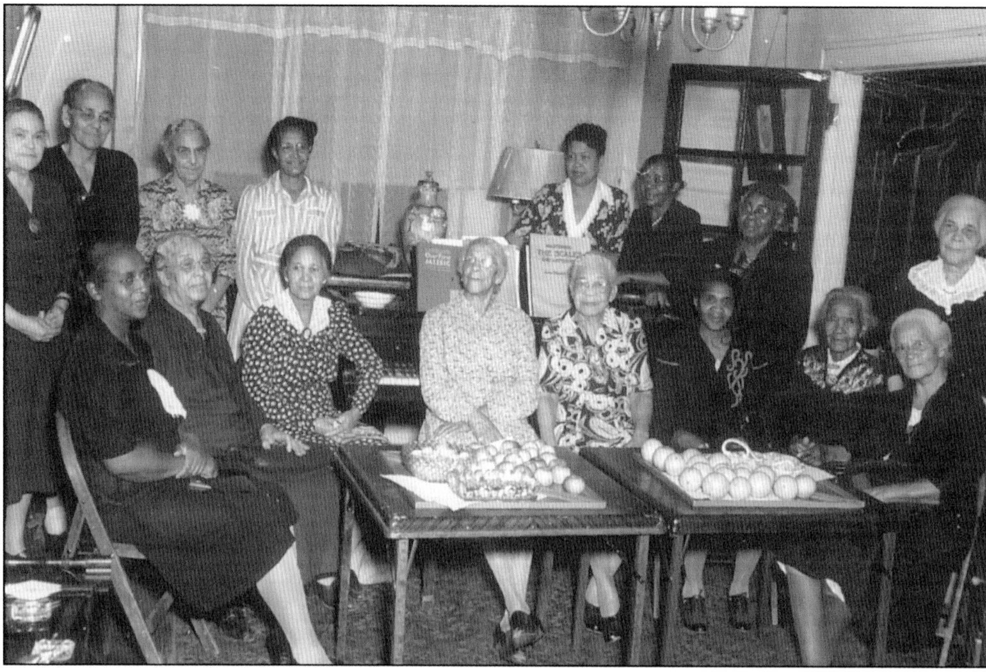

This is a 1943 gathering of the White Rock Baptist Church Missionary Circle at the home of Grizelle Hubbard at 612 Dupree Street. Members present were, from left to right, as follows: (seated) Mamie Weaver, Tempie Whitted, Ora Reynolds, Hattie Shepard, Emma Russell, Minnie Lyon, Belle Logan, and Mary Wyatt; (standing) Hallie White, Louvenia Eaton, Maggie Smith, Rochie Brown, Grizelle Hubbard, Martha Williams, and visitors Flossie Dunston and Carrie Austin. (Courtesy of Andre D. Vann.)

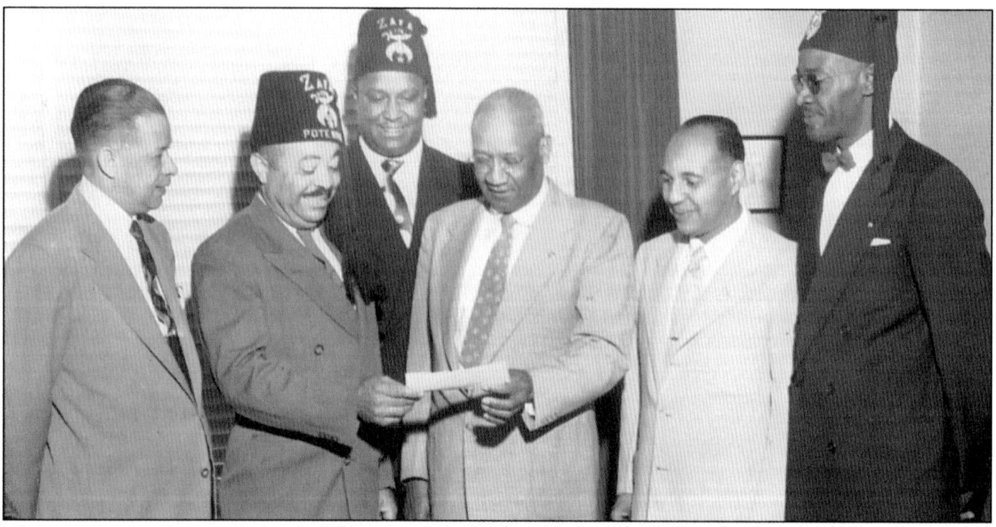

This is a 1950 photograph of Zafa Temple Potentate Frank Burnette, second from the left, and an unidentified member presenting a financial contribution to John Avery's Boys Club board member William J. Kennedy Jr., North Carolina Mutual executive. They are, from left to right, as follows: John Wheeler, president of Mechanics and Farmers Bank; Burnette; unidentified; Kennedy; John S. Stewart, president of Mutual Savings and Loan; and Lee Smith, director of John Avery's Boys Club. (Courtesy of James Stewart / Andre D. Vann.)

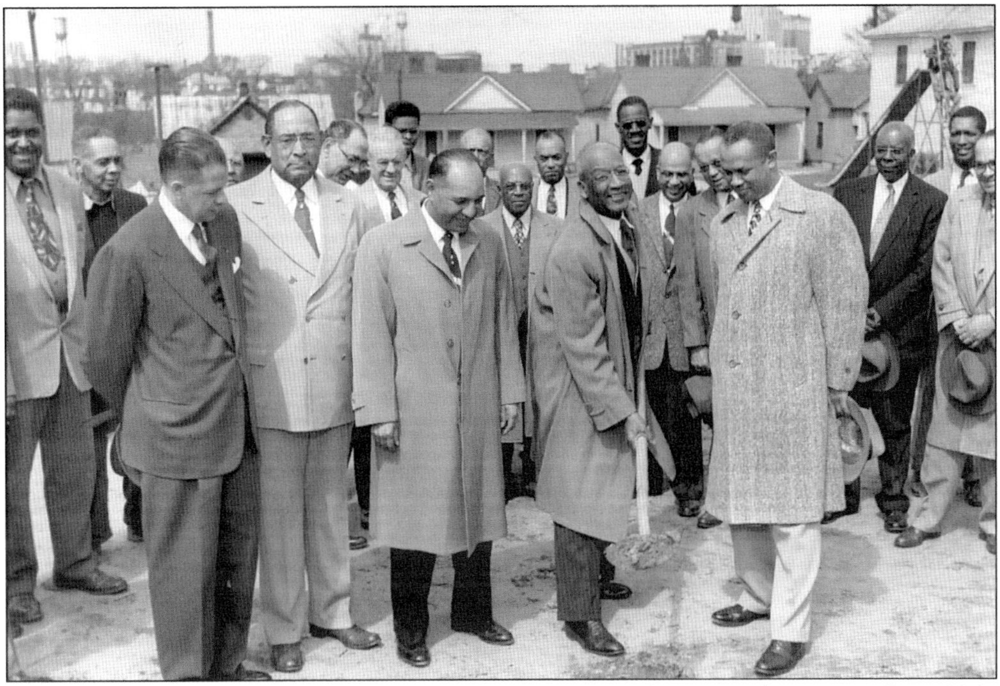

This is a 1955 photo of the ground-breaking ceremony for the new John Avery's Boys Club, which was organized in 1939. They are, from left to right, as follows: John H. Wheeler, Reverend Dr. Charles McLester, John Stewart, William J. Kennedy, and James J. "Babe" Henderson. (Courtesy of Andre D. Vann.)

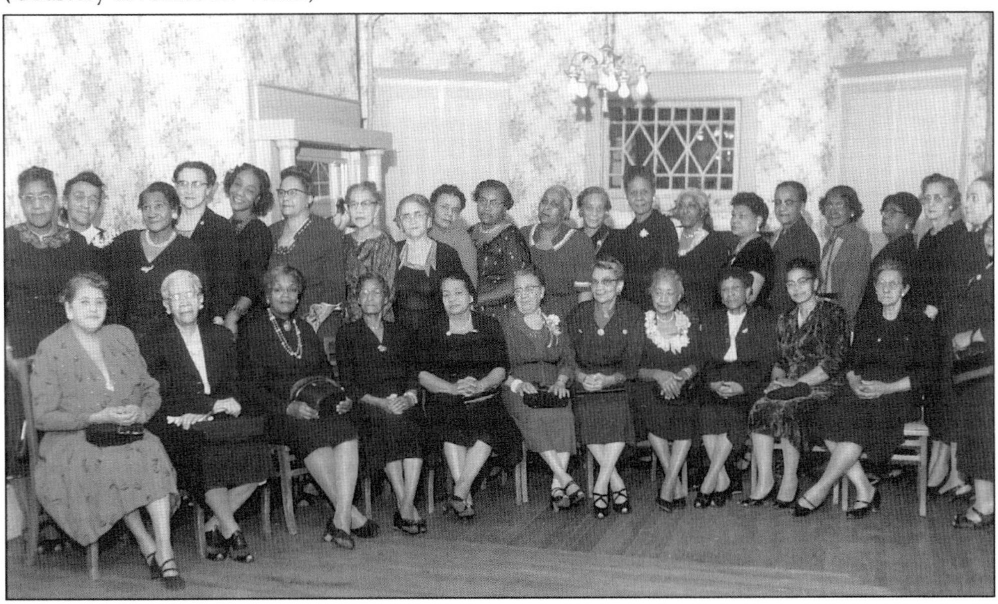

This is a 1951 photo of the Daughters of Dorcas Club, which was organized in 1917 by Matilda Townsend, Sarah Felder, Ada Leach, Bessie Doby, Lillian Thompson, Bessie Pratt, and Maggie Lennon. The club was formerly called the Busy Woman's Club and was organized at the home of Janie Spaulding at 509 Fayetteville Street. The club fostered various philanthropic endeavors in the Hayti community. (Courtesy of Viola Pindle / Andre D. Vann.)

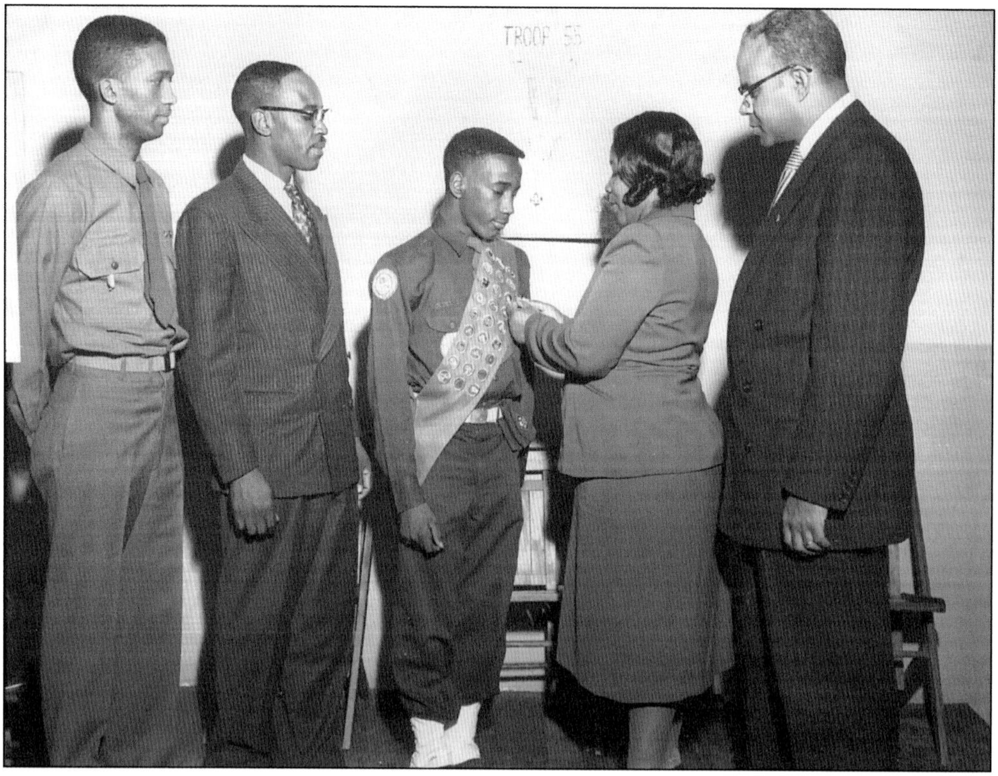

This 1953 photo shows members of Troop 55 at the White Rock Baptist Church. Scouting began under the leadership of Reverend Miles Mark Fisher in the early 1930s. (Courtesy of Andre D. Vann.)

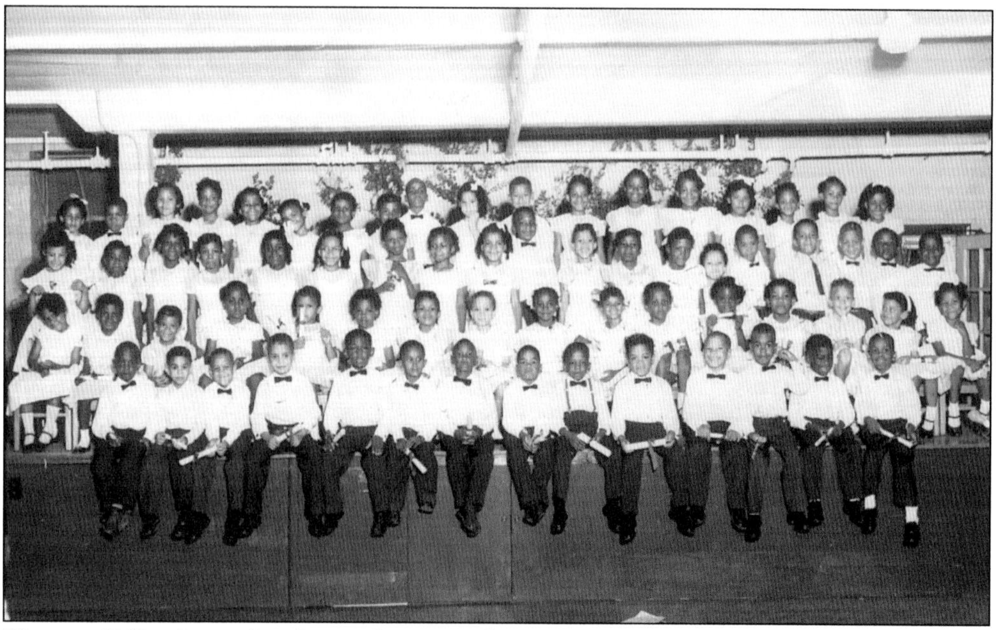

This is a 1950s photo of students taking a graduation picture with diplomas as they graduated from the St. Joseph's A.M.E. Church Day Care Center. (Courtesy of Andre D. Vann.)

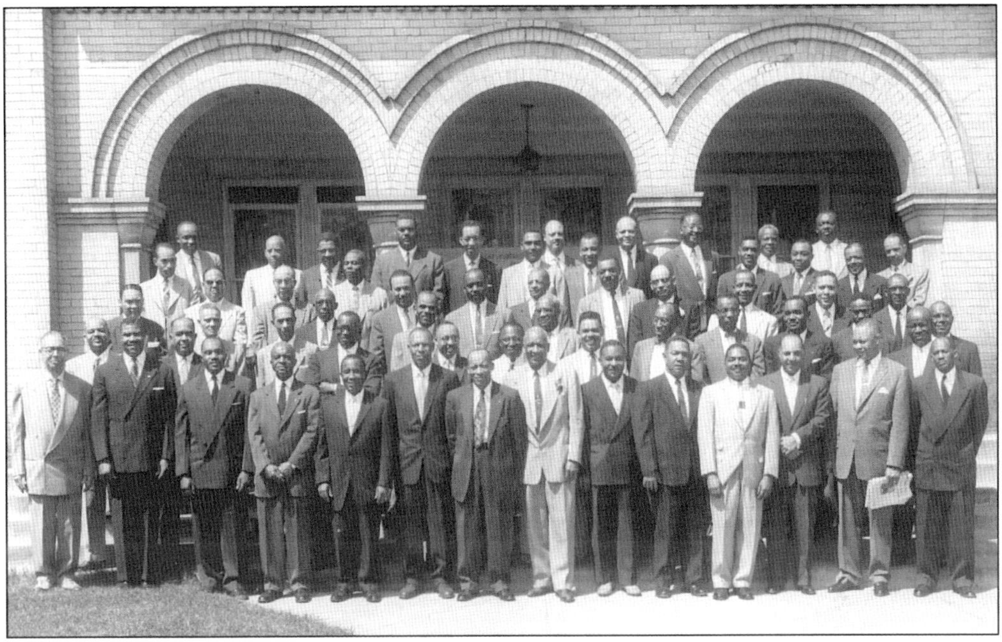

In 1957 members of the Aaron M. Moore Bible class pose on Easter Sunday on the steps of the White Rock Baptist Church on Easter Sunday. The Moore Bible Class became one of the outstanding church schools in the state and nation from its founding as the Baraca Class in 1910 to the present. The name was later changed to the Moore-Kennedy Bible Class in honor of William J. Kennedy, who served as a teacher of the class from 1920 until 1975. (Courtesy of Andre D. Vann.)

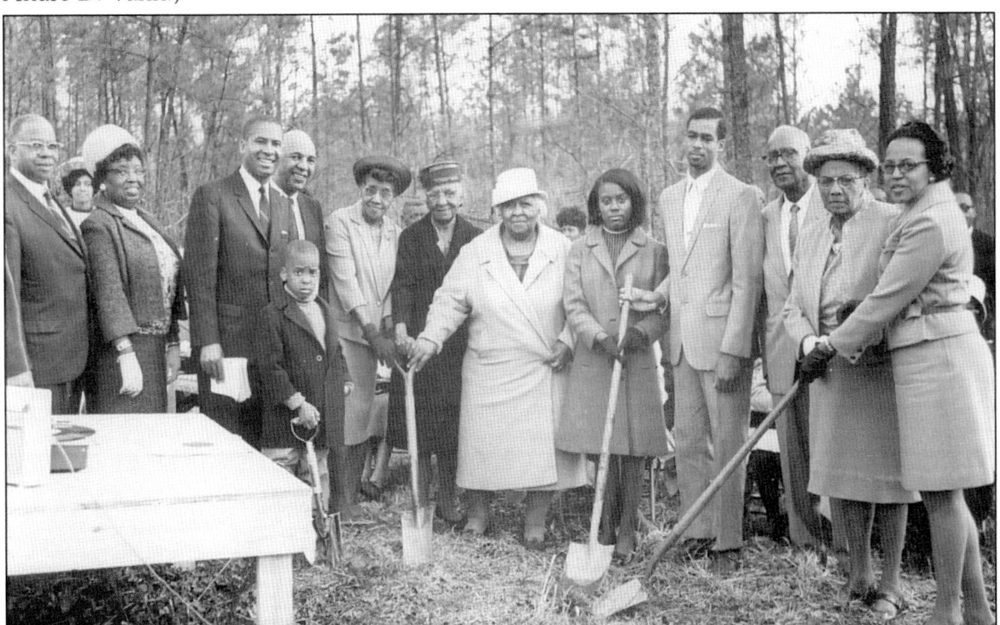

Ground-breaking ceremonies were held on March 30, 1969, for the new White Rock Baptist Church at 3400 Fayetteville Street. In 1971 the congregation moved to its new location after 75 years at the corner of Mobile and Fayetteville Street. (Courtesy of Andre D. Vann.)

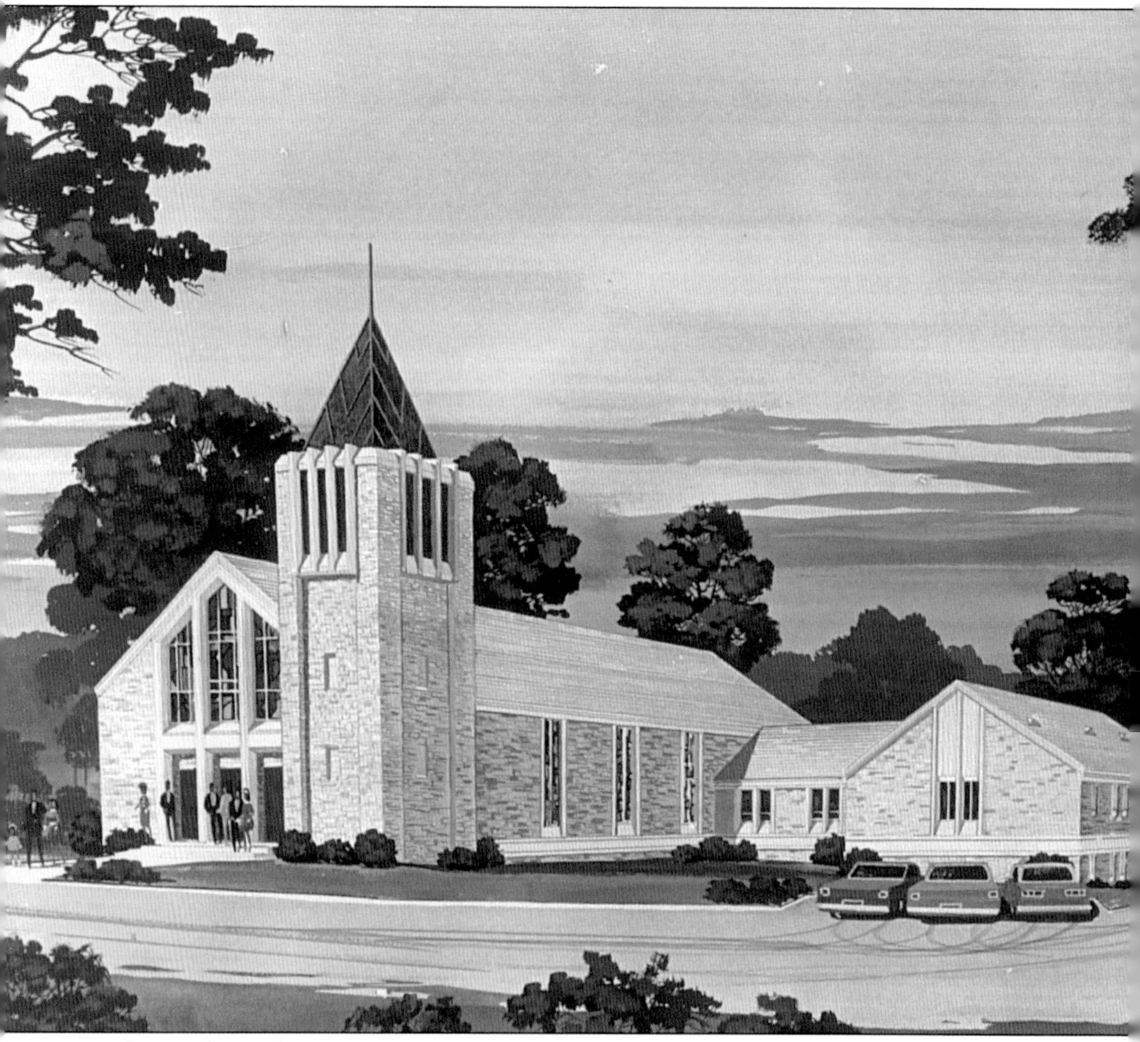

This is the architects rendering of the new White Rock Baptist Church. (Courtesy of Andre D. Vann.)

Four

EDUCATION AND POLITICS

Without doubt, it is an unshirkable duty of every parent to join with existing agencies in the community to see to it that his child shall be provided with the best opportunities for the development of the potentialities with which he is endowed. To do less is a lack of wisdom, and a breach of faith with the future.

—Dr. C. Elwood Bouleware, president of the Durham City P.T.A. Council (black), a professor at North Carolina College, in 1951 at the North Carolina Congress of Colored Parents and Teachers, Inc. meeting at Hillside High School.

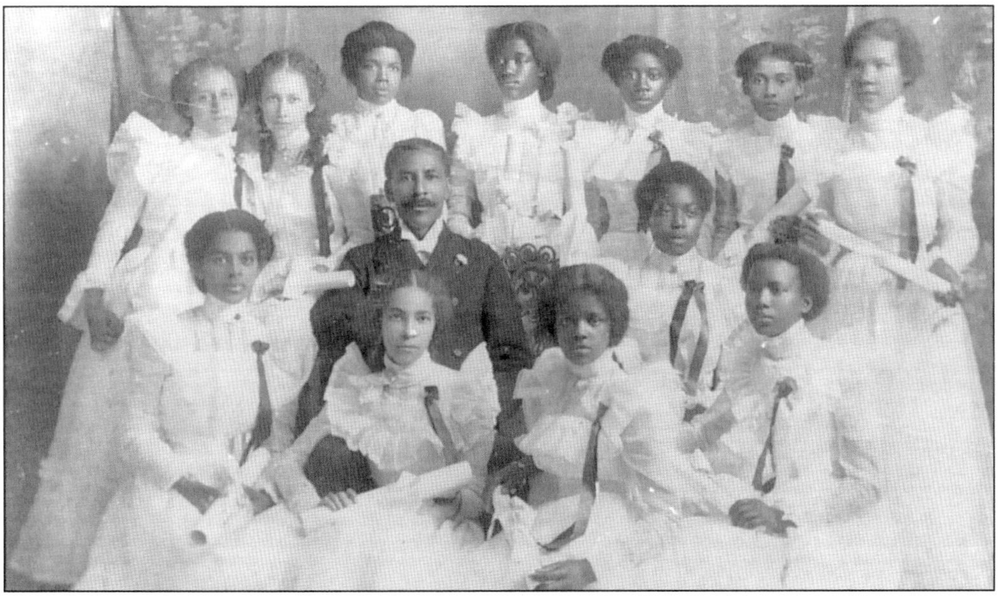

This is a 1900 photo of graduates of the Whitted High School in Durham. Seated in the center is Principal William Gaston "Prof" Pearson (1858–1947) surrounded by his students. Pearson began teaching at the Whitted School in the fall of 1886. He also was the first principal of Hillside High School and served actively in that capacity until 1940, when he became Principal Emeritus. Professor Pearson served unofficially as Durham's "Colored Superintendent"" for over 30 years and was a real estate and business executive. (Courtesy of Andre D. Vann.)

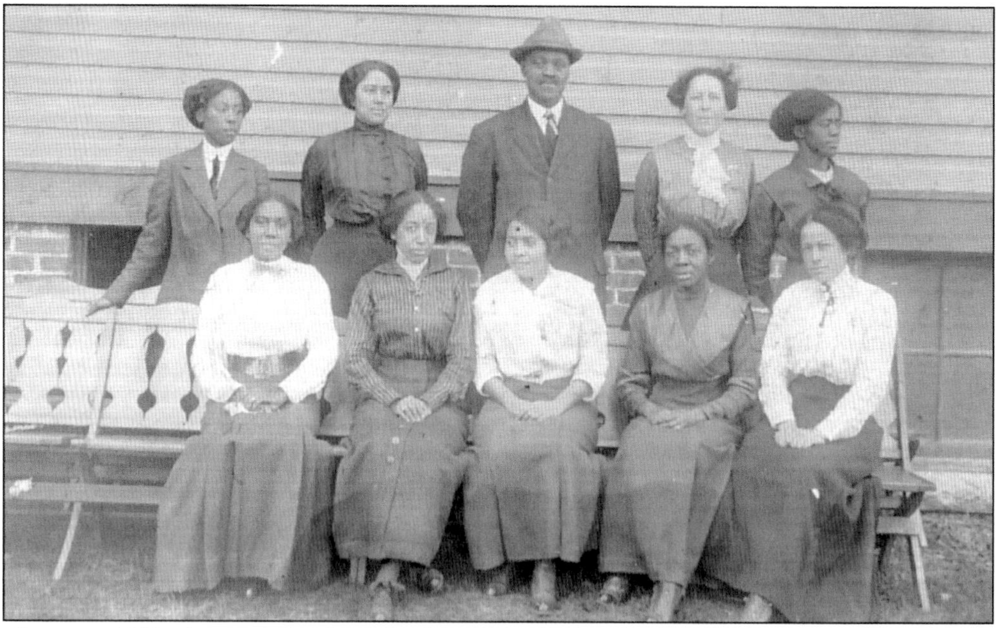

This is a 1909 photo of the faculty of the East End School with Principal P.W. Dawkins (1862–1913) in the center. On the first row, extreme left, is Nannie Faucette Cooper, and on the second row, extreme left, is Maggie Poole Bryant, both longtime residents of Hayti. (Courtesy of Maggie Bryant / Andre D. Vann.)

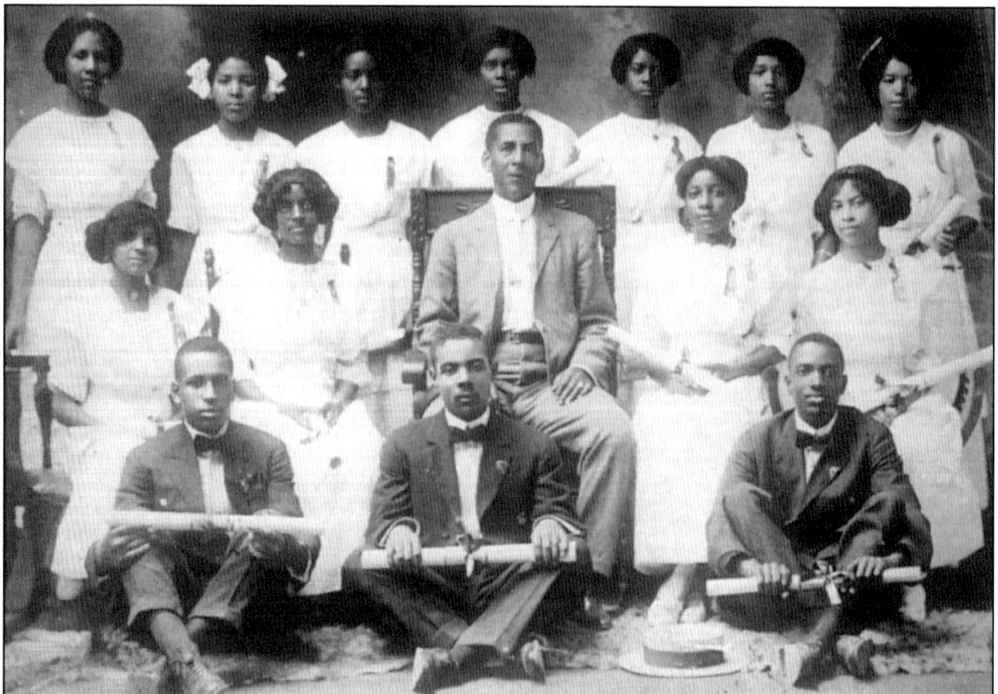

This is a 1913 photo of graduates of the Whitted High School in Hayti. Principal Pearson is surrounded by his students. The W.G. Pearson School was named in his honor for his years of dedication to the educational arena. (Courtesy of Maggie Bryant / Andre D. Vann.)

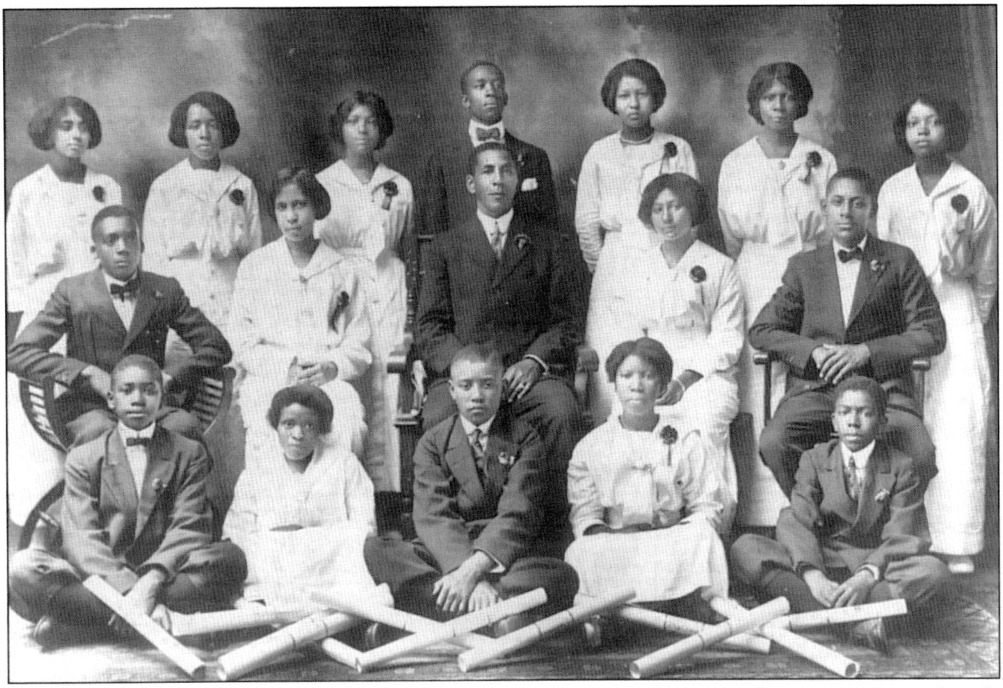

In this 1917 graduation photo, students of Whitted High School students are pictured with Principal Pearson, seated in the center. (Courtesy of Lavinia Parker / Andre D. Vann.)

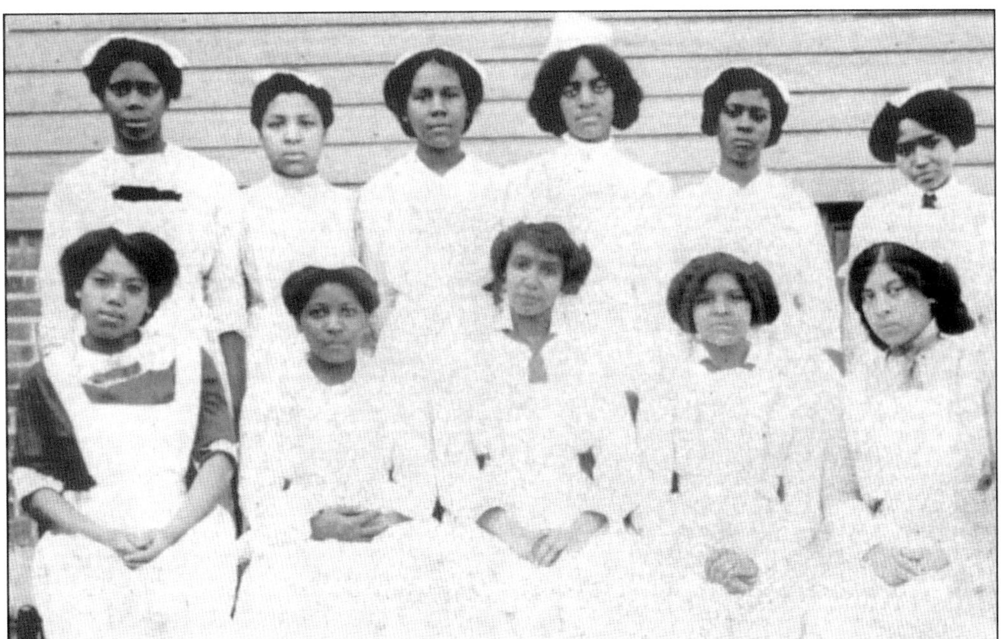

This is a 1915 group photo of female students enrolled at the National Religious Training School at Chautauqua, which was founded in 1910 by Dr. James E. Shepard. The school is now known as North Carolina Central University. (Courtesy of Gazella Lipscomb / Andre D. Vann.)

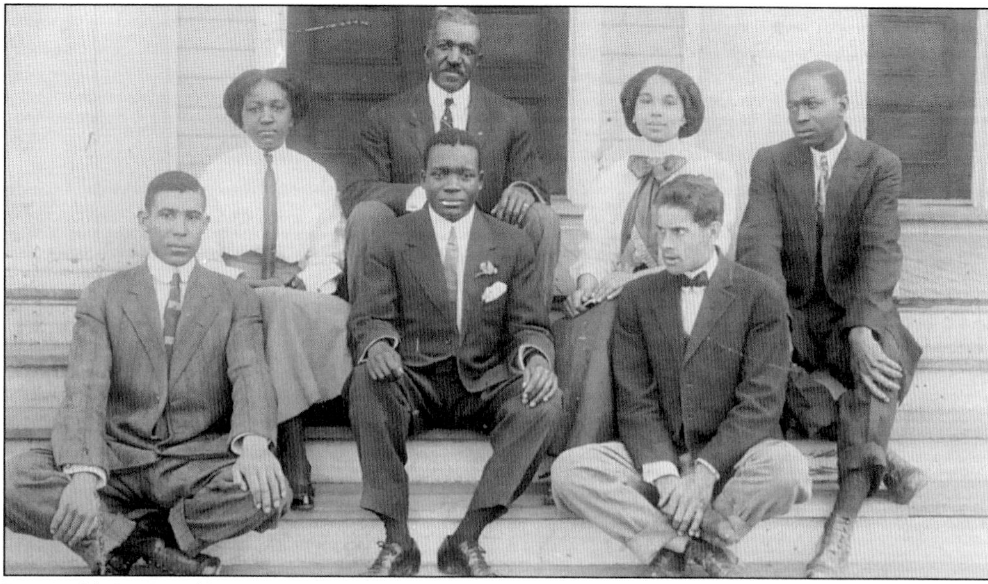

Dr. Cadd G. O'Kelly, center, is surrounded by students on the steps of the Avery Auditorium on the campus of the National Religious Training School at Chautauqua. (Courtesy of Maggie Bryant / Andre D. Vann.)

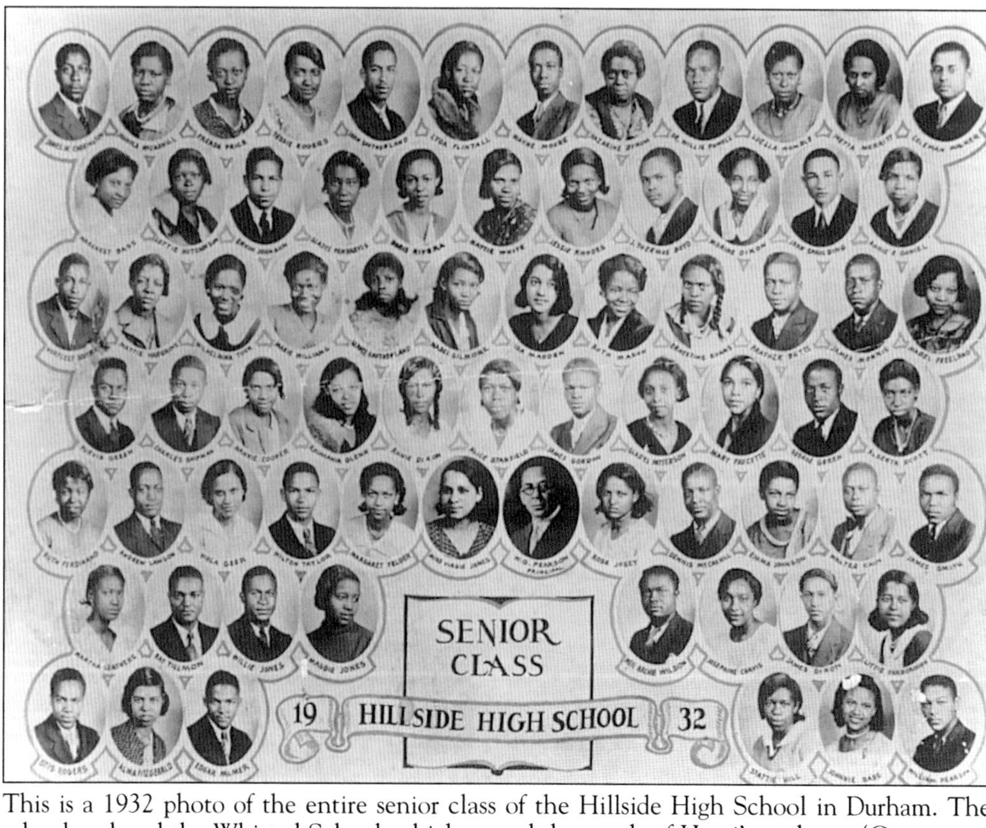

This is a 1932 photo of the entire senior class of the Hillside High School in Durham. The school replaced the Whitted School, which served the needs of Hayti's students. (Courtesy of Ernestine Evans Young / Andre D. Vann.)

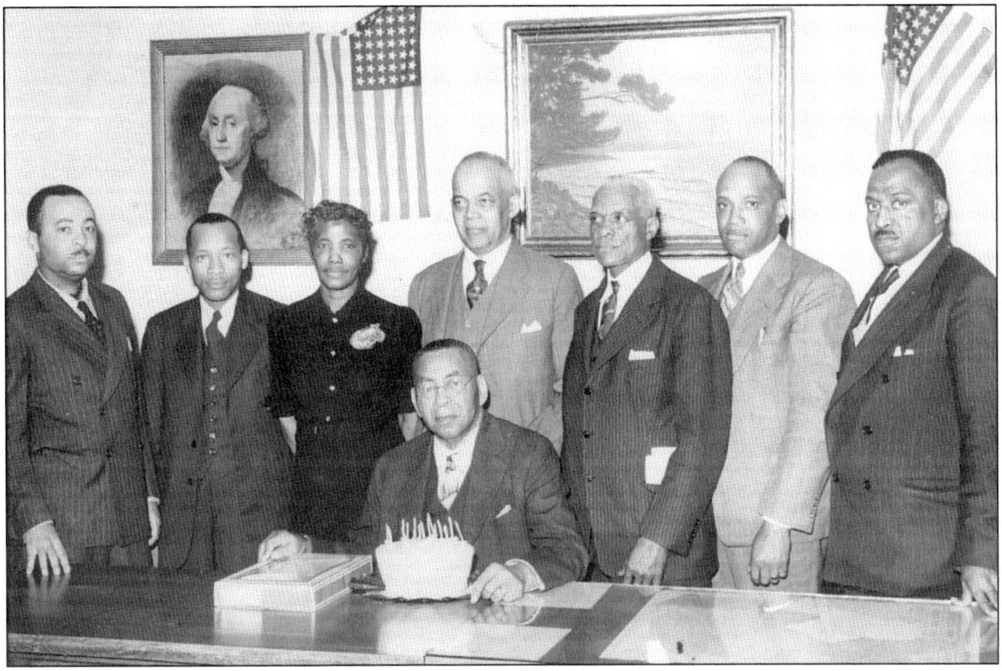

This is a 1940s photo of black principals of Durham. They are, from left to right, as follows: F.G. Burnette, J.M. Schooler, C.T. Russell, J.W. Davidson, unidentified, N.A. Cheek, F.D. Marshall, and Dr. W.G. Pearson (seated). (Courtesy of Andre D. Vann.)

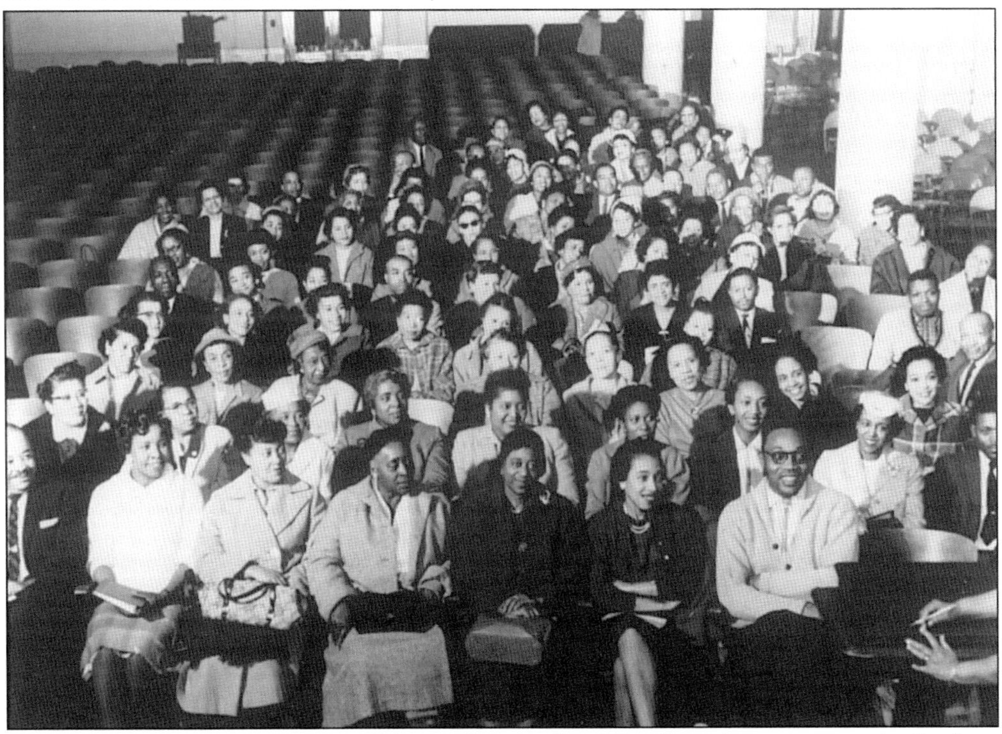

This is a 1951 photo of members of the Durham Colored Teachers Association in the Durham City Schools. (Courtesy of Andolia Eaton / Andre D. Vann.)

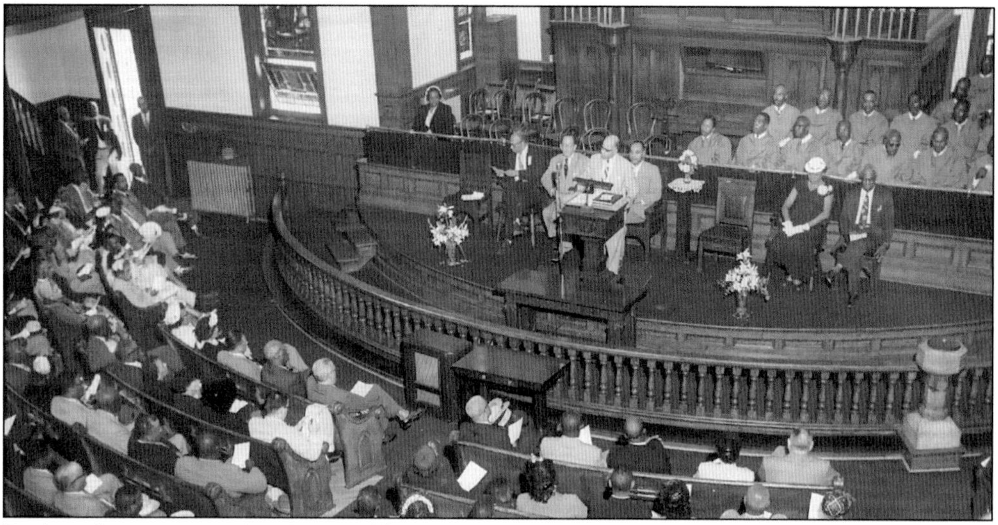

Durham businessman Asa T. Spaulding Sr. is shown addressing the mass meeting at the St. Joseph's A.M.E. Church on May 23, 1954, in the wake of the *Brown vs. Board of Education* decision of Topeka, Kansas, on May 17, 1954. The decision ruled unanimously that racial segregation in public schools was unconstitutional. Other speakers included, from left to right, the following: Louis Austin, editor of the *Carolina Times*; Rencher N. Harris, Durham City Council member; John S. Stewart, chairman of the Durham Committee on the Affairs of Negroes; Dr. Rose Butler Browne, professor at North Carolina College; and Reverend Dr. A.S. Croome. (Courtesy of Andre D. Vann)

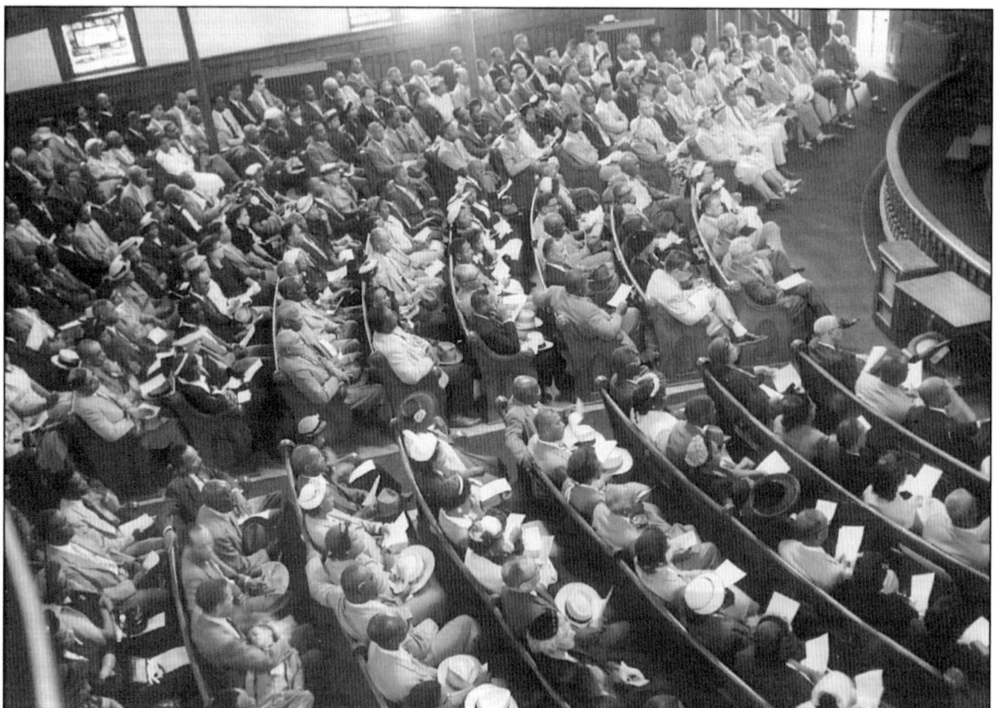

This is a scene from the May 23, 1954 mass meeting held at St. Joseph's A.M.E. Church. (Courtesy of Andre D. Vann.)

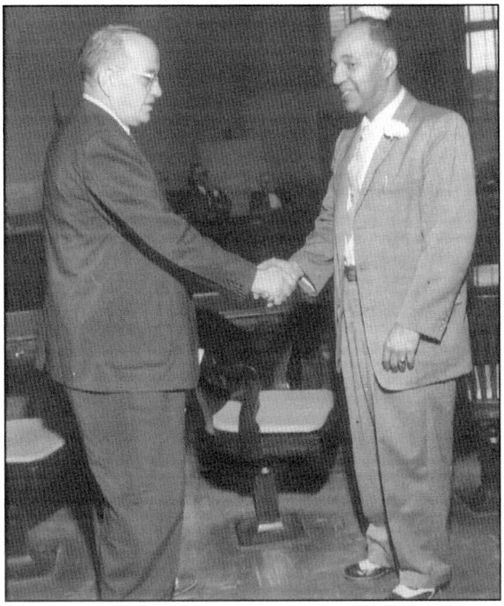

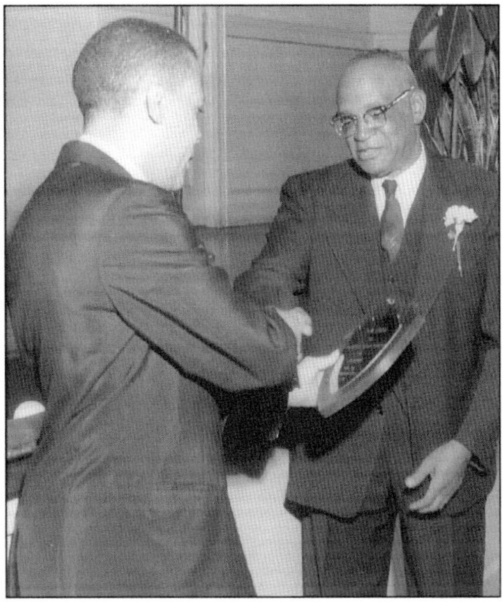

Left: Rencher N. Harris (1900–1965), left, is shown extending congratulations to John S. Stewart (1910–1997), right, who was sworn in as the second black member of the Durham City Council. Stewart served from 1957 until 1973 on the city council. Harris was elected the first black member of the Durham City Council in 1953 and served until 1957 and decided not to run for reelection. In 1958, Harris was appointed by the city council to the board of education, becoming the first black to be appointed to the board of education. (Courtesy of Ellis Allen / Andre D. Vann.)
Right: Nathaniel A. Cheek Jr. (1895–1980) was presented an award upon retirement in 1961 as principal of the W.G. Pearson Elementary School. Cheek began teaching in North Carolina public schools in 1926 and was principal of Pearson Elementary from 1939 until 1961. He was a graduate of Shaw University in Raleigh and Columbia University in New York. (Courtesy of Andre D. Vann.)

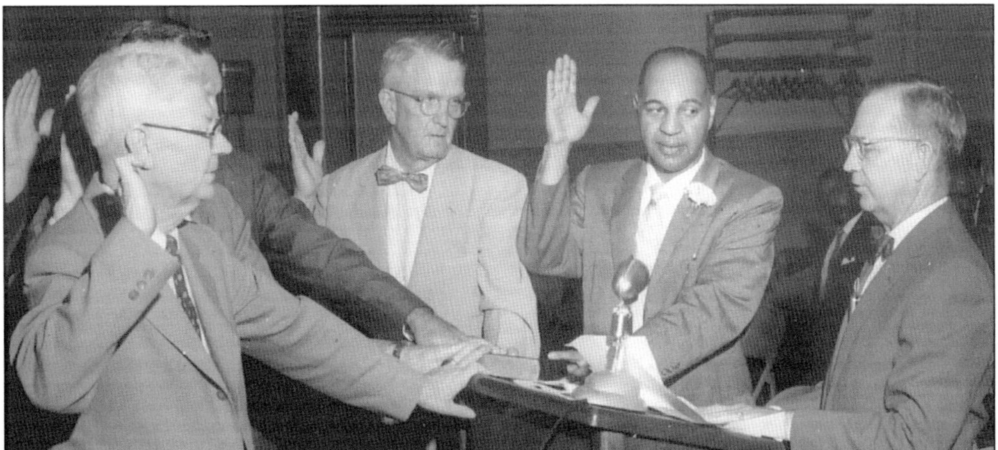

On May 20, 1957, John S. Stewart (1910–1995), second from the right, takes the oath of office as the second black elected member of the city council. He also was president of Mutual Savings and Loan Association and had previously served as chairman of the Durham Committee on the Affairs of Black People from 1943 until 1957. (Courtesy of Ellis Allen / Andre D. Vann.)

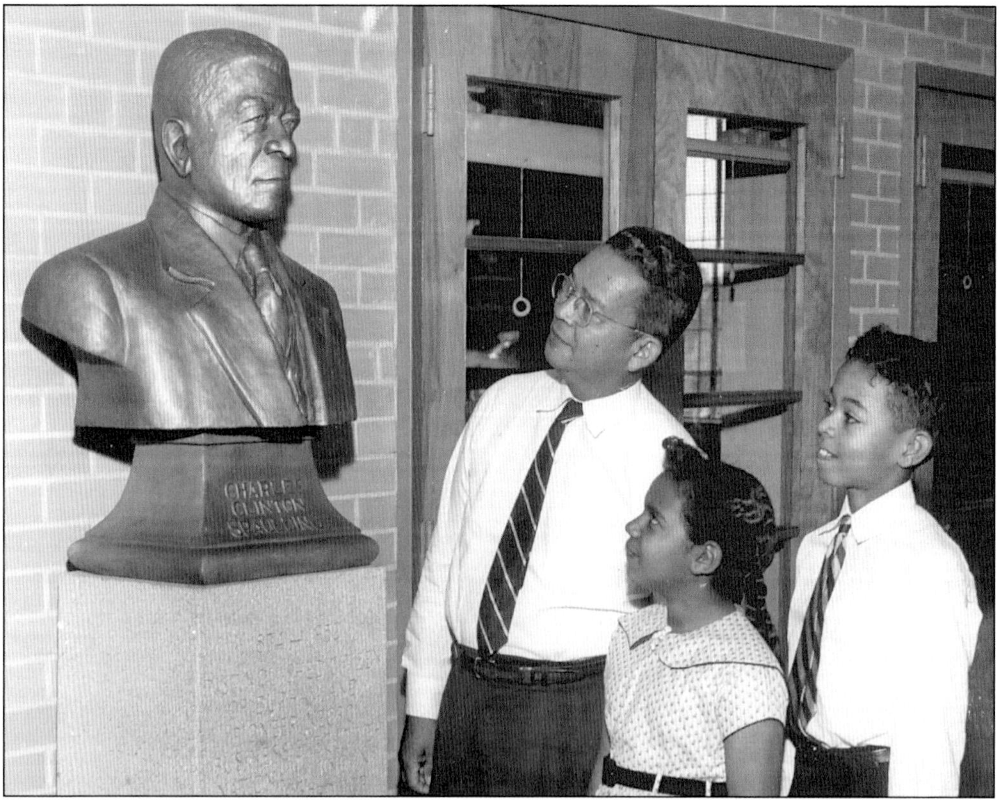

Principal L.E. Davis, first principal of the C.C. Spaulding Elementary School, with Janetta Stewart and James Turner admire the bust of C.C. Spaulding that adorns the hallway of the school. (Courtesy of *Herald Sun*.)

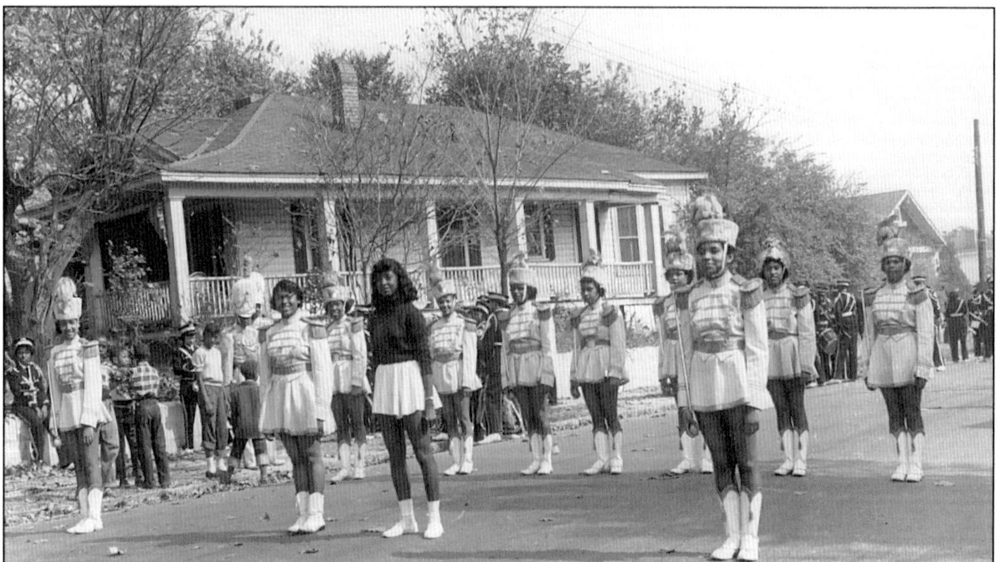

Hillside High School students perform for residents on Fayetteville Street. (Courtesy of Andre D. Vann.)

Five

How Hayti Lived and Played

Hayti has served as the economic, cultural, civic, and political backbone of the New South.

—Andre D. Vann, in an address at the Durham County Public Library in 1999.

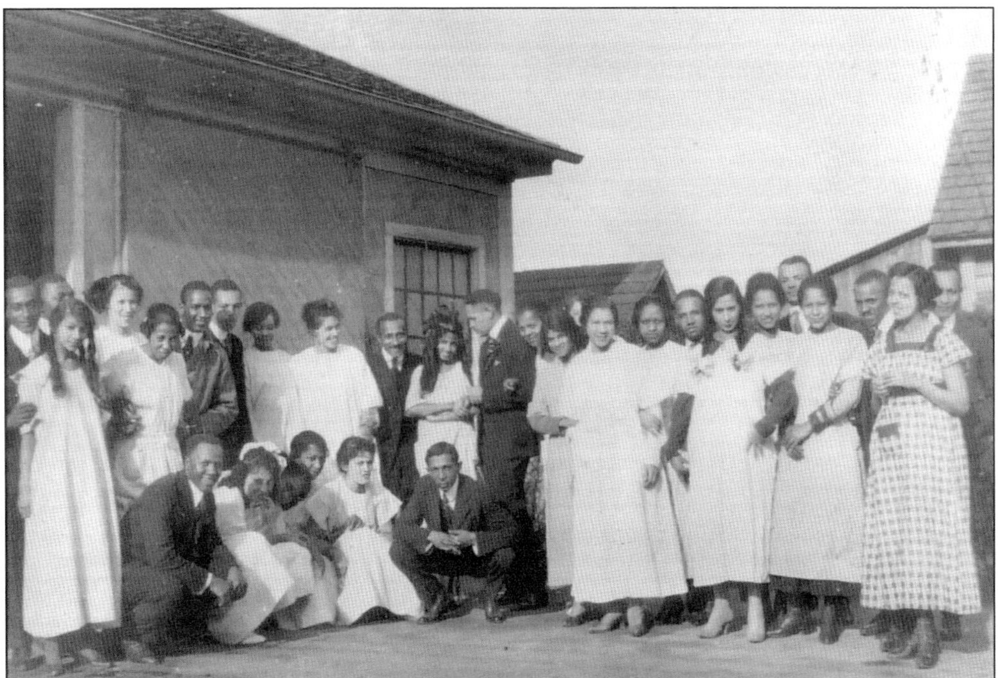

Clyde Donnell and Martha Merrick, daughter of John and Martha Merrick, were married on December 10, 1899. Here friends and family members surrounded the couple. (Courtesy of Andre D. Vann.)

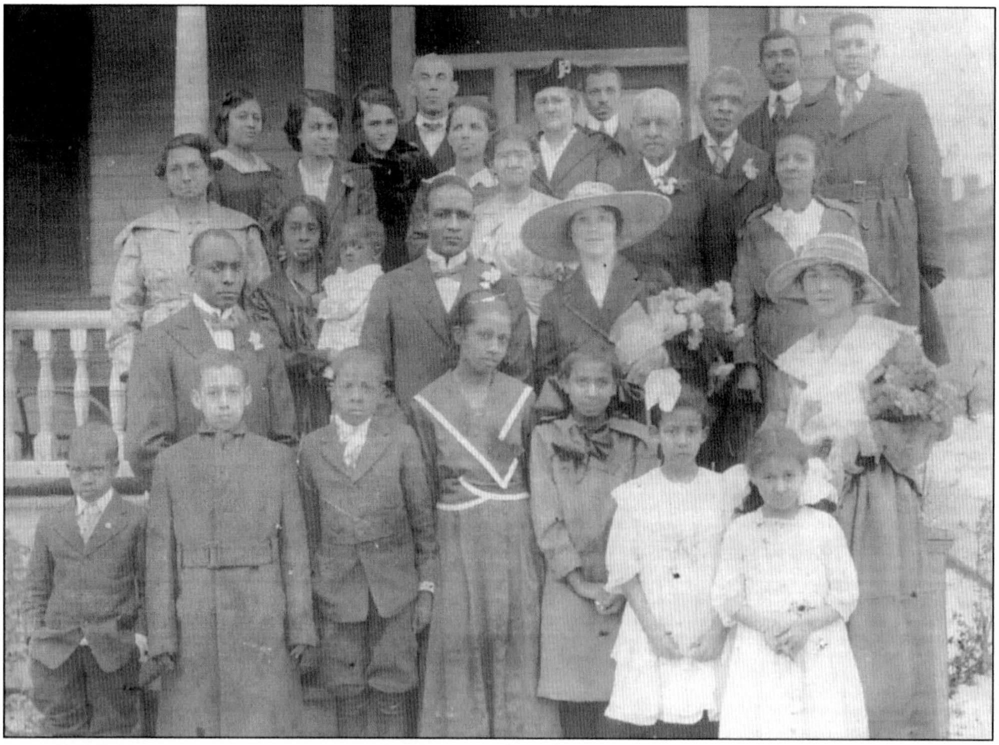

This photograph was taken on December 27, 1917, on the steps of Charles C. Spaulding's house at 1006 Fayetteville Street. The occasion was the marriage of North Carolina Mutual Life Insurance Executive William J. Kennedy Jr. and Margaret Lillian Spaulding, sister of C.C. Spaulding. The couple is in the center surrounded by family members. (Courtesy of Andre D. Vann.)

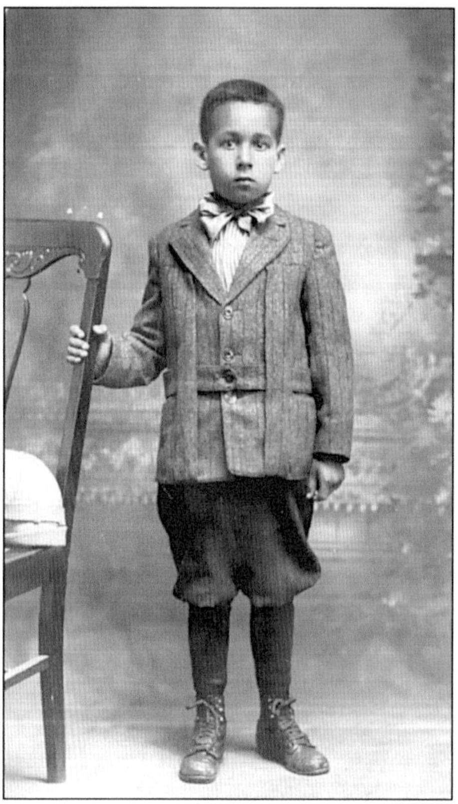

This is an early photo of Lemuel Alonzo Spaulding (1904–1955), son of Alonzo Gaston and Janie Marie Spaulding. (Courtesy of James Stewart.)

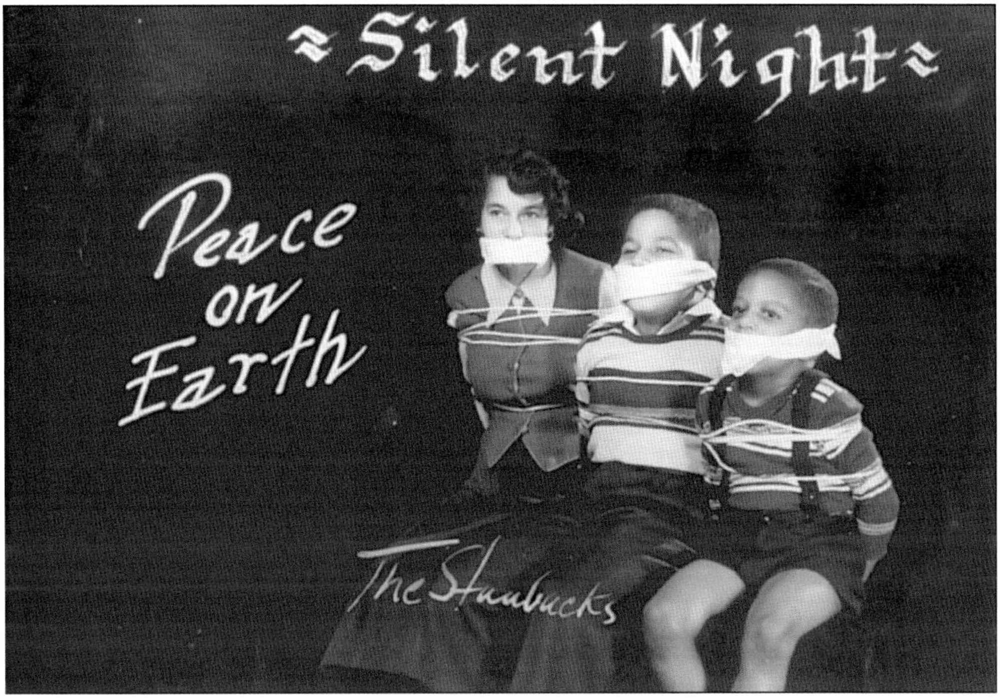

Durham photographer Charles Stanback took this opportunity to extend Christmas greetings to friends by sending this postcard. (Courtesy of Charles Stanback / Andre D. Vann.)

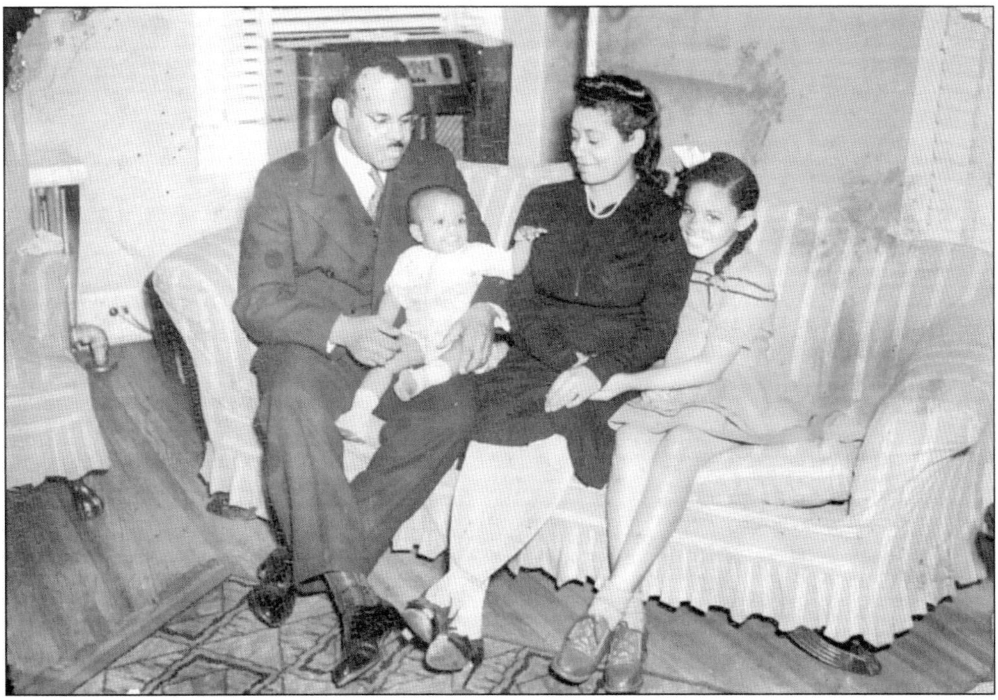
Mr. William A. and Josephine Dobbs Clement are seen here with son William Clement Jr. and Alexine Clement Jackson. The Clements were active participants in the civic, educational, and business affairs in Hayti and Durham. (Courtesy of Andre D. Vann.)

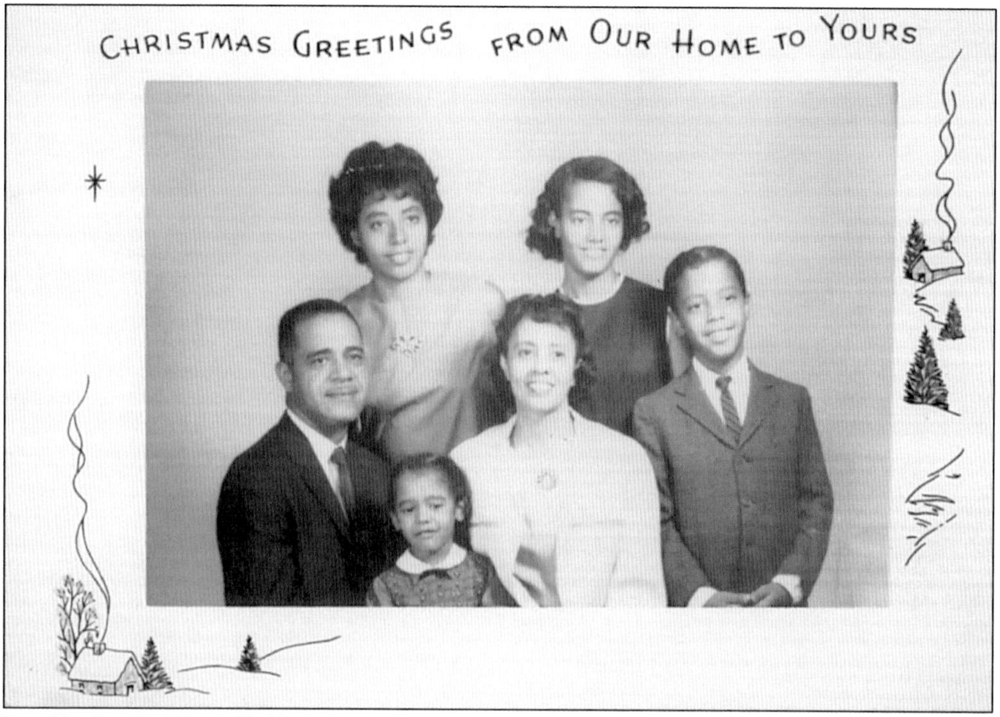

Dr. Charles D. Watts (left) and Constance Merrick Watts (center) are shown surrounded by children in this early Christmas greeting card photograph. Dr. Watts was a member of the board of trustees and chief surgeon at Lincoln Community Health Center and also the medical director and vice president of the North Carolina Mutual Life Insurance Company. (Courtesy of Andre D. Vann.)

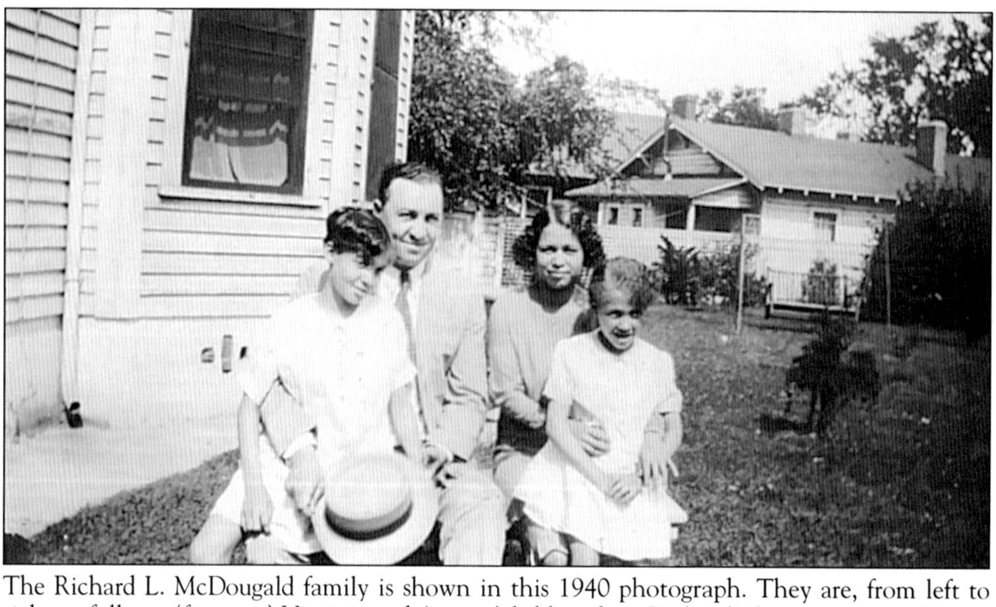

The Richard L. McDougald family is shown in this 1940 photograph. They are, from left to right, as follows: (first row) Virginia and Arona (children from Richard's first marriage to Mattie L. Moore, daughter of Dr. A.M. Moore); (last row) R.L. McDougald and wife, Dorothy Everette. (Courtesy of Andre D. Vann.)

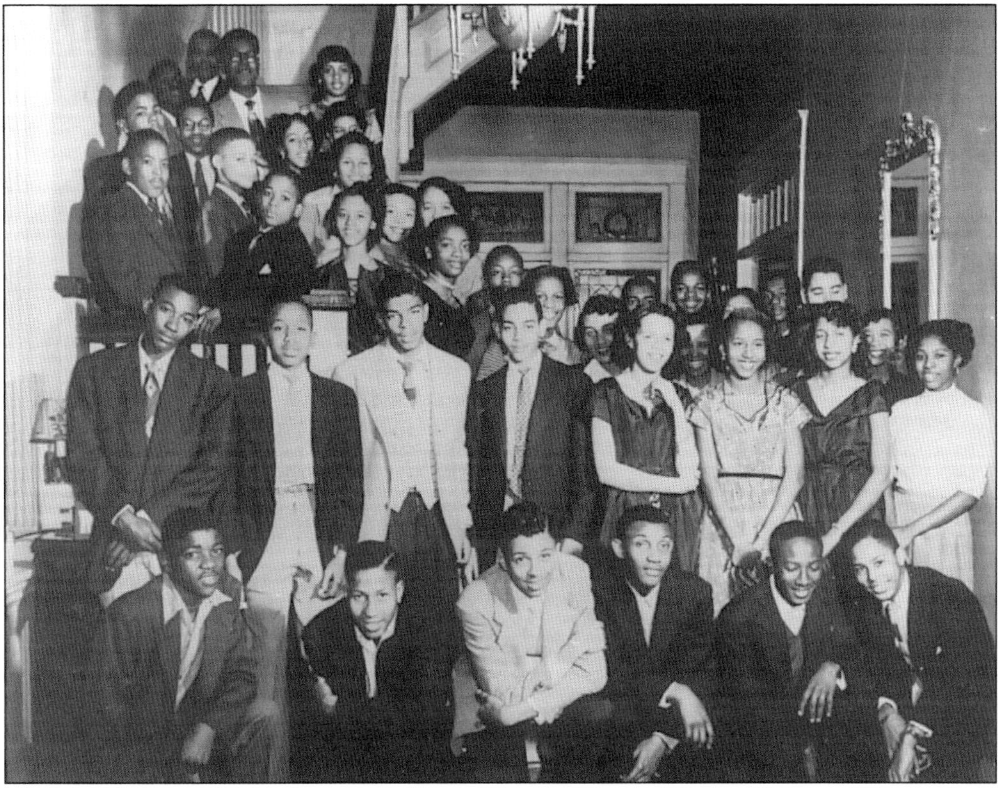

This photograph was taken on the occasion of the 15th birthday of John C. "Skeepie" Scarborough III on September 14, 1952, at the Scarborough Mansion at 1406 Fayetteville Street. The guests assembled represent members of the Hillside High School Classes of 1954, 1955, and 1956. (Courtesy of Skeepie Scarborough / Andre D. Vann.)

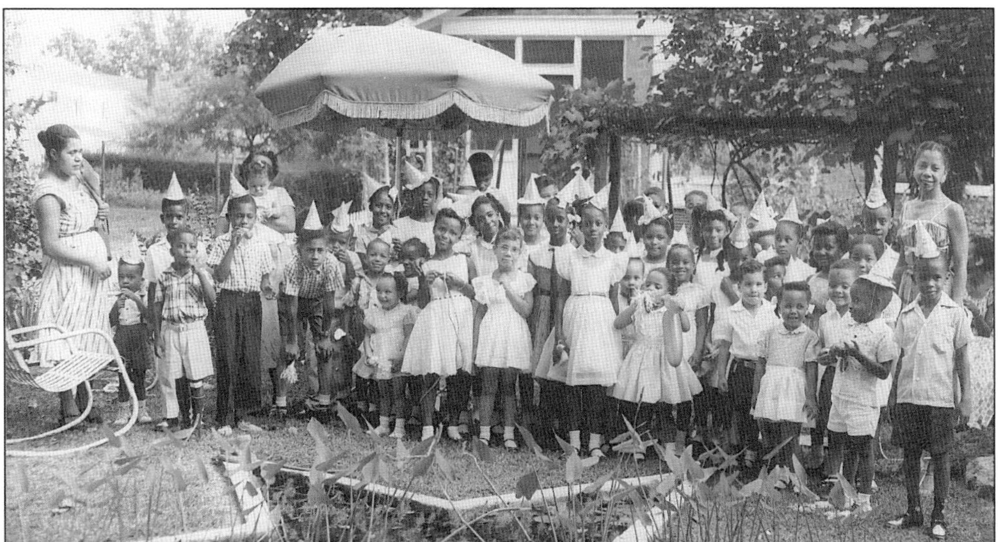

Hayti children enjoy a birthday party at the home of the Rencher N. Harris family on Formosa Avenue. (Courtesy of Ellis Allen / Andre Vann.)

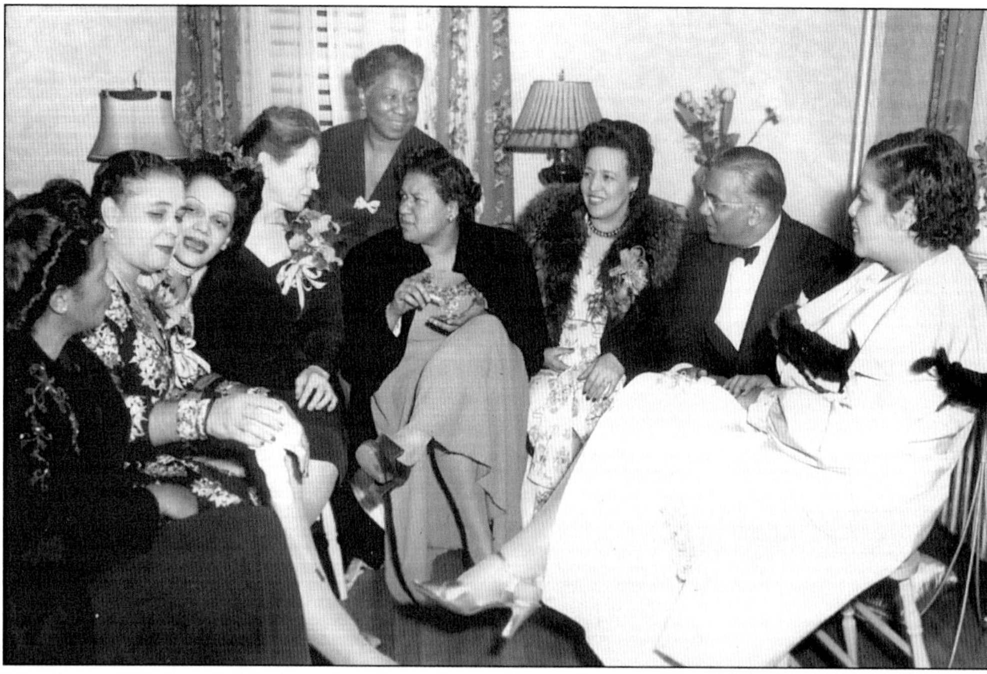

Members of Durham's black society hosted an affair in honor of Jessie Mae Vann, editor of the *Pittsburgh Courier* (fourth from left), who is shown chatting with Dr. Helen G. Edmonds of North Carolina College. (Courtesy of Andre D. Vann.)

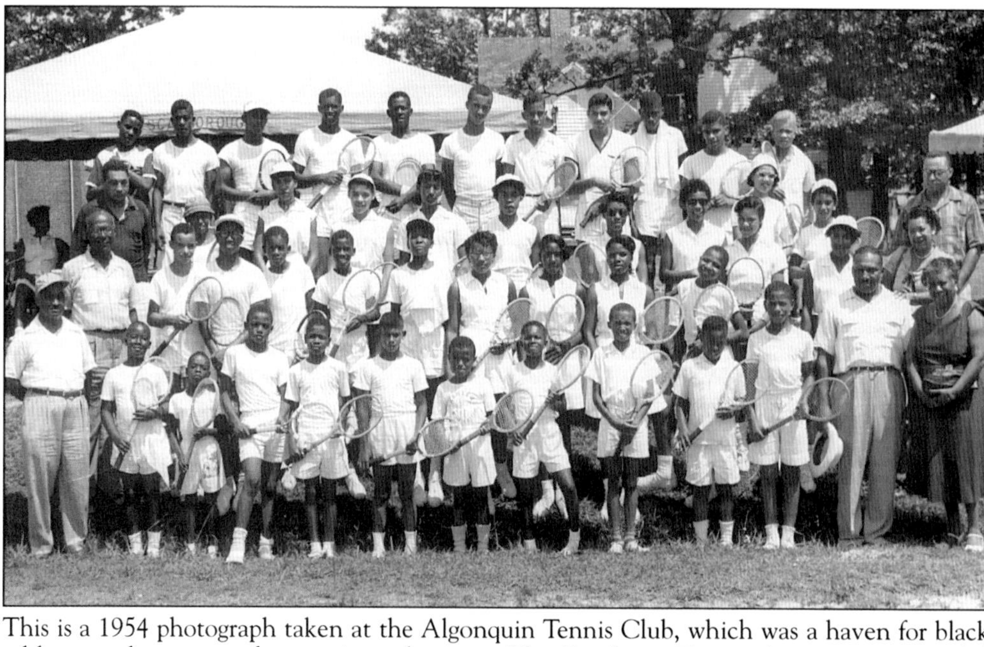

This is a 1954 photograph taken at the Algonquin Tennis Club, which was a haven for black athletes and a mecca for tennis enthusiasts. The Southern Tennis Association provided instruction, equipment, supplies, and paid lodging and travel expenses for budding tennis players. On the front row, ninth from the left, is Arthur Ashe and Mrs. Bessie A. Whitted, a great supporter of social activities for youth in Durham. (Courtesy of Alex Rivera / Andre D. Vann.)

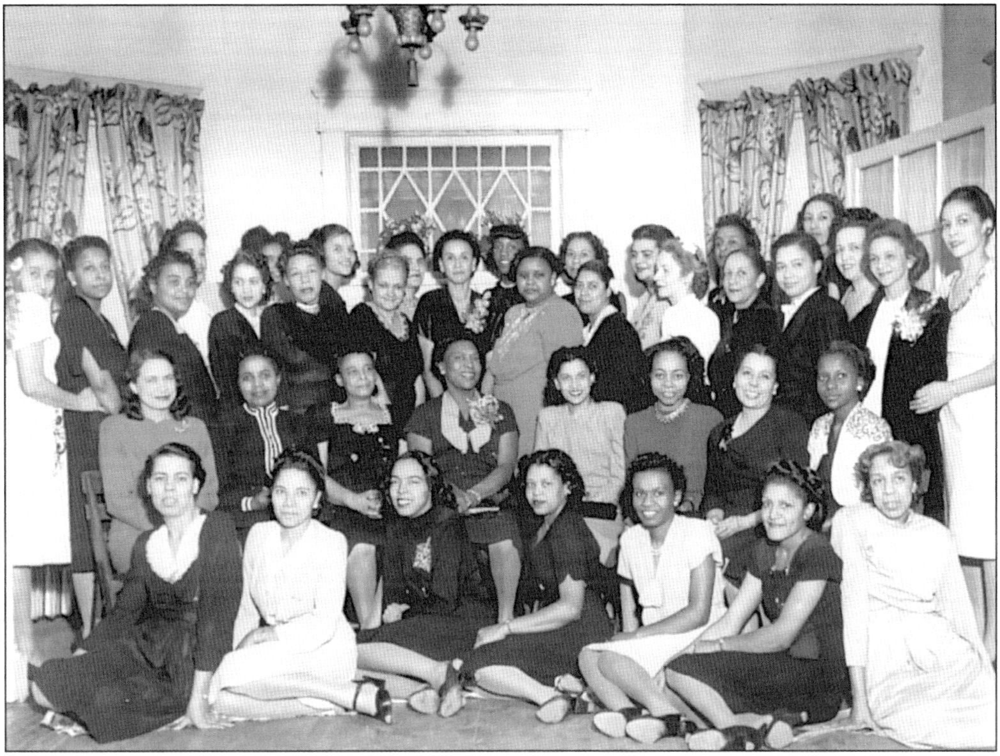

This is a 1950s photograph of members of the Alpha Zeta Omega Chapter of the Alpha Kappa Alpha Sorority, Inc. meeting at the spacious Scarborough Mansion at 1406 Fayetteville Street, the home of Clydie Fulwood and Hattie Bell Strong Scarborough. (Courtesy of Skeepie Scarborough / Andre D. Vann.)

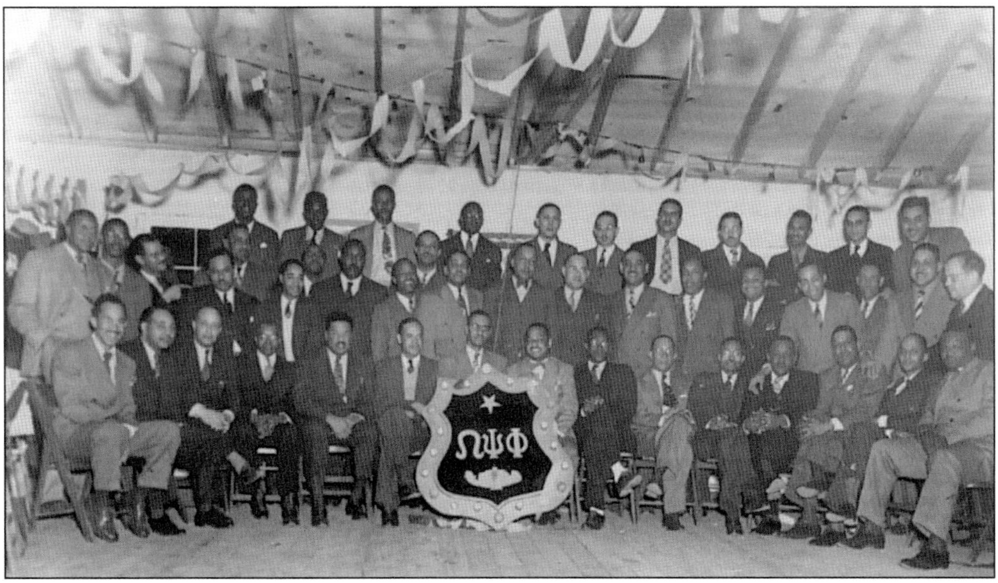

This is a 1950 photograph of members of the Beta Phi Chapter of Omega Psi Phi Fraternity, Inc. The chapter was founded in the home of Rencher N. Harris on Formosa Avenue. (Courtesy of Skeepie Scarborough / Andre Vann.)

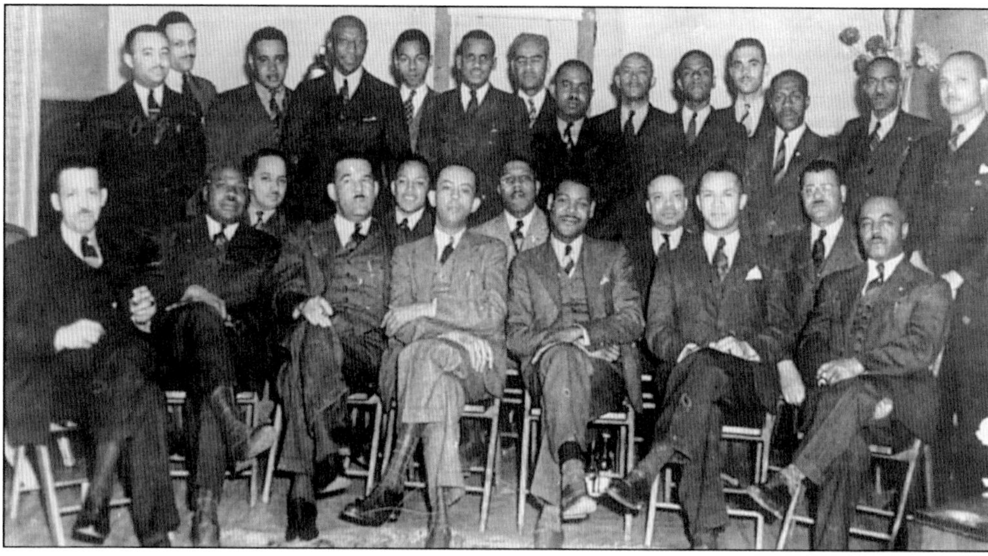

Members of the Durham Alumni Chapter of Kappa Alpha Psi Fraternity, Inc. are seen in this 1940 photograph taken at the Algonquin Tennis Club. The alumni chapter was chartered on September 12, 1921, as the first alumni chapter of any fraternity in the city. The founders were Leo Bruce, Lee Bynum, A. Moore Shearin, and Conrad O. Pearson, all members of the Delta Chapter at Wilberforce, Ohio. In 1923, the following citizens of Durham were initiated or affiliated with the chapter: James E. Shepard, William Gaston Pearson, Charles C. Spaulding, Edward R. Merrick, Stanford L. Warren, John Avery, and many others. Seated at the far left on the front row is A. Moore Shearin, who served as the past Grand Polemarch (national president) of the Kappa Alpha Psi Fraternity, Inc. (Courtesy of Lenzie Barnes / Andre D. Vann.)

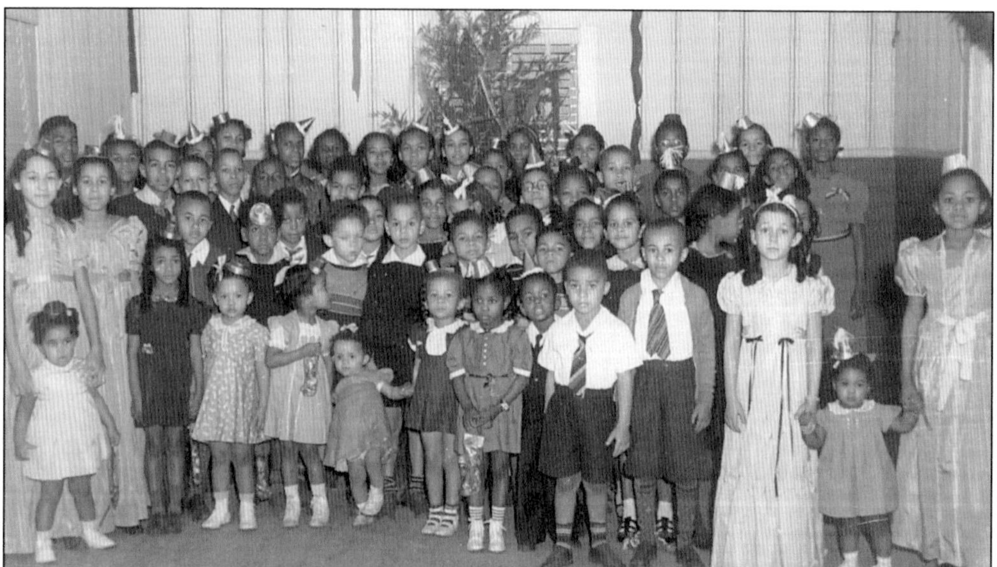

This is a 1940s photograph of middle-class youth at the Algonquin Tennis Club in Hayti. The club served as a social center for the children of employees of the North Carolina Mutual Life Insurance Company, North Carolina College (now NCCU), Lincoln Hospital, and other black businesses. (Courtesy of Andre D. Vann.)

Frank Wright was a leader and organizer of the Bull City Night Hawks Dance Orchestra, which provided dance music in Durham and surrounding areas from the 1930s to the 1960s. The Bulls City Night Hawks was organized about 1933 by Wright and Wellington Black and recruited semi-professional or part-time musicians to perform at dances for high schools, colleges, benefits, and charities throughout North Carolina, South Carolina, and Virginia. (Courtesy of Dorothy Faucette Parker.)

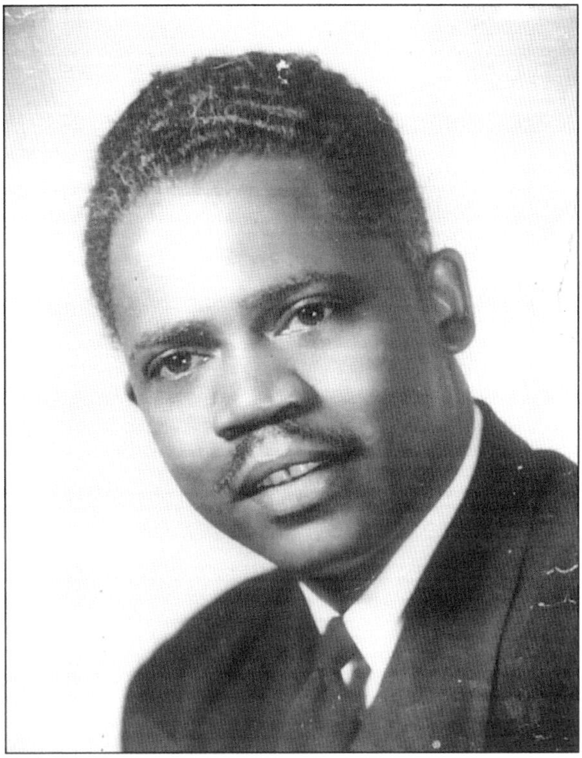

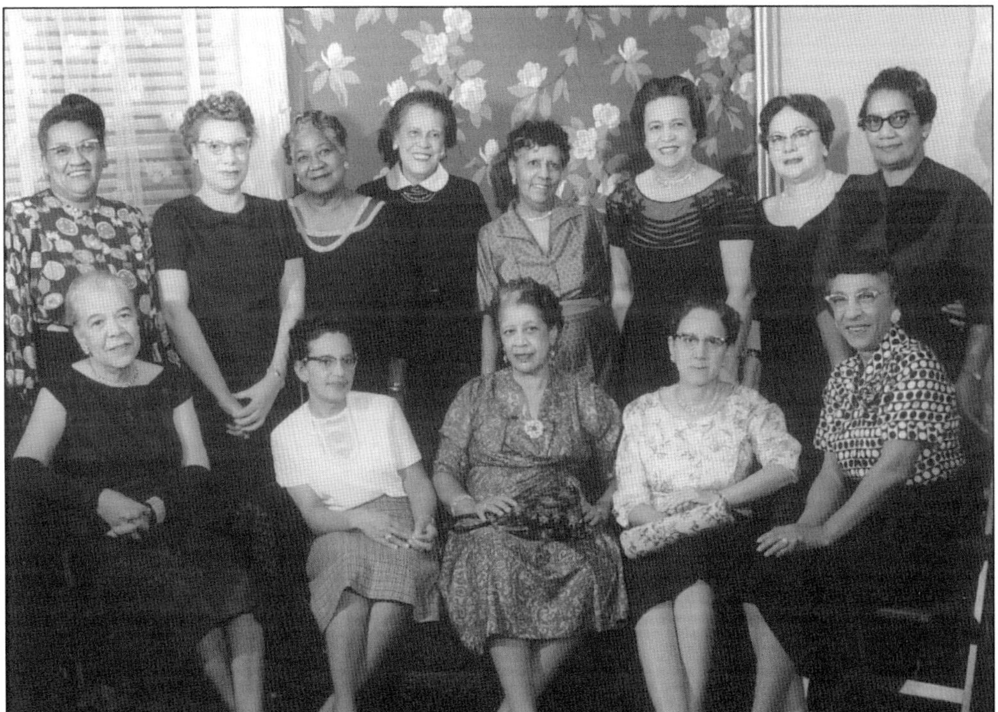

This 1960s photograph shows members of the Gourmet Bridge Club, which was begun during the early 1930s. (Courtesy of Andre D. Vann.)

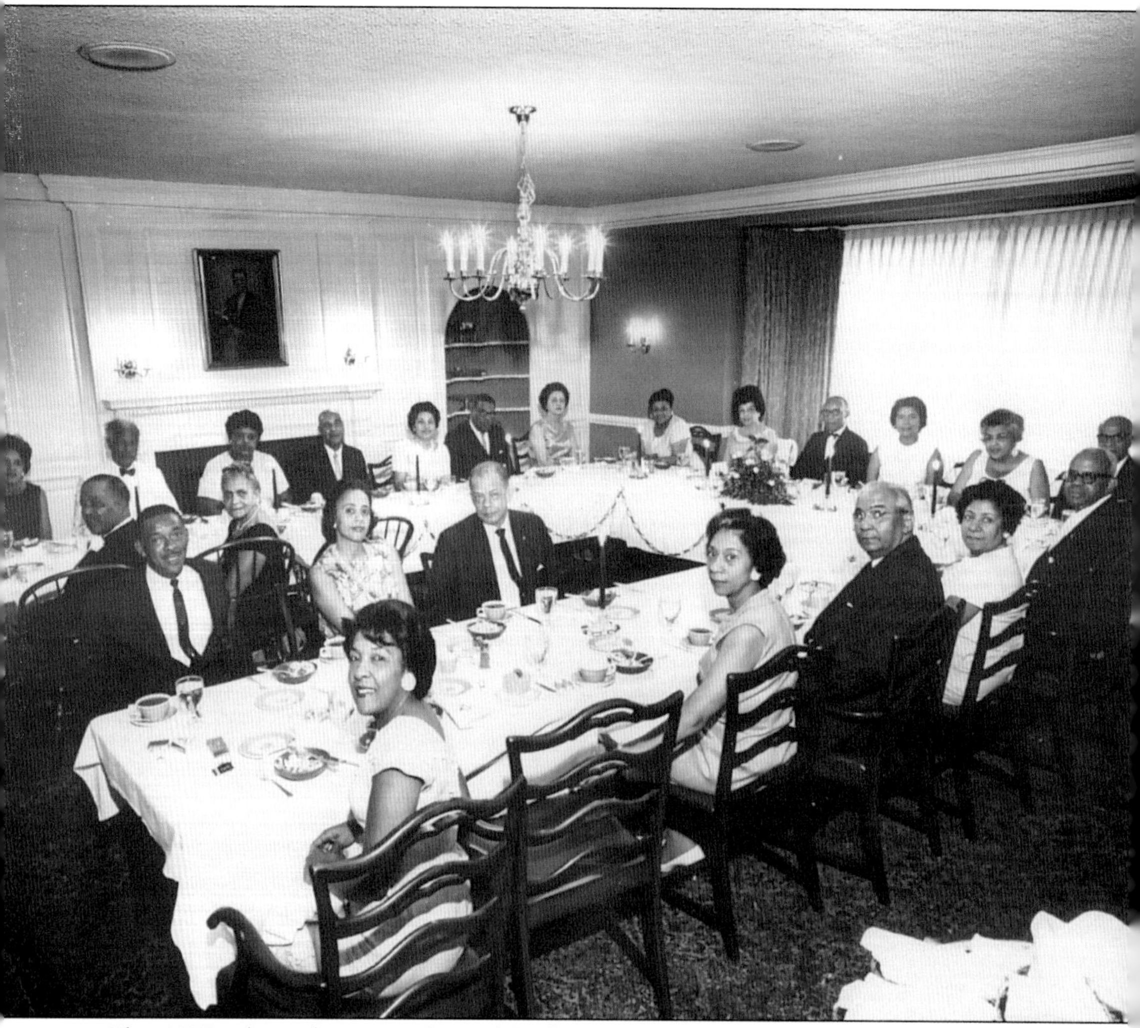

This 1970s photo shows members of Durham's Links Chapter hosting an affair in honor of Helen G. Edmonds, national president of the Link's, Inc. (Courtesy of Andre D. Vann.)

Six

Black Business and the Profession

Go to Durham. . . . You need the inspiration. Go to Durham and see Negro business with an aggregate capital of millions. Go to Durham and see twenty-two Negro men making modern history. Among your New Year's resolves, resolve to go to Durham!

—From a 1928 article written by the editor of the *St. Luke Herald*, a black weekly in Richmond, Virginia.

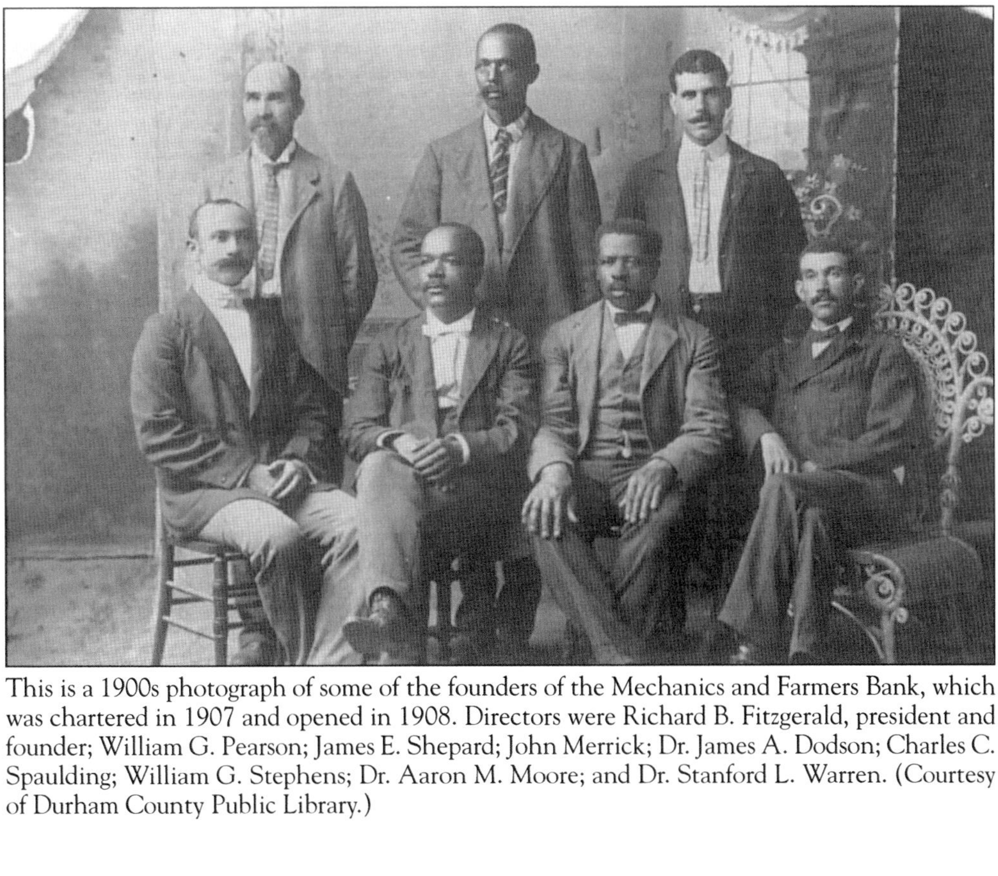

This is a 1900s photograph of some of the founders of the Mechanics and Farmers Bank, which was chartered in 1907 and opened in 1908. Directors were Richard B. Fitzgerald, president and founder; William G. Pearson; James E. Shepard; John Merrick; Dr. James A. Dodson; Charles C. Spaulding; William G. Stephens; Dr. Aaron M. Moore; and Dr. Stanford L. Warren. (Courtesy of Durham County Public Library.)

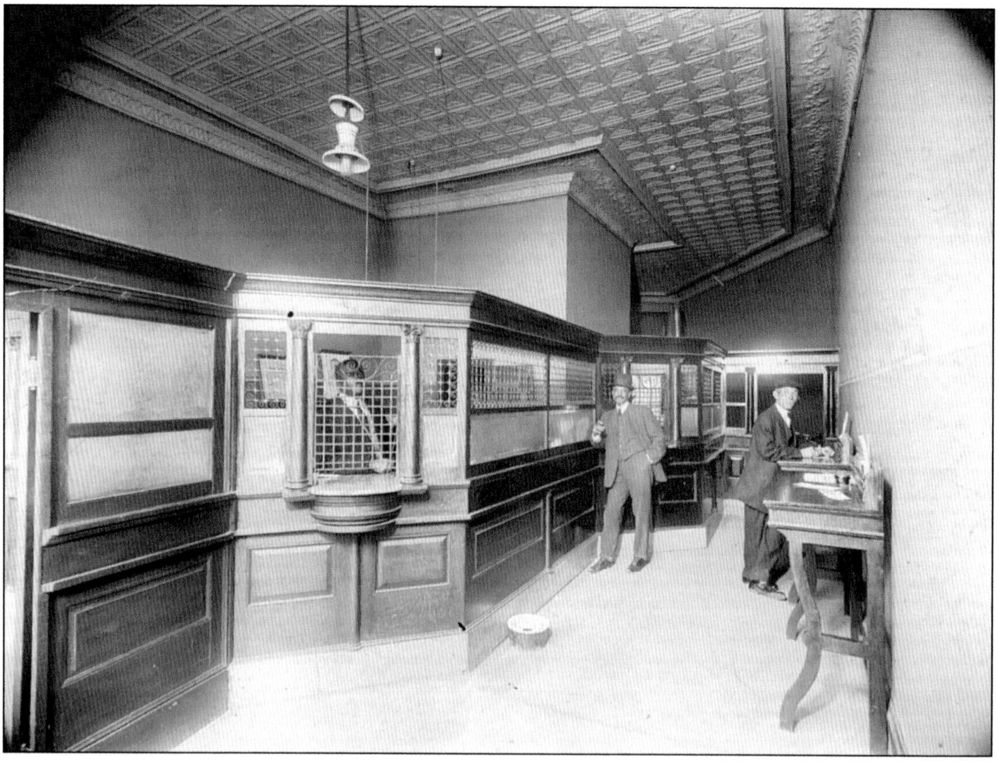

John Merrick (left) and Dr. Aaron M. Moore are featured in this 1915 photograph inside the Mechanics and Farmers Bank of Durham, located on Parrish Street. (Courtesy of Andre D. Vann.)

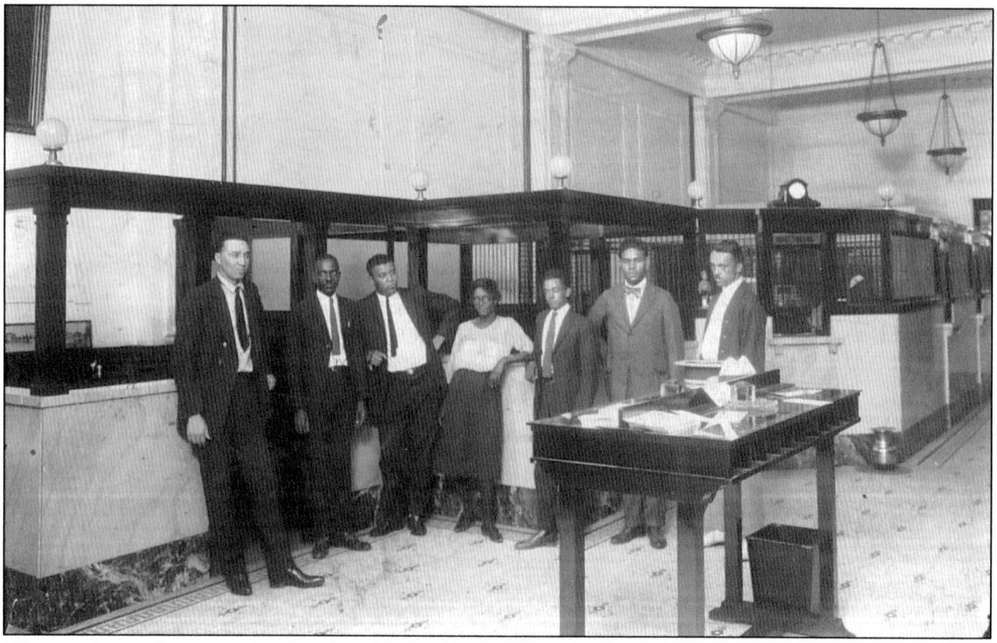

This is a 1918 photograph of Richard L. McDougald and other bank employees of the Mechanics and Farmers Bank. (Courtesy of Andre D. Vann.)

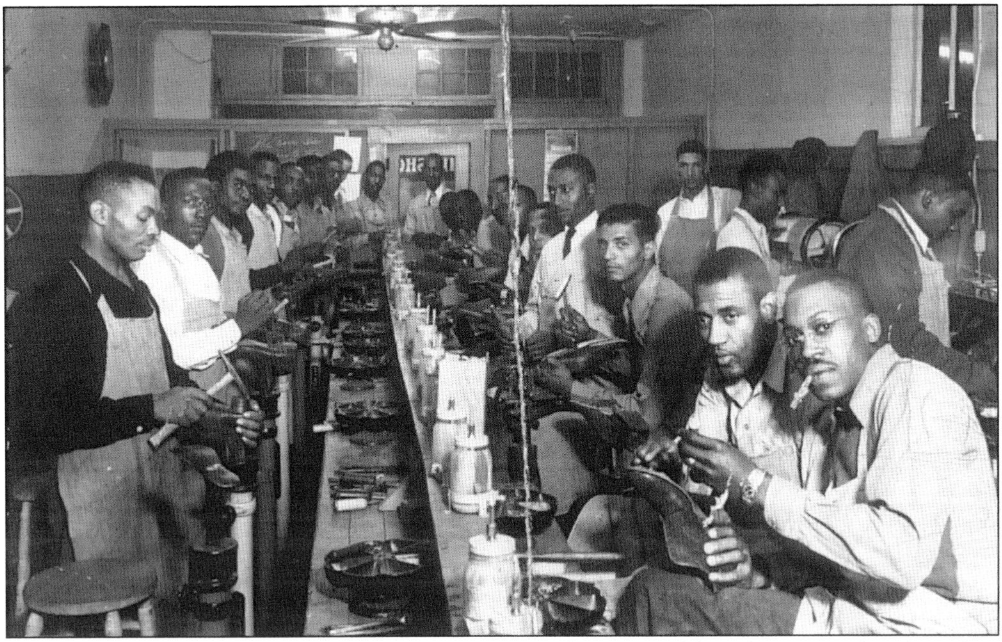

This 1940 photograph shows apprentices working along a workbench equipped with a shoe repair apparatus at Shelly's Modern Shoe Shop and Shoe School, located at 520 Pettigrew Street. The blackboard in the back to the left states, "The race is given to the swift." (Courtesy of Durham County Public Library.)

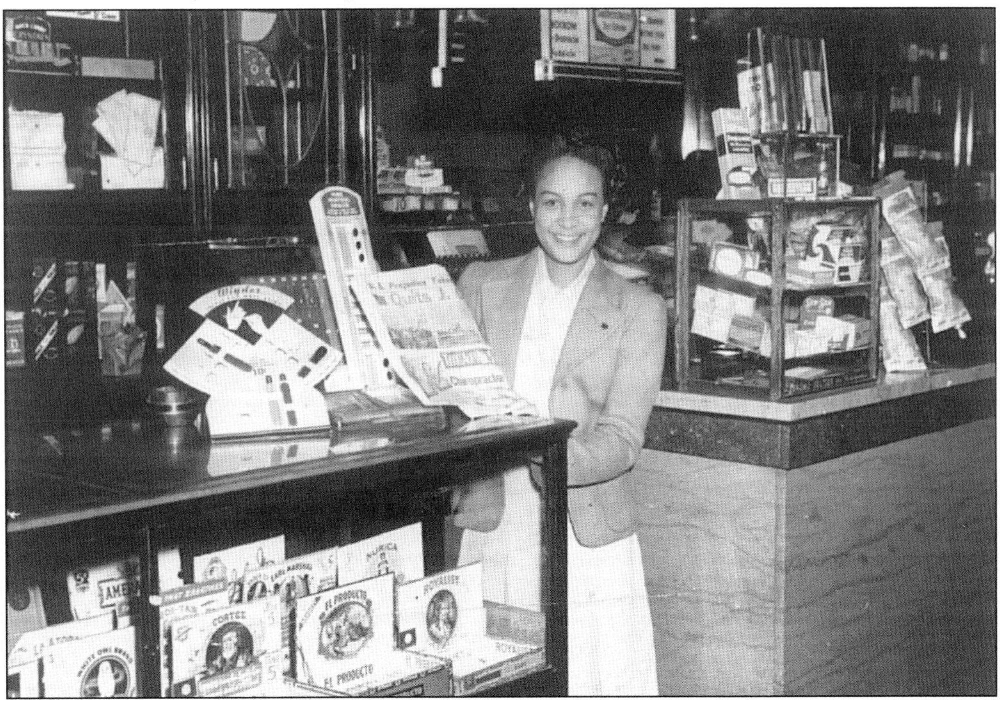

In this 1940 photograph, Gloria Garrett Pratt, daughter of Dr. York David and Julia Williams Garrett, is pictured with newspapers beside a tobacco counter inside the Biltmore Drug Store in the Biltmore Hotel on Pettigrew Street. (Courtesy of the Durham County Public Library.)

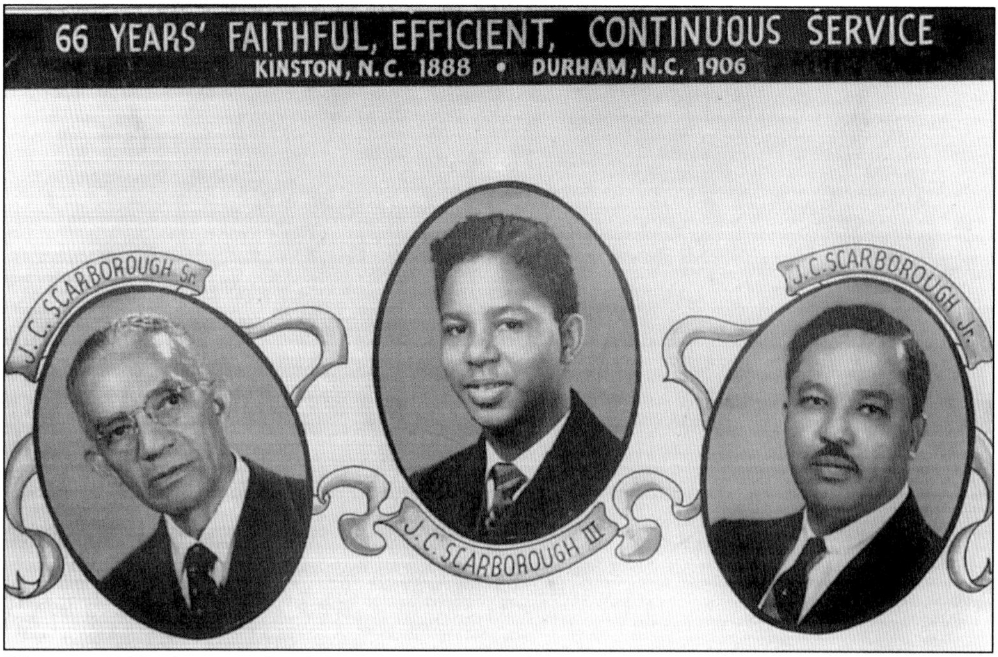

This is a 1952 photograph of three generations of morticians in the Scarborough family, who were the founders of the Scarborough & Hargett Funeral Service, which was started in Durham in 1906. This business has been in continuous operation for decades and served as the first professional funeral service in the city. (Courtesy of John C. "Skeepie" Scarborough.)

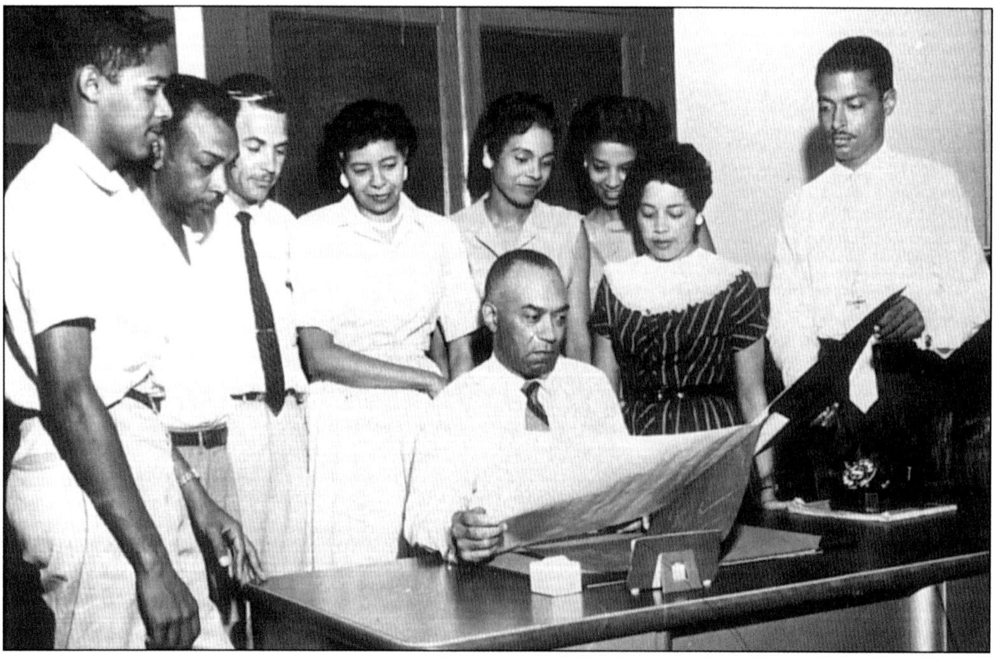

Henry McKinley Michaux Sr. (1897–1986), president of Union Insurance and Realty Company, is seen seated in the center surrounded by employees and his son, Henry M. "Mickey" Michaux Jr., pictured at the extreme right. Michaux's business was located at 814 Fayetteville Street. (Courtesy of Durham County Public Library.)

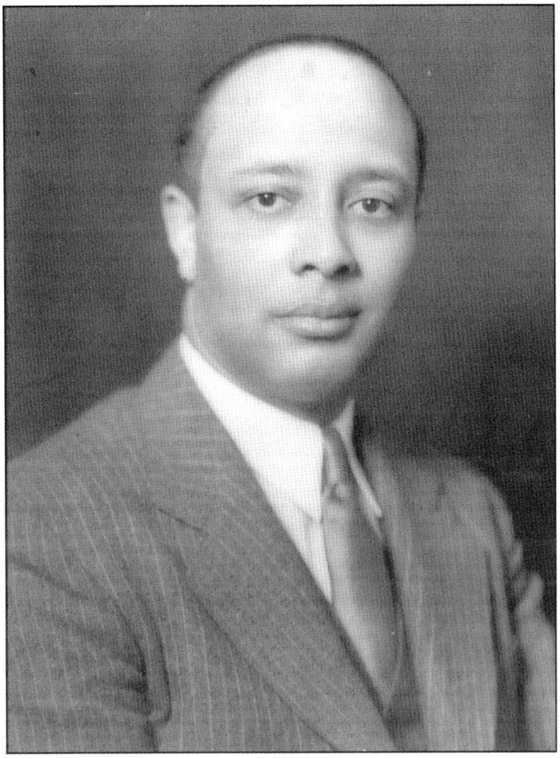

Joseph Waverly Goodloe (1906–1990), featured in this 1940s photograph, was born in Durham, North Carolina, the son of Allen L. and Rosa Goodloe. He graduated from Hampton Institute and began his professional career in 1926 at the Home Office at North Carolina Mutual Life Insure Company. He held many positions on the official staff of the company and served as president from 1968 to 1972. Besides being a trustee at the White Rock Baptist Church, Goodloe served on the boards of Mutual Savings and Loan, Mechanics and Farmers Bank, John Avery's Boys Club, and the Omega Psi Phi Fraternity. He was married to Betty W. Goodloe. (Courtesy of Andre D. Vann.)

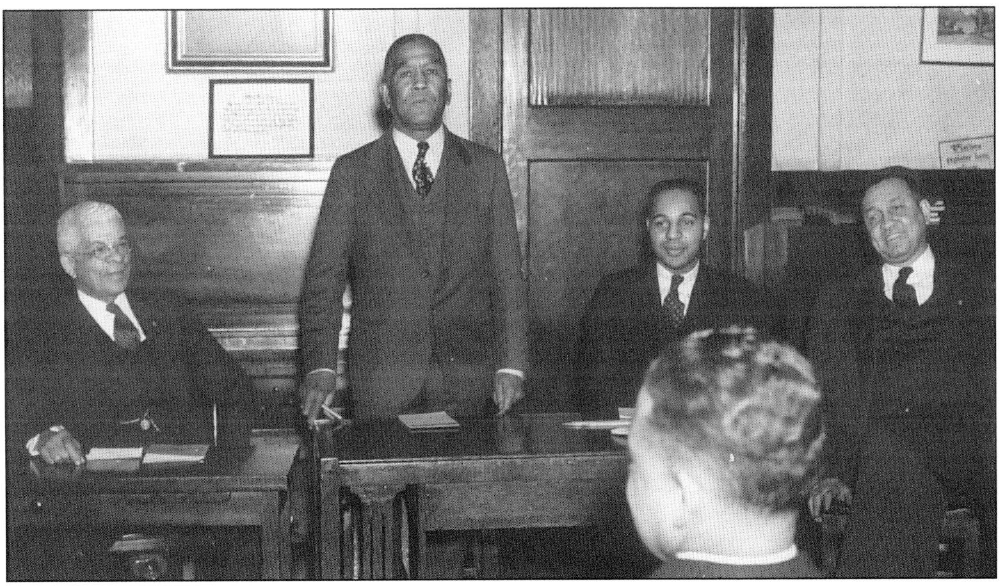

Frank L. McCoy (1875–1951), business executive and insurance pioneer, came to Durham in 1920 to become a life underwriter for North Carolina Mutual Life Insurance Company and fire underwriter for Bankers Fire Insurance Company. From 1921 until his death, McCoy served as secretary manager of the Mutual Building and Loan Association. He was a member and Omega Psi Phi Fraternity, Algonquin Club, and the Volkamenia Club. Pictured here are, from left to right, the following: Charles C. Spaulding Sr., Frank McCoy, John S. Stewart, and Richard L. McDougald. (Courtesy of Andre D. Vann.)

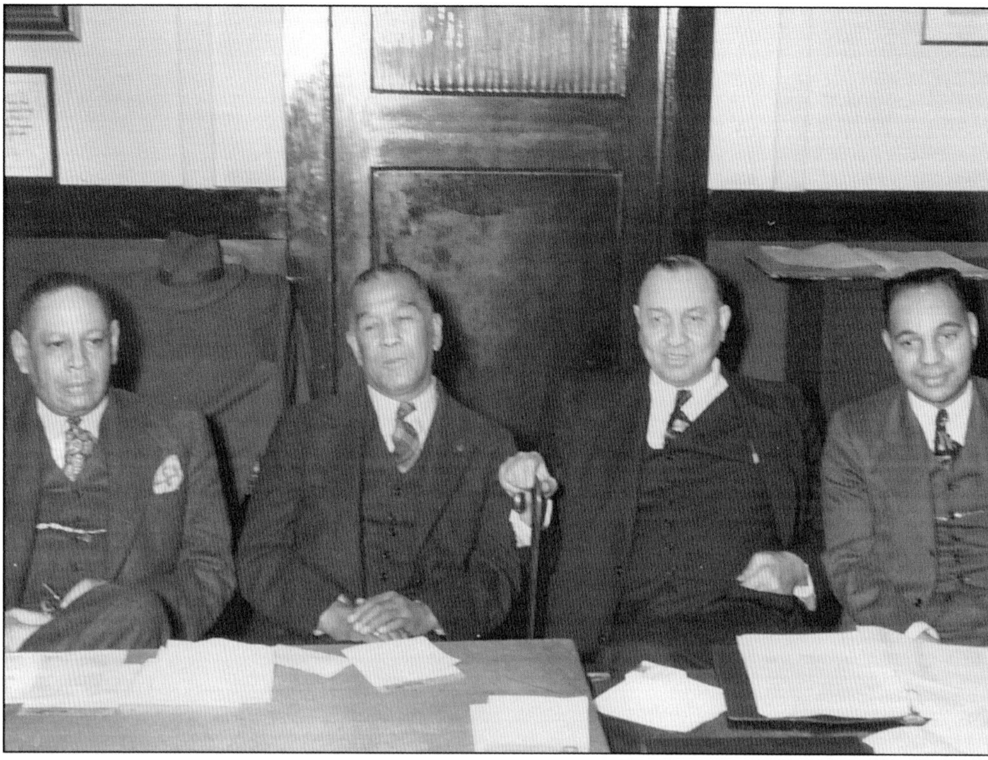

This is a 1944 meeting of influential business leaders in Hayti. Seated, from left to right, are the following: Dr. Clyde Donnell, Frank McCoy, Richard L. McDougald, and John S. "Shag"" Stewart. (Courtesy of Andre D. Vann.)

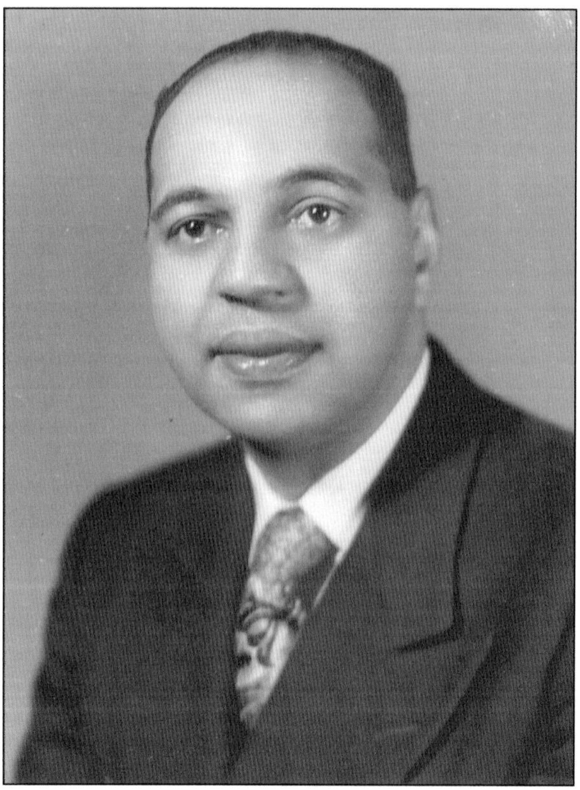

John S. Stewart came to Durham in 1935 and served as secretary-treasure of the Mutual Savings and Loan Association at 144 West Parrish Street. He was born in Atlanta, Georgia, and graduated from Atlanta University with an A.B. degree. In 1936, he married Otelia Spaulding and was the father of three: Ethel Marie, Janetta Sylvester, and James Alonzo Stewart. He served as the chairman of the Durham Committee on Negro Affairs and on the boards of Bankers Fire Insurance Co., Mechanics and Farmers Bank, and Southern Fidelity. (Courtesy of Andre D. Vann.)

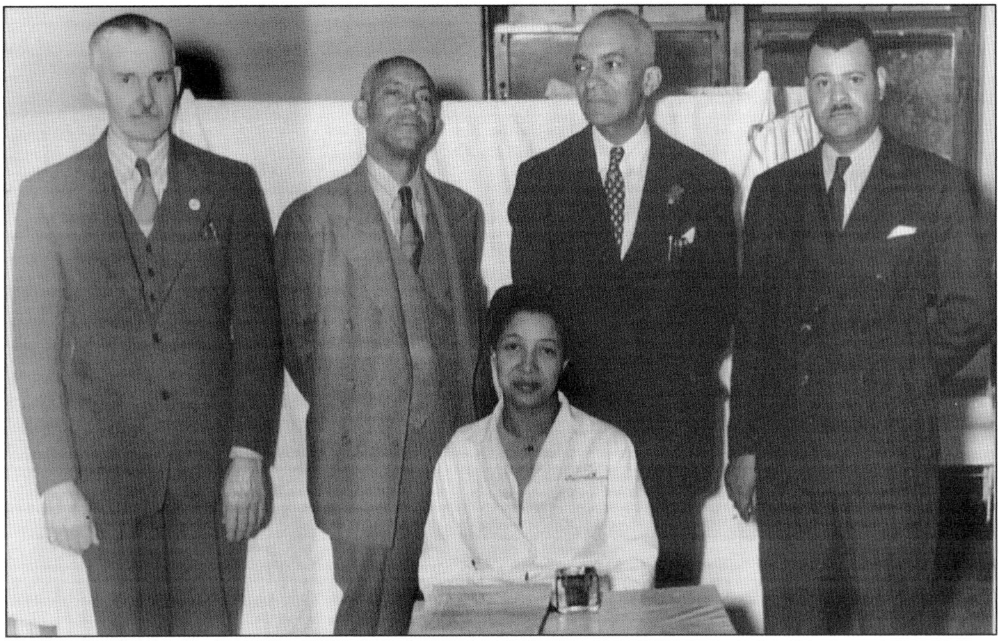

Seen here in 1944 at Lincoln Hospital are members of Durham's medical community. From left to right are as follows: Dr. Norris, Dr. Alexander S. Hunter, Dr. John V. Cordice, Dr. Leo Bruce, and Laura Bruce (the records clerk at Lincoln Hospital). (Courtesy of Janet H. Lynch / Andre D. Vann.)

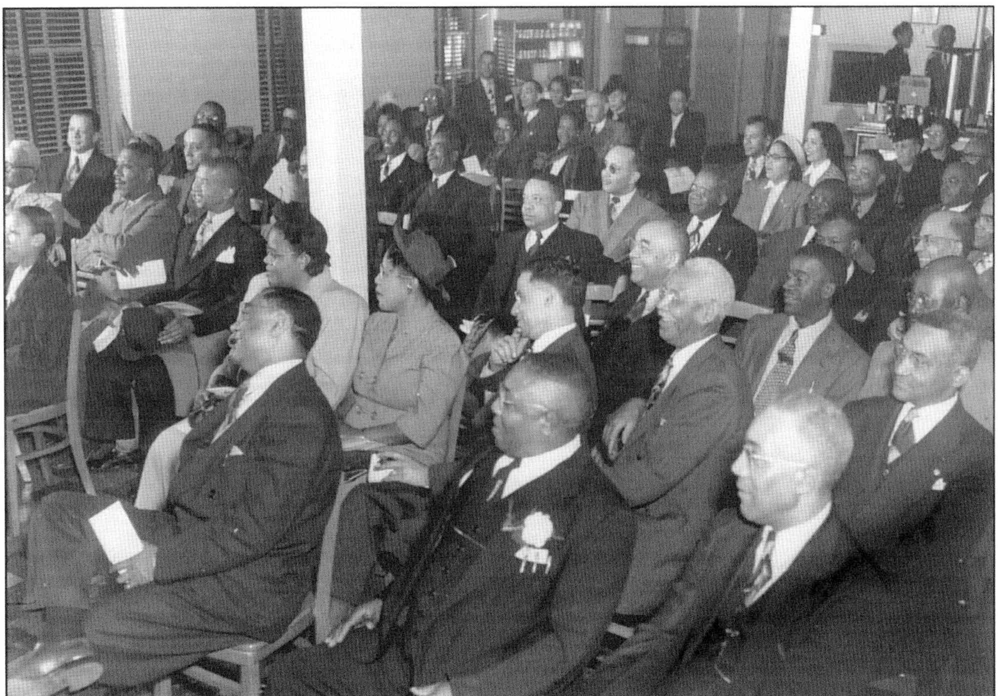

In this picture, Mutual Saving and Loan Association shareholders assemble for their annual meeting. (Courtesy of Andre D. Vann.)

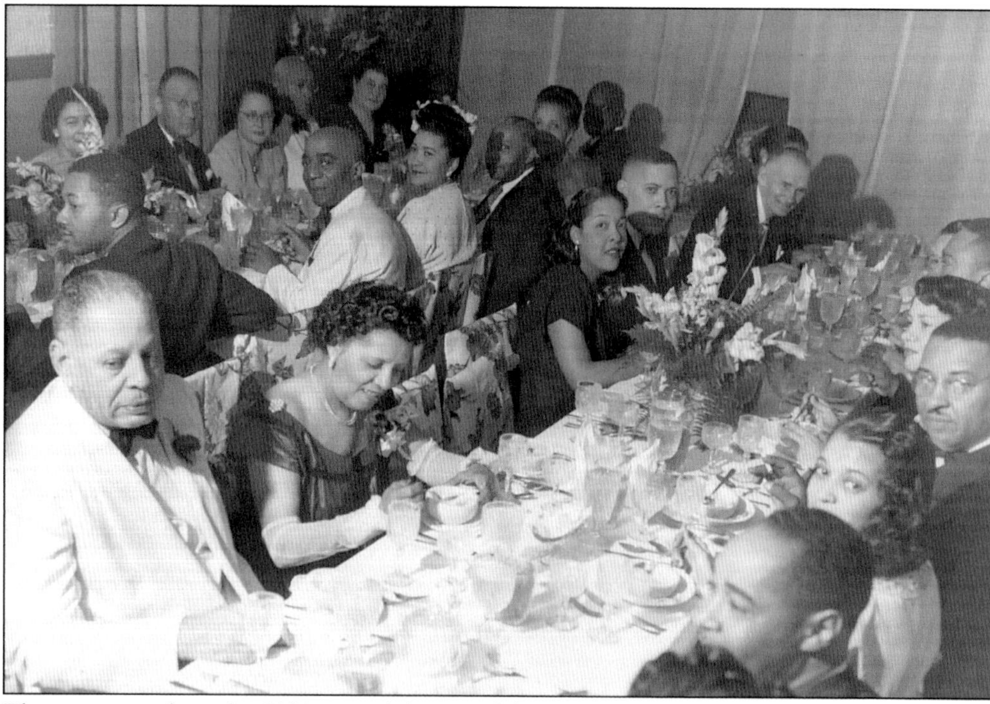

This is a scene from the 1951 annual dinner of the Durham Academy of Medicine, Dentistry, and Pharmacy. (Courtesy of Andre D. Vann.)

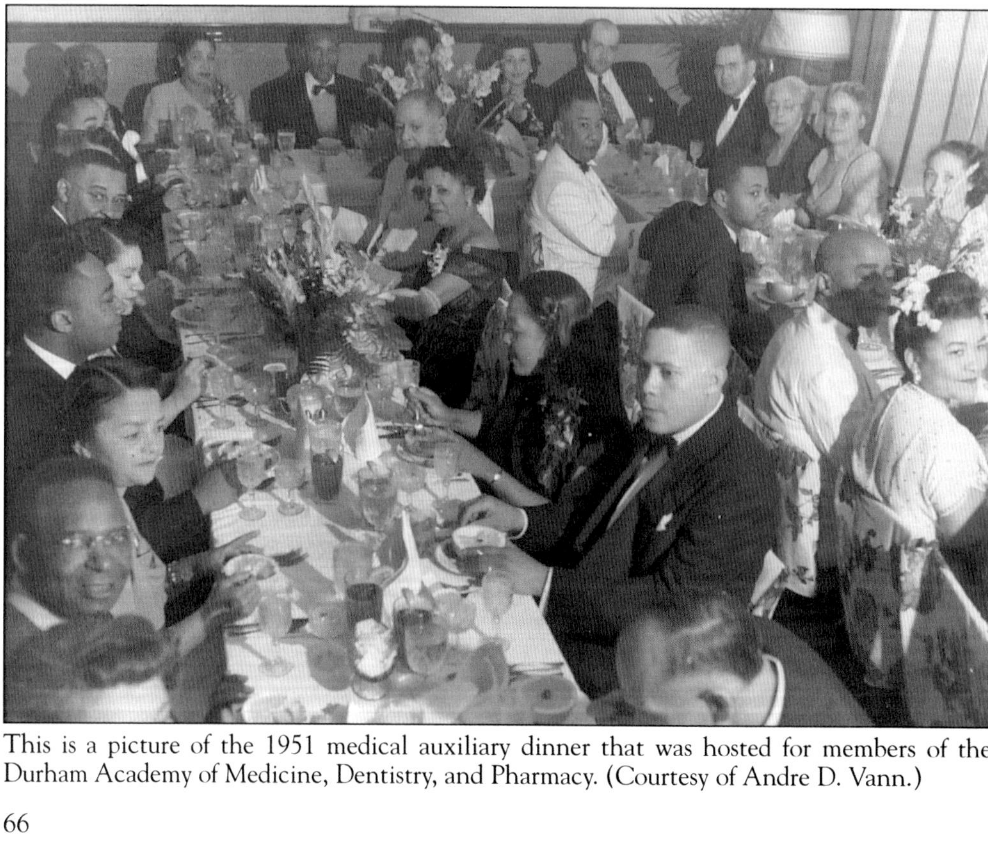

This is a picture of the 1951 medical auxiliary dinner that was hosted for members of the Durham Academy of Medicine, Dentistry, and Pharmacy. (Courtesy of Andre D. Vann.)

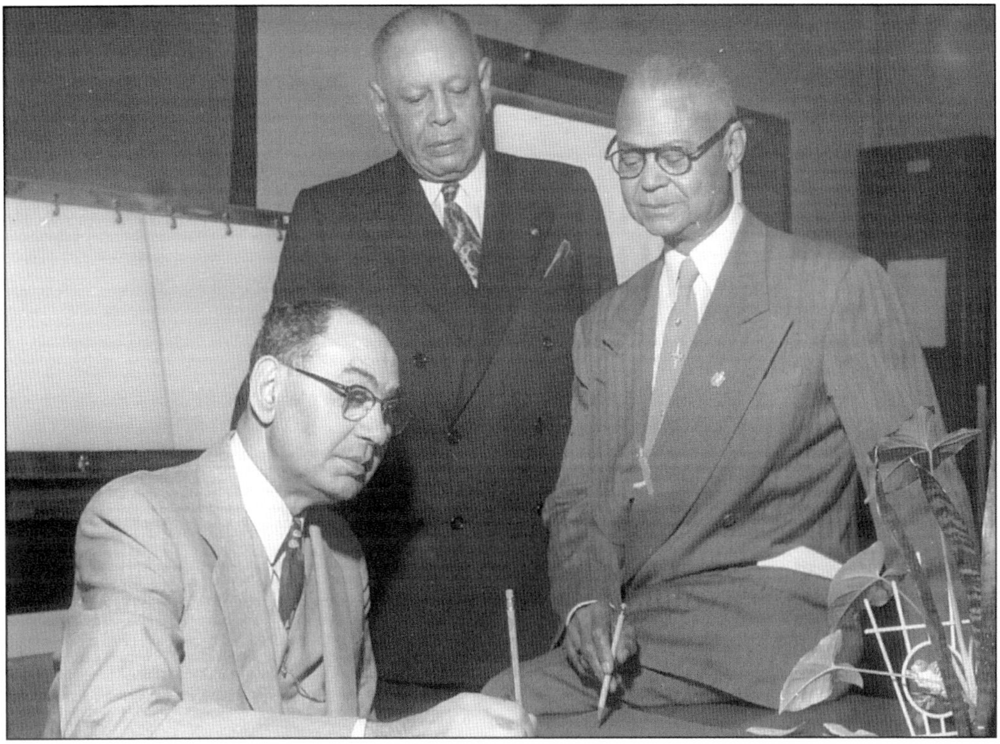

Featured in this 1950s photo are Lincoln Hospital officials conversing during a Lincoln Hospital clinic. They are, from left to right, as follows: William M. Rich, director; Dr. Clyde Donnell, chairmen of the board; and Dr. McCauley, board member. (Courtesy of Andre D. Vann.)

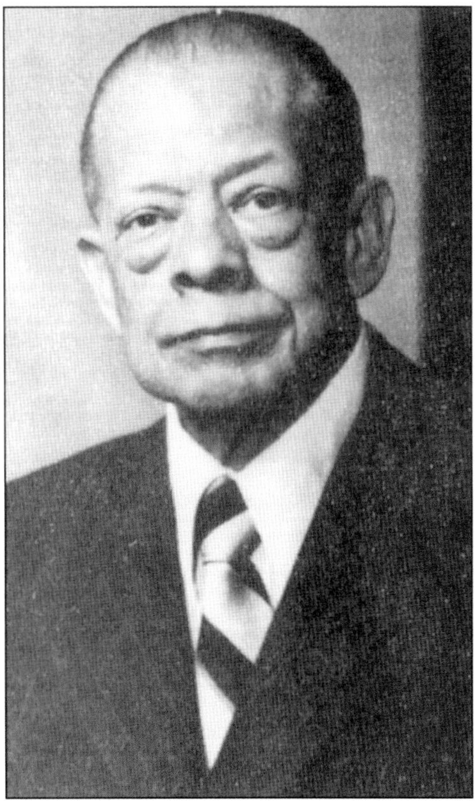

John Hervey Wheeler (1908–1978), businessmen and statesmen, was born in Kittrell, North Carolina, was educated in Atlanta, and graduated from Morehouse College in Atlanta. Wheeler was affiliated with various civic, political, academic, and business organizations. In 1929 he became a teller at the Mechanics and Farmers Bank and gradually was promoted to the presidency in 1952, following the death of C.C Spaulding. He served as president of the bank for over 25 years. He was the first black to head the Southern Regional Council and, as a lawyer, brought the first integration suit to the State of North Carolina. He was best known as the chairman of the Durham Committee on the Affairs of Black People and served as the president of the National Negro Bankers Association. (Courtesy of Andre D. Vann.)

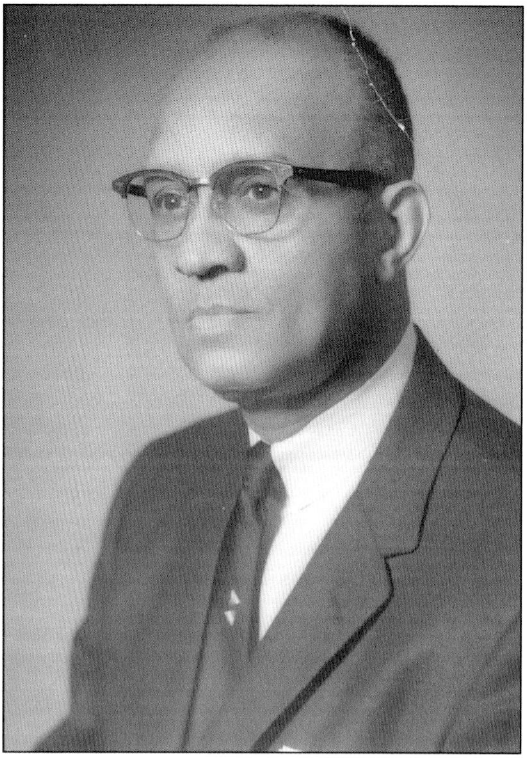

Dr. Robert P. Randolph (1909–1996), a physician on the staff at Lincoln Hospital, came to Durham during the 1930s following his graduation from medical school at Howard University. He served as the chief of staff and surgeon at the hospital. (Courtesy of Frances Dyer.)

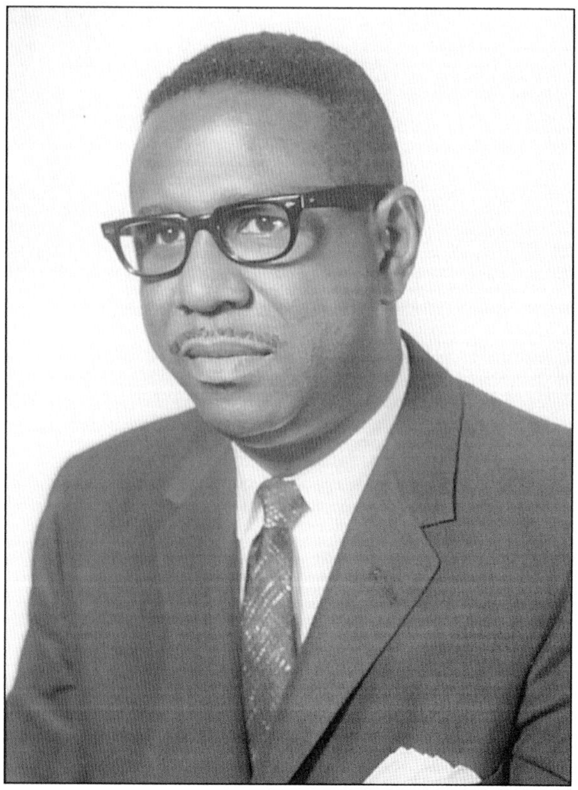

Dr. Robert E. Dawson (born in 1918), a Rocky Mount native, came to Durham in 1946 after receiving a M.D. Degree from Meharry Medical College in 1943 and after serving his internship and residency at Homer G. Phillips Hospital in St. Louis. From 1946 until 1955, he was a member of the attending staff in opthamology at Lincoln Hospital. From 1950 to 1964, he was a member of the attending staff at NCCU. In 1955, he joined the United States Air Force and later returned to Durham to become chief of opthamology at Lincoln. Dr. Dawson is a Mason, a Shriner, a member of the Alpha Phi Alpha Fraternity, Inc, a fellow of the American College of Surgeons, and a past president of the National Medical Association. (Courtesy of Robert Dawson / Andre D. Vann.)

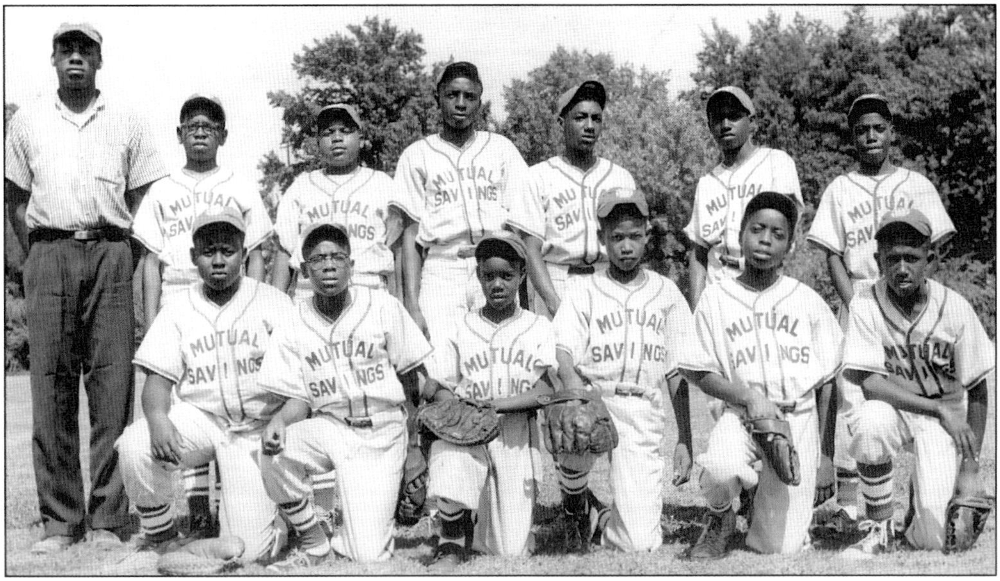

During the 1950s, the Mutual Savings and Loan Association became the proud sponsors of this Little League community baseball team. (Courtesy of Andre D. Vann.)

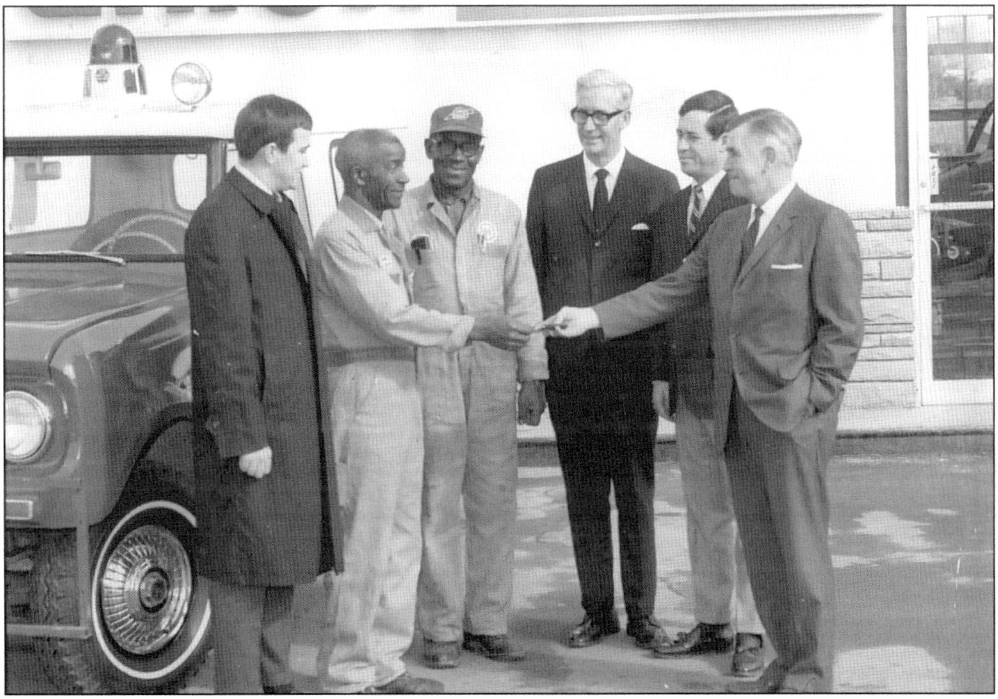

Durham businessmen Theodore Roosevelt Speight (born in 1908), second from left, came to Durham in 1932 with only 83¢ and took a job at a service station. In 1938 he opened Speight's Auto Service Center at Pettigrew and Fayetteville Street. Speight closed the station on Pettigrew Street in 1966 because of the encroachment of urban renewal and the construction of the Durham Freeway. Speight's Auto Service Center later moved to the lower end of Fayetteville Street and is the only surviving auto shop from Hayti. The business is still in existence today. (Courtesy of Theodora S. Manley.)

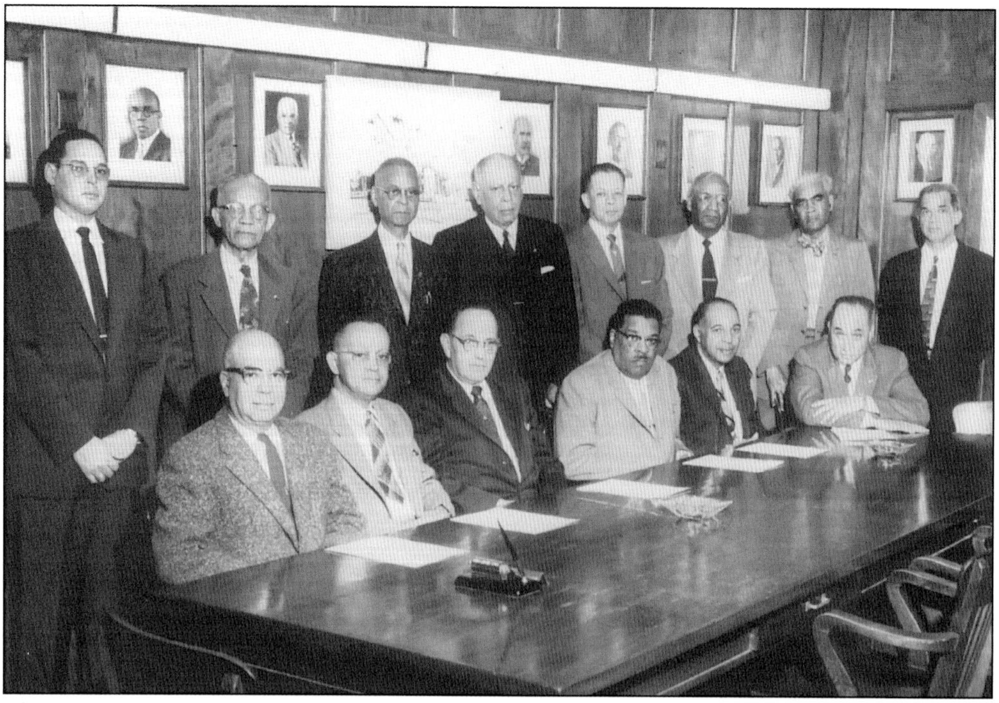

This is a 1950s photograph of members of the board of directors of the Mechanics and Farmers Bank. (Courtesy of Andre D. Vann.)

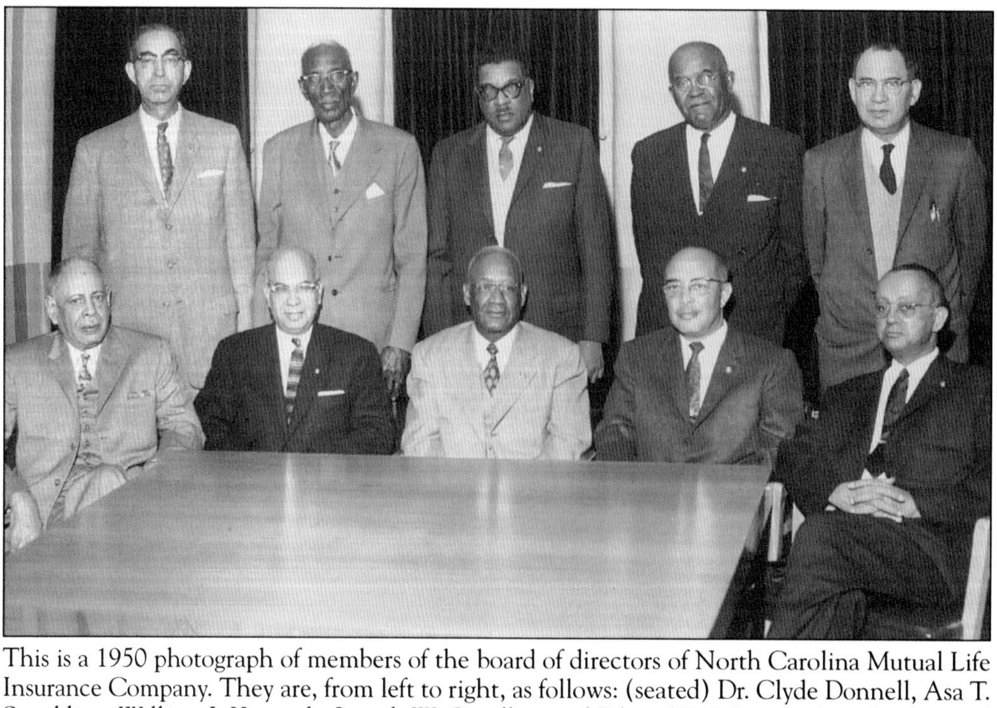

This is a 1950 photograph of members of the board of directors of North Carolina Mutual Life Insurance Company. They are, from left to right, as follows: (seated) Dr. Clyde Donnell, Asa T. Spaulding, William J. Kennedy, Joseph W. Goodloe, and Edward R. Merrick; (standing) David Crockett Deans, William H. Harvey, Charles C. Spaulding Jr., Arthur E. Spears, and William M. Rich. (Courtesy of Andre D. Vann.)

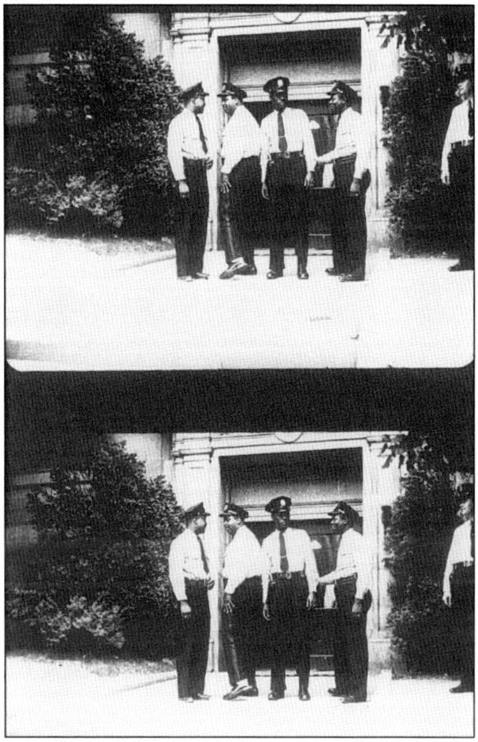

This is an early photograph of Durham's first black police officers, which were hired as a result of a request by C.C. Spaulding for black police officers in Hayti to help diffuse racial tensions between black citizens and white police officers. (Courtesy of Durham County Public Library.)

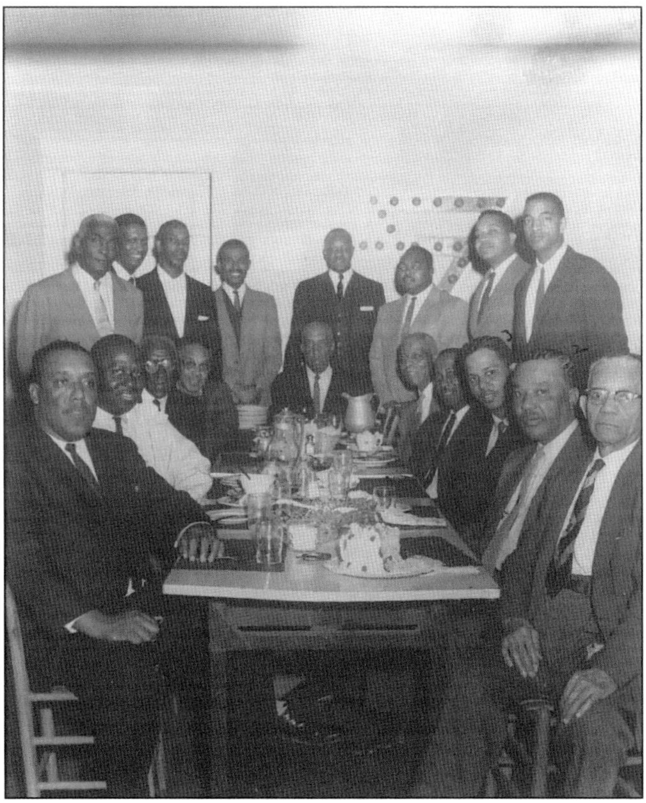

This photograph was taken on February 13, 1962, and is a group photo of members of the One O'Clock Luncheon Club, which was affiliated with the Durham Business and Professional Chain. (Courtesy of John C. "Skeepie" Scarborough / Andre D. Vann.)

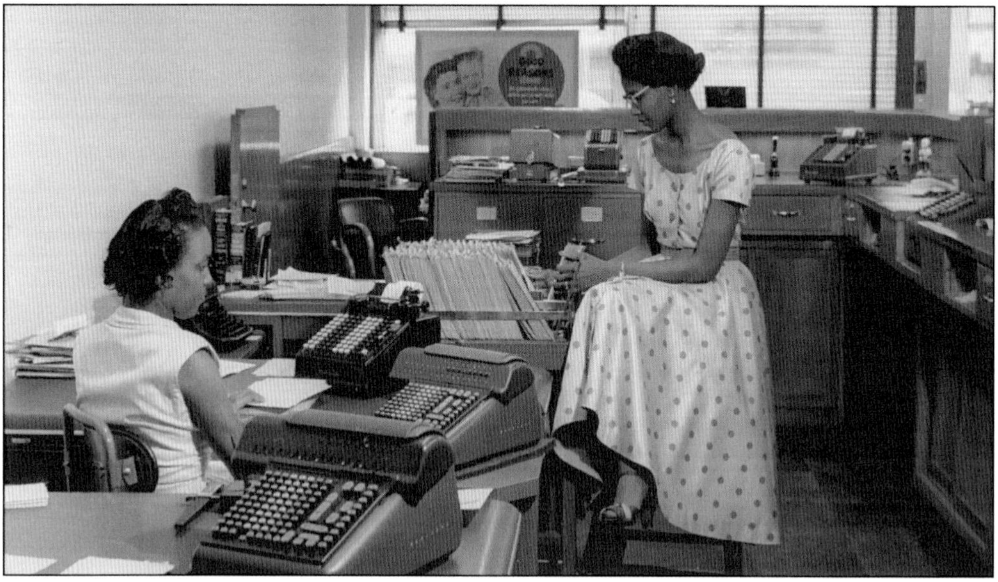

Josephine Shearin Strayhorne and an unidentified clerk are captured in this photograph inside the Mutual Savings and Loan Association, located at 122 West Parrish Street in downtown Durham. (Courtesy of Andre D. Vann.)

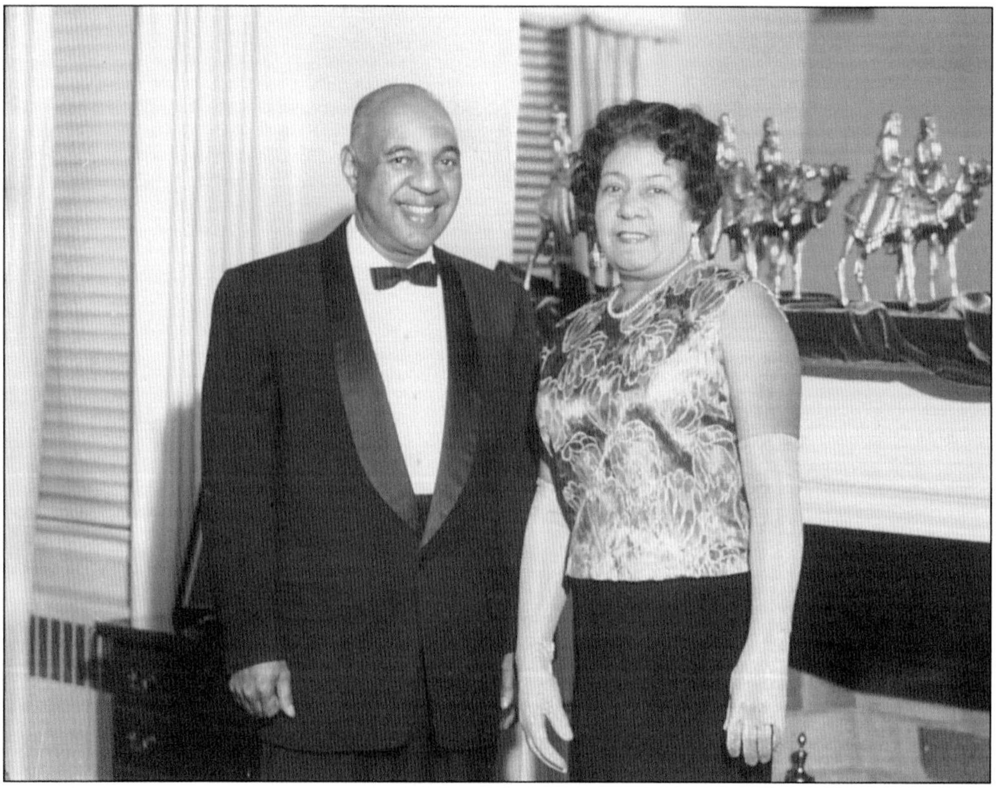

John S. "Shag" Stewart and Otelia Spaulding Stewart were both prominent members of Hayti's black middle class. Stewart was the president of Mutual Saving and Loan Association and was active in various civic affairs. (Courtesy of James Stewart / Andre D. Vann.)

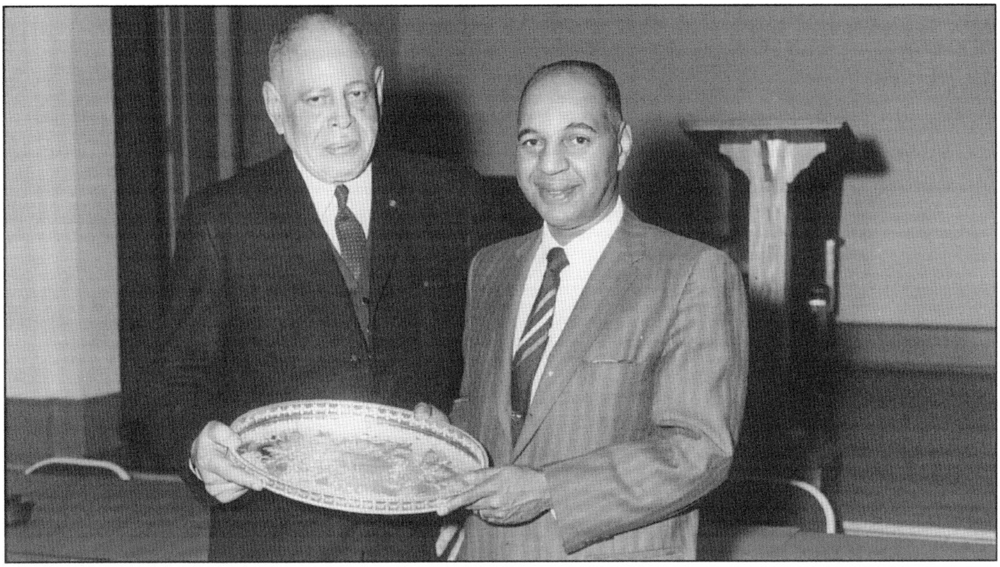

Dr. Clyde Donnell, a physician and businessman, is shown receiving a silver platter from John S. "Shag" Stewart for his years of service on the board of Mutual Savings and Loan Association. (Courtesy of Andre D. Vann.)

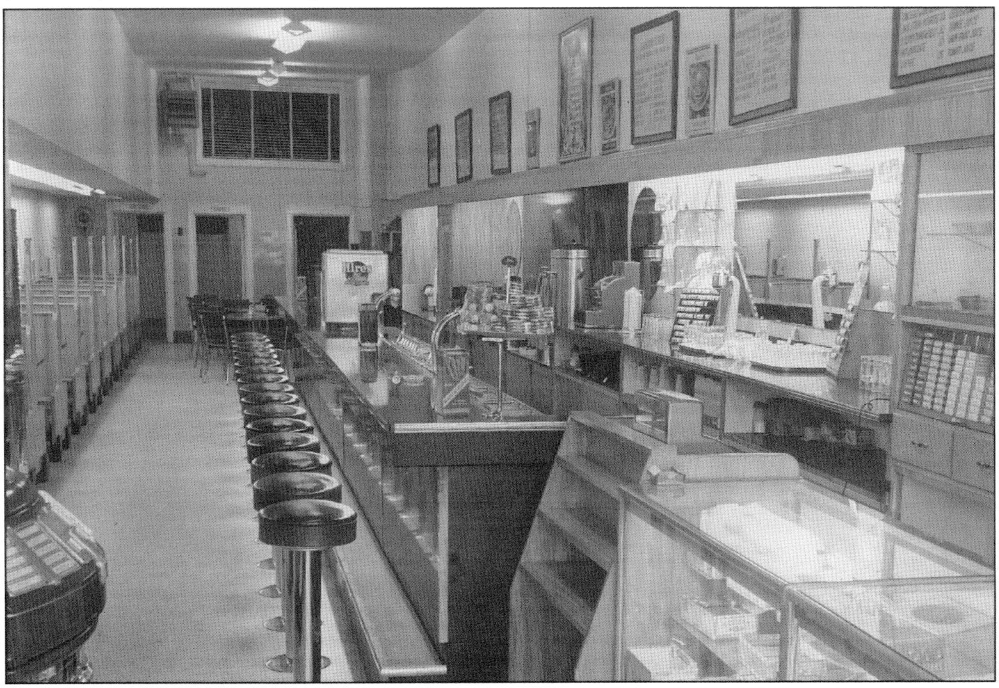

This is a 1949 interior view of the Donut Shop, which was founded by William Gaston Pearson II and his wife, Jessie Logan, in July 1947. Located at 336 East Pettigrew Street, this business was hailed as "The South's Finest Eating Establishment," and was the center of many social gatherings in Hayti. The Donut Shop is in the main section and had a seating capacity for 68 customers. The adjacent room, known as "The Jade Room," which had a beautiful pea green and pink combination of colors, accommodated 100 customers. (Courtesy of Jesse Logan Pearson / Andre D. Vann.)

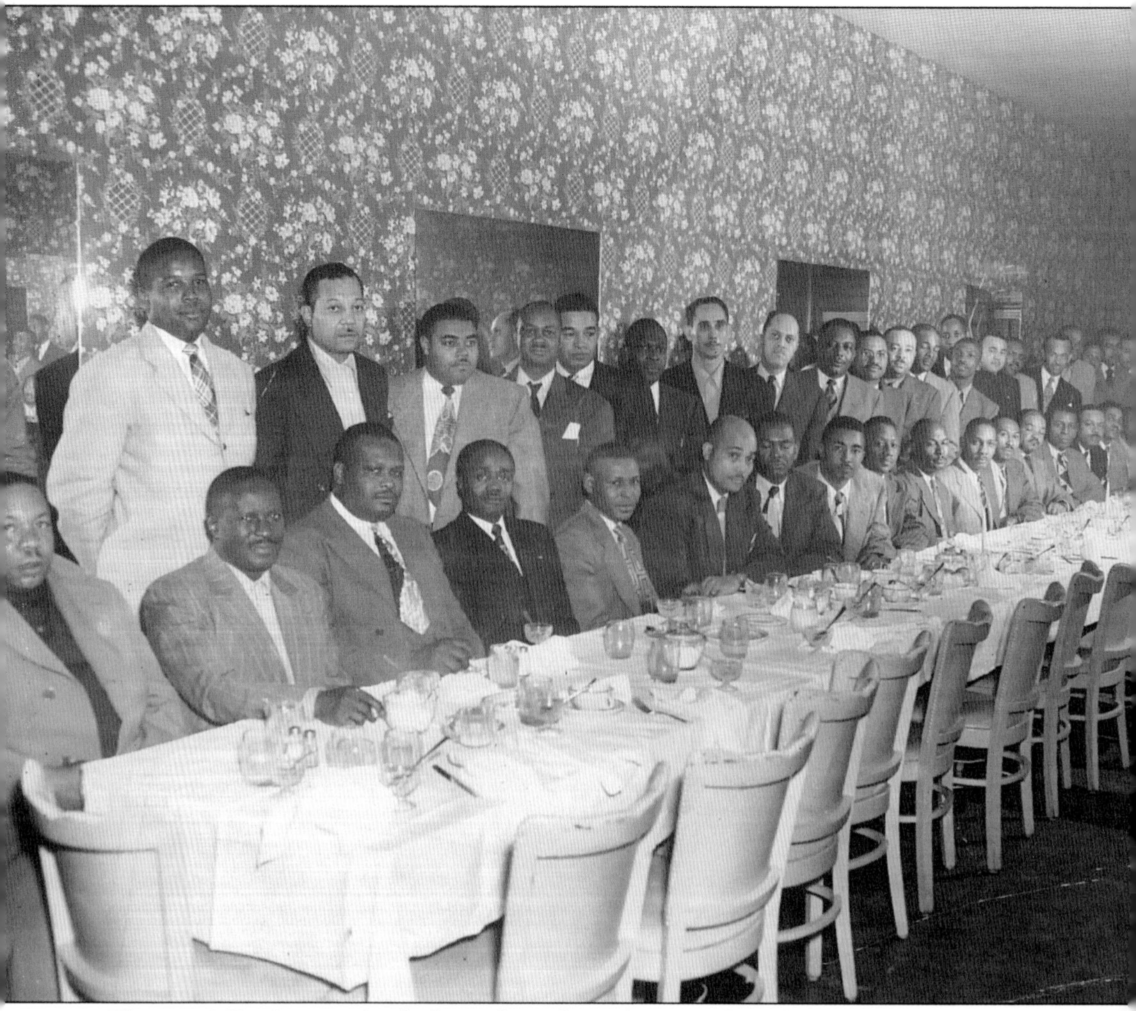

This is a 1960s photograph of referees throughout the state of North Carolina meeting in the Jade Room of the Donut Shop on Pettigrew Street. (Courtesy of Gladys Rennick / Andre D. Vann.)

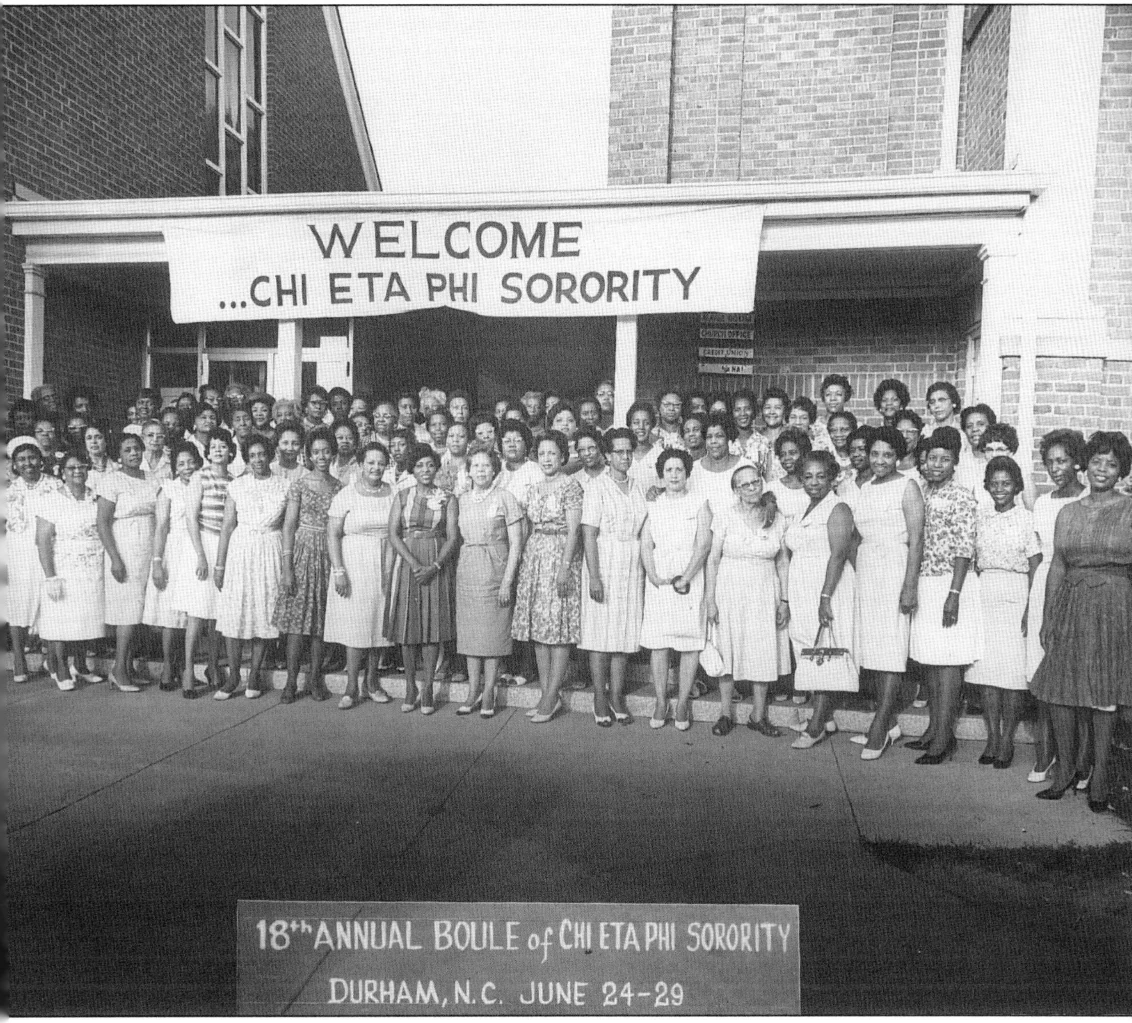

The Pi Chapter of Chi Eta Phi Nurse Sorority hosted their annual meeting in Durham at the Mt. Vernon Baptist Church on June 24–29, 1963. (Courtesy of Andre D. Vann.)

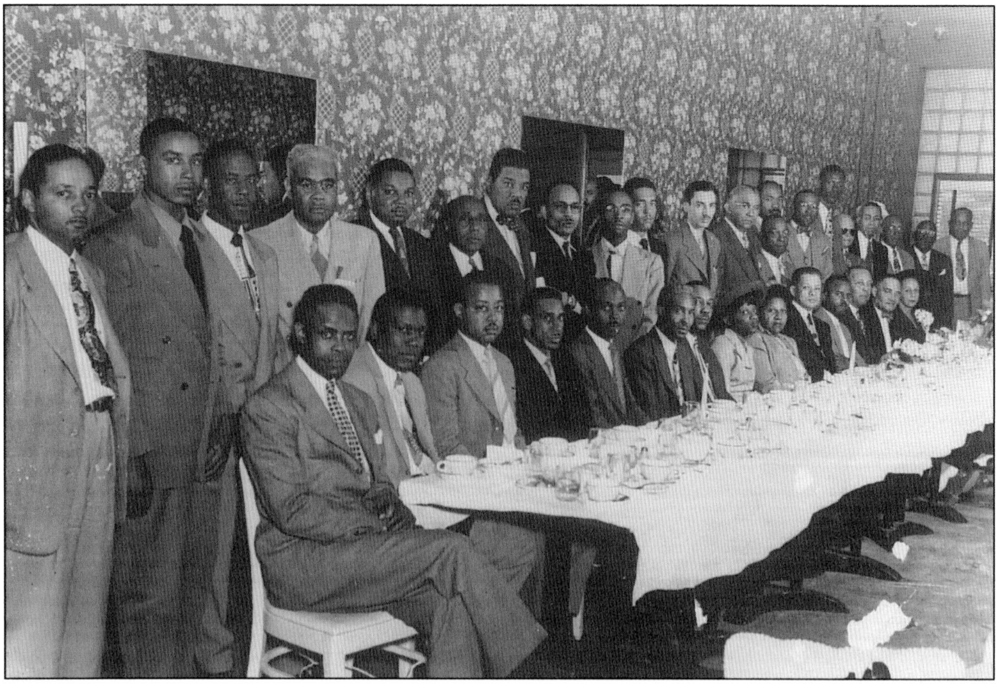

This is a 1950s photograph of members of the North Carolina Lawyers Association, which was organized in Durham in 1954. The black lawyers banned together to pursue the common goals of justice for minorities and poor people, to develop legal strategies, and to provide professionalism in the black Bar. This meeting is being held in the Jade Room of the Donut Shop. Note the presence of attorney Floyd B. McKissick Sr. (back row, second from the left), who distinguished himself as a national civil rights attorney, as a civil rights spokesman, and as an author. He also served as the national chairman of the Congress of Racial Equality. (Courtesy of Gladys H. Rennick / Andre D. Vann.)

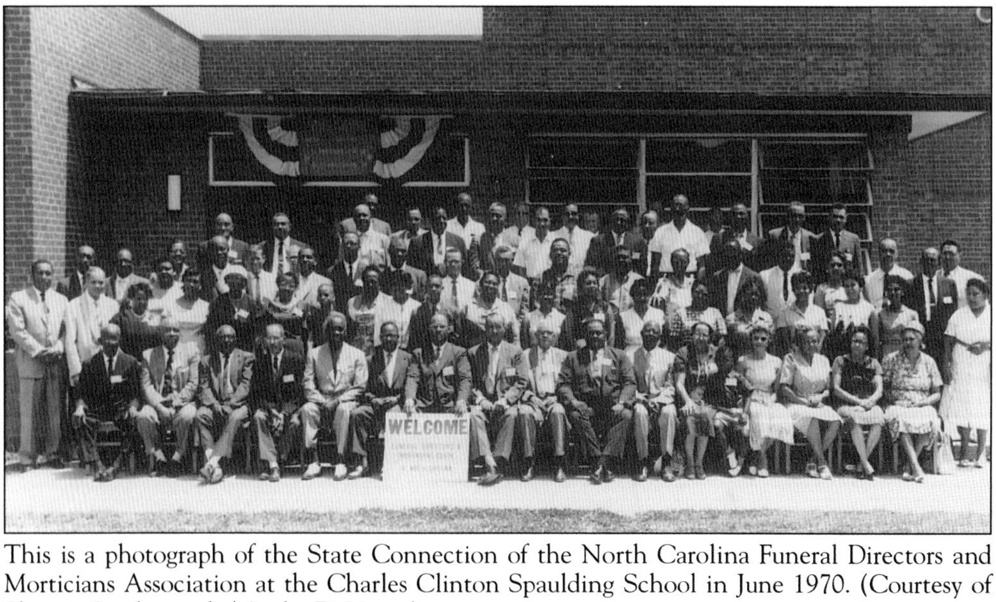

This is a photograph of the State Connection of the North Carolina Funeral Directors and Morticians Association at the Charles Clinton Spaulding School in June 1970. (Courtesy of Skeepie Scarborough / Andre D. Vann.)

Seven

CIVIL RIGHTS

The Battle for Freedom Begins Every Morning.

—The late John Hervey Wheeler (1908–1978),
chairman of the Durham Committee on the Affairs of Black People.

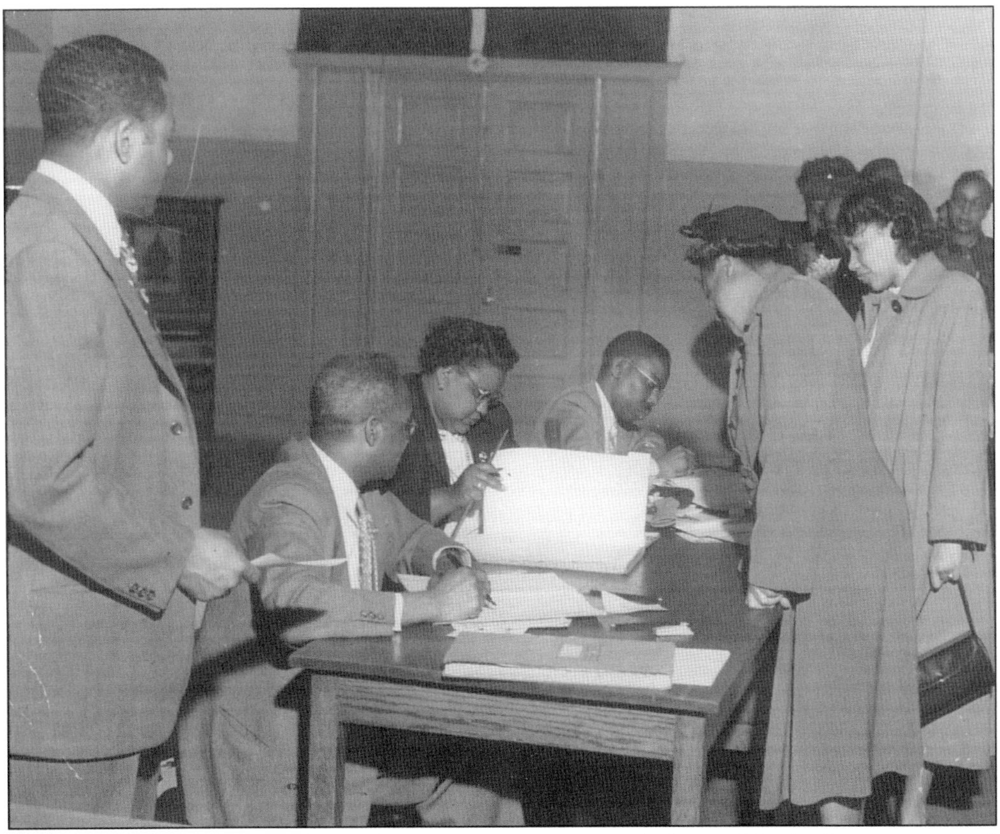

Durham residents, through the Durham Committee on the Affairs of Blacks, have maintained high levels of political participation through the use of the ballot. This 1950 photograph shows pictures of blacks seeking to vote at the Pearson School Precinct. (Courtesy of Andre D. Vann.)

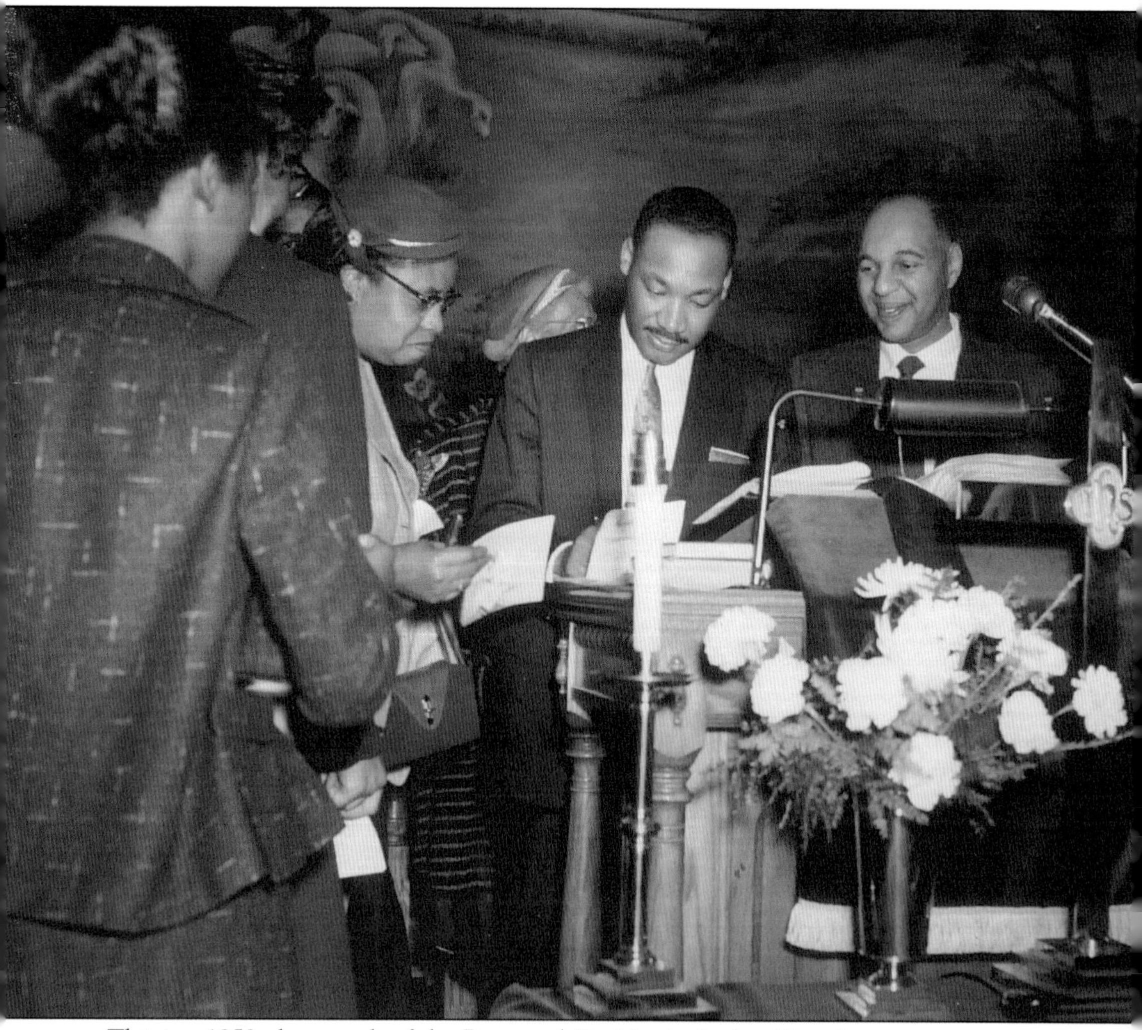

This is a 1958 photograph of the Reverend Dr. Martin Luther King Jr. at a voter registration rally at the Saint Mark African Methodist Episcopal Zion Church. At right is City Councilman John Sylvester "Shag" Stewart, president of the Mutual Community Saving and Loan Bank. (Courtesy of Andre D. Vann.)

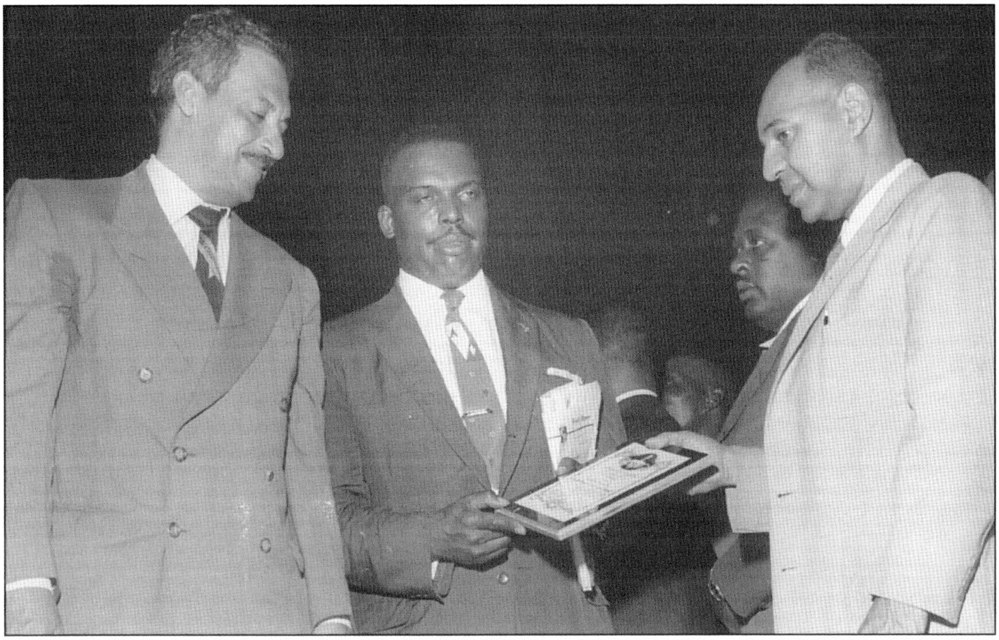

Thurgood Marshall, left, was chief counsel for the NAACP from 1938 until his appointment to the federal court and eventually to the United States Supreme Court. Marshall watches Kelly Alexander, head of the North Carolina Conference of State Branches, NAACP, as he presents John Stewart with life membership in this 1956 photograph. (Courtesy of Andre D. Vann.)

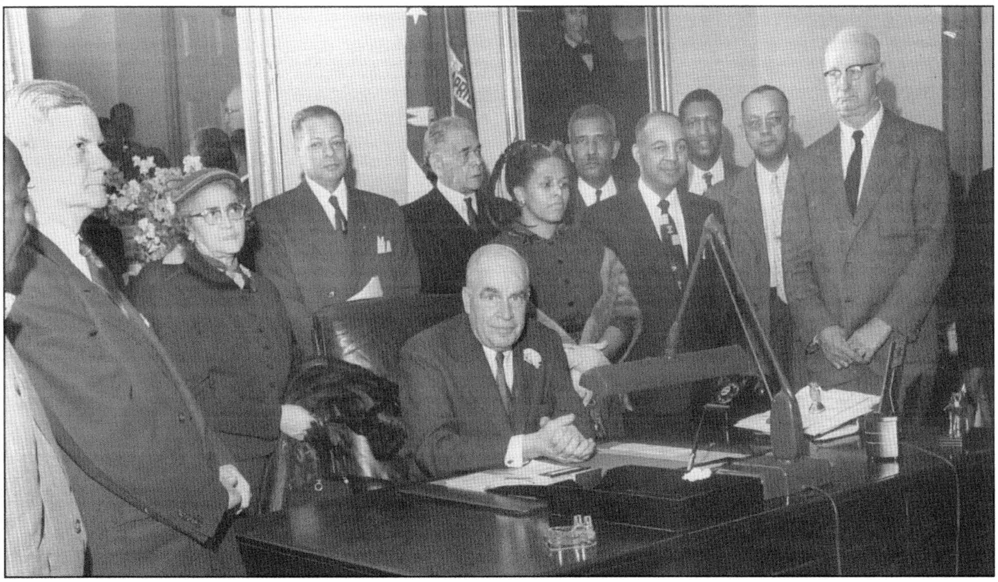

In 1954 black leaders met with Governor Luther Hodges to protest the defiance of *Brown vs Board of Education* decision to desegregate the public schools. The governor explained that there was no defiance to the *Brown* decision and that the State of North Carolina was proceeding with all deliberate speed and that they were moving as fast as they could. The black leaders are, from left to right, as follows: Alexander Barnes, unidentified legislator, Lyda Merrick, John H. Wheeler, Dr. G.W. Carnes, Ms. J.J. Hannibal, William L. Greene, John S. Stewart, Nathaniel White, Edward Merrick, and State Senator Claude Currie of Durham. (Courtesy of Alex Rivera.)

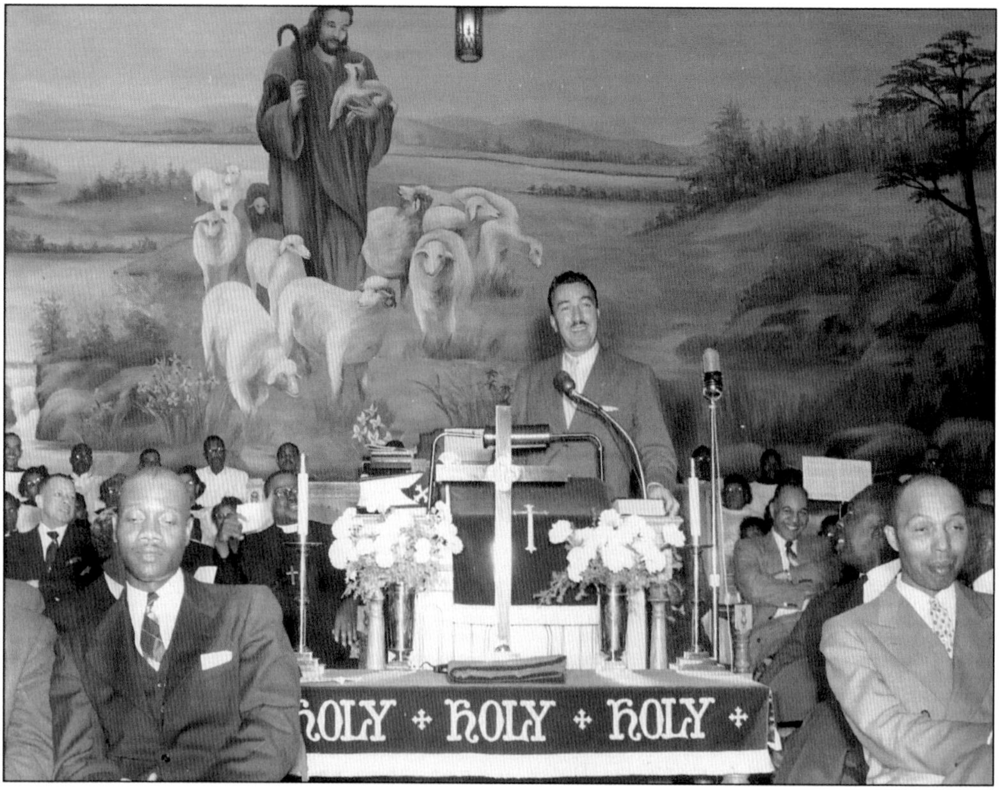

In 1959, the Reverend Adam Clayton Powell Jr. is shown rendering a soul-stirring speech at a voter registration rally held at the Saint Mark A.M.E.Z. Church. In 1932, Reverend Powell Jr. came to White Rock Baptist for a trial sermon but was passed over because the ladies of the church declared that he was too flashy for White Rock. The pulpit remained empty until Reverend Miles Mark Fisher came in 1933. (Courtesy of Andre D. Vann.)

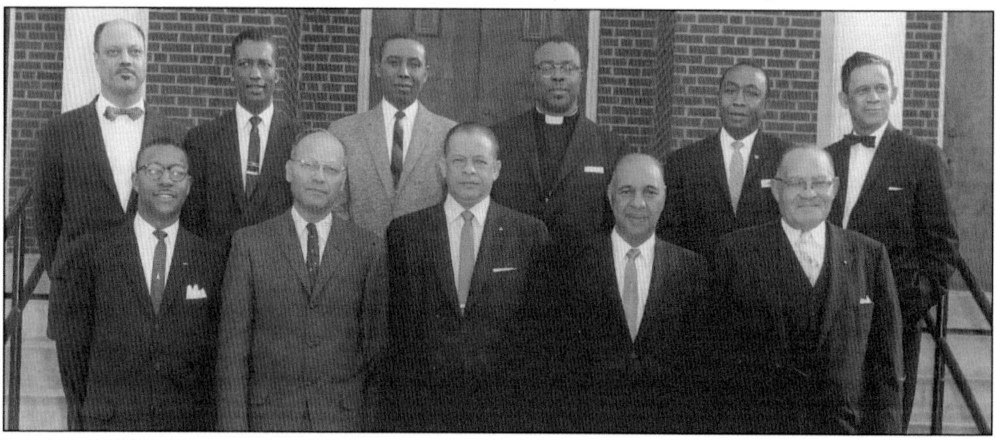

In this 1950s photograph of the executive committee of the Durham Committee on the Affairs of Negroes, taken on the steps of St. Mark's A.M.E.Z. Church, the men are, from left to right, as follows: (front row) William Marsh, Dr. C.E. Bouleware, John Wheeler, John S. Stewart, and attorney Hugh M. Thompson; (back row) D. Eric Moore, Nathaniel White, Floyd B. McKissick, Reverend Reuben Speaks, Leroy B. Frasier, and Ellis Jones. (Courtesy of Andre D. Vann.)

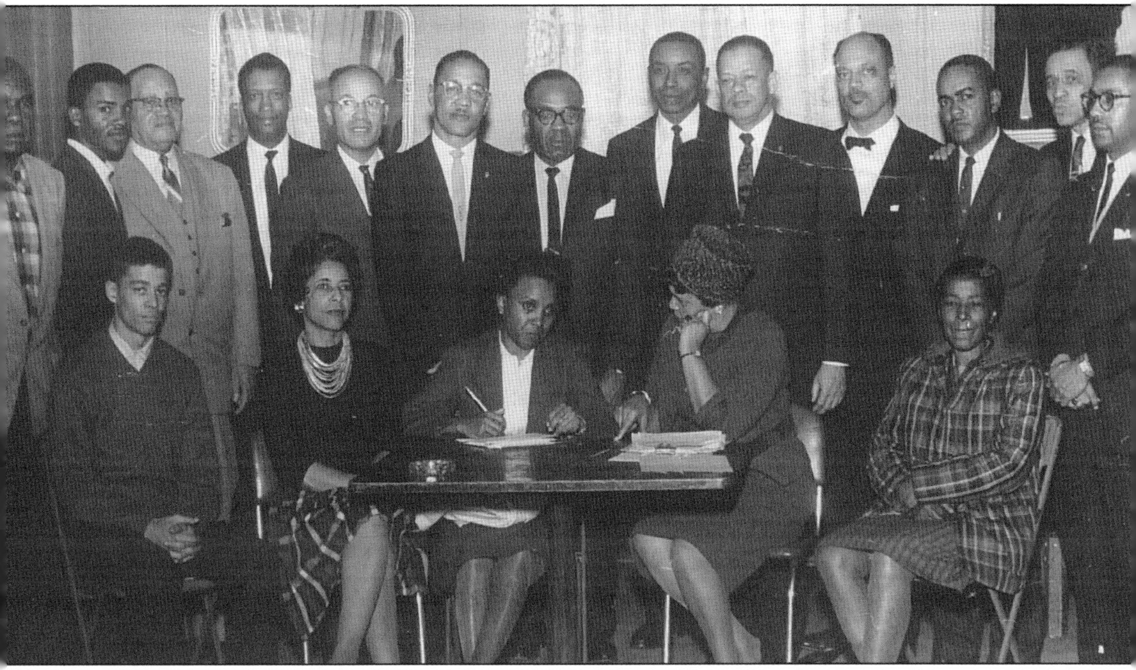

The Durham Committee on the Affairs of Negroes members gathered for this groups photograph, which is representative of the black population of Hayti. The organization was begun in 1935 and has served as the most progressive power and voter machinery in the New South. (Courtesy of Andre D. Vann.)

This is a 1940s photograph of attorney Conrad Odell Pearson (1920–1984), who was reared in Durham by his grandparents, George Washington Pearson Sr. and Cynthia Barbee Pearson, both of whom were former slaves. Pearson attended Durham schools, graduating from Whitted School in 1918, and studied at Wilberforce University in Wilberforce, Ohio, graduating in 1924. After receiving the J.D. degree from Howard University School of Law in 1932, Pearson returned to Durham to practice law. A pioneer lawyer in the struggle for civil rights, he filed an action in 1933 on behalf of Thomas R. Hocutt against the University of North Carolina. This case was the forerunner of all civil rights actions brought in the desegregation of state-supported universities throughout the South. In 1933 he was brought to trial in the case of *State vs. Tucker*, in which Pearson noted the exclusion of black people from juries, pointing out that no black man had served on a jury in North Carolina since 1900. As a result, blacks subsequently served on both petty and grand juries throughout the state. He was a member of the Masons, Kappa Alpha Psi, and the St. Joseph's A.M.E. Church. He died in 1984 and is interred in Beechwood Cemetery. (Courtesy of Andre D. Vann.)

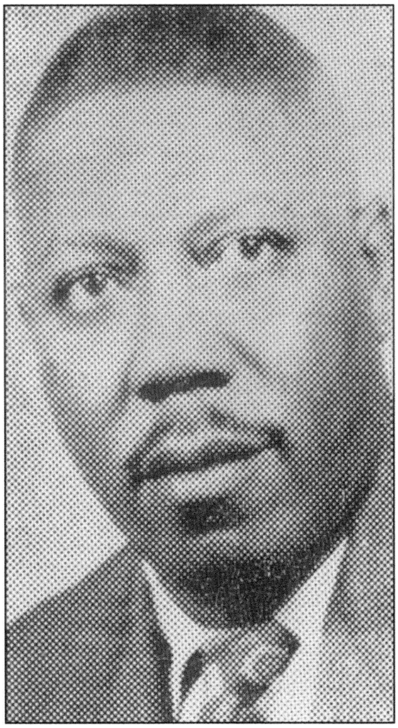

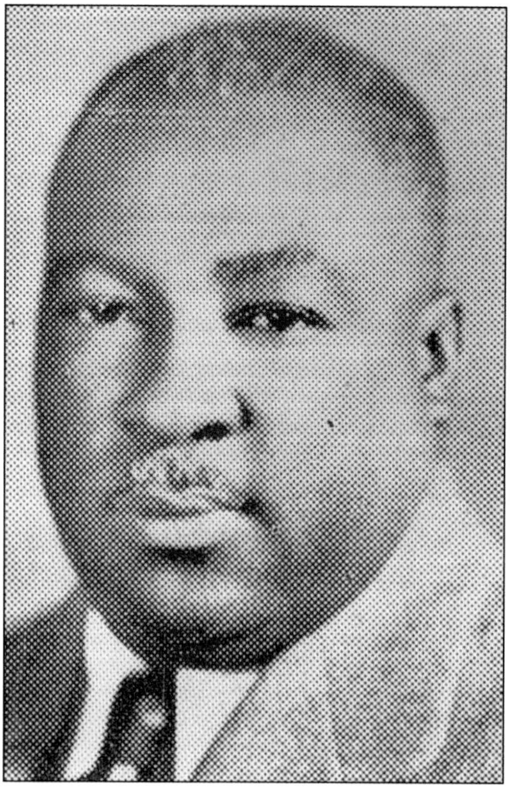

Attorney Caswell Jerry Gates (1895–1970) was one of Durham's most noted lawyers. He was a native of Durham and an early graduate of Shaw University in Raleigh; he later received the Bachelor of Laws Degree from Boston University. Gates taught in the Vance County School System and later journeyed back to Durham in 1927, after being admitted to the Bar. From 1927 until 1970, he practiced continuously as an advocate for the rights of minorities. He held membership in the NAACP, Phi Beta Sigma Fraternity, and was a member of the St. Joseph's A.M.E. Church. He died in 1970 and is interred in the Beechwood Cemetery in Durham. (Courtesy of Andre D. Vann.)

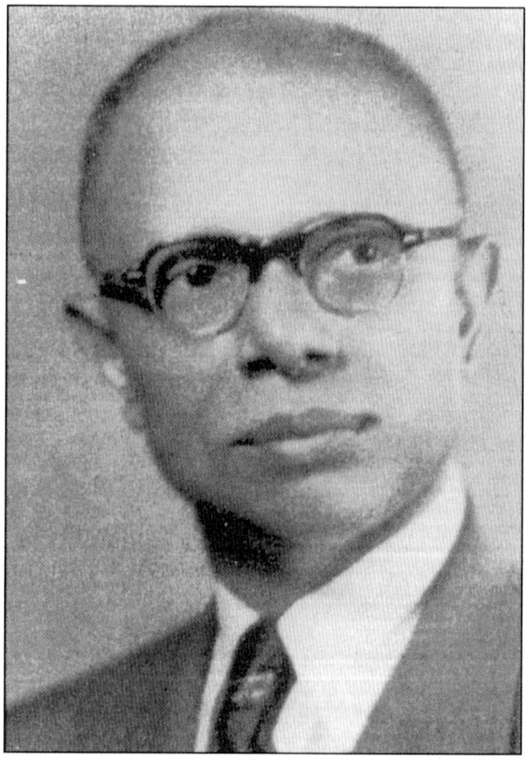

This is a c. 1950s photograph of Louis Ernest Austin (1898–1971), who was a native of Enfield, North Carolina. He attended the National Training School and Chautauqua, where he later was awarded an honorary LL.D. degree. Austin worked as an insurance agent for the North Carolina Mutual Life Insurance Company until 1926. When he founded the militant newspaper, the *Carolina Times*, he dedicated the paper, whose motto is "The Truth Unbridled," to justice and equality for all blacks in the Durham community. Austin's office served as the headquarters for many civil rights efforts in the local community. He was the driving force behind Raymond Hocutt's legal challenge of the University of North Carolina at Chapel Hill's segregation policy. Austin also fought to hire black firemen, policemen, and bus drivers; he crusaded for equal pay for black teachers and paved streets and adequate streetlights in black communities. (Courtesy of Vivian Austin Edmonds.)

Eight

The North Carolina Mutual Life Insurance Company

As long as it is God's Will, I Want this Institution to move; For men to support their families; And God will let it Live. That is what I am interested about and God knows it. I want this institution to live and she will! God bless you all.

—From the last speech delivered by John Merrick,
co-founder of NCMLIC, at the 20th anniversary of the company, June 19, 1919.

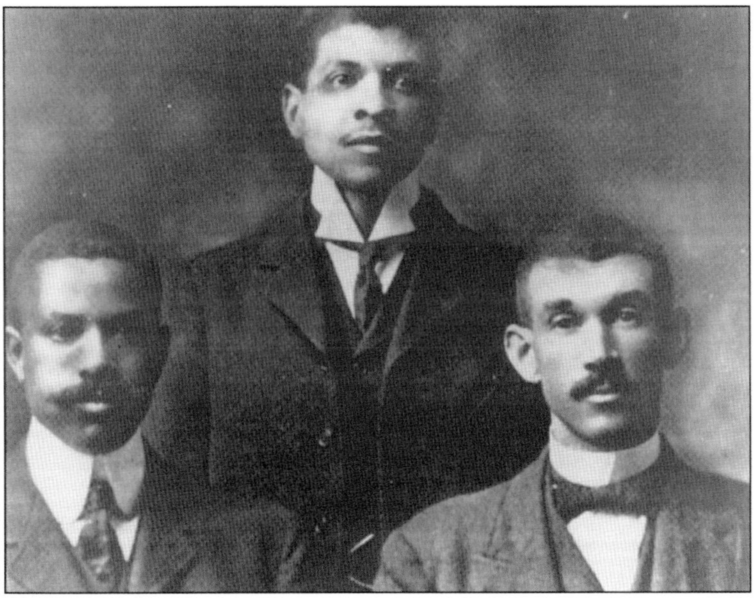

This photograph captures the North Carolina Mutual Life Insurance Company under the leadership of the triumvirate around 1900. From left to right, they are as follows: John Merrick, president; Charles C. Spaulding, general manager; and Dr. Aaron M. Moore, secretary, treasurer, and medical director. (Courtesy of North Carolina Division of Archives and History.)

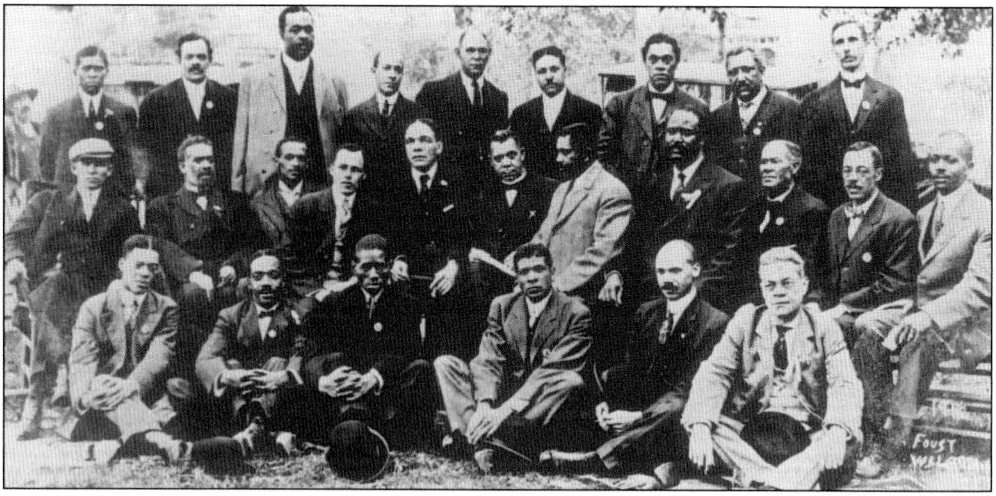

Booker T. Washington and his entourage visited North Carolina Mutual Life Insurance Company in 1910 on a tour through towns and cities in North Carolina. The climax of the tour was Durham, where Washington's philosophy of self-help was evident in the various economic enterprises in Hayti. Washington (center second row) is pictured with John Merrick (to his right), C.C. Spaulding Sr. (first row center), and James E. Shepard (second row, third from the left). (Courtesy of Durham County Public Library.)

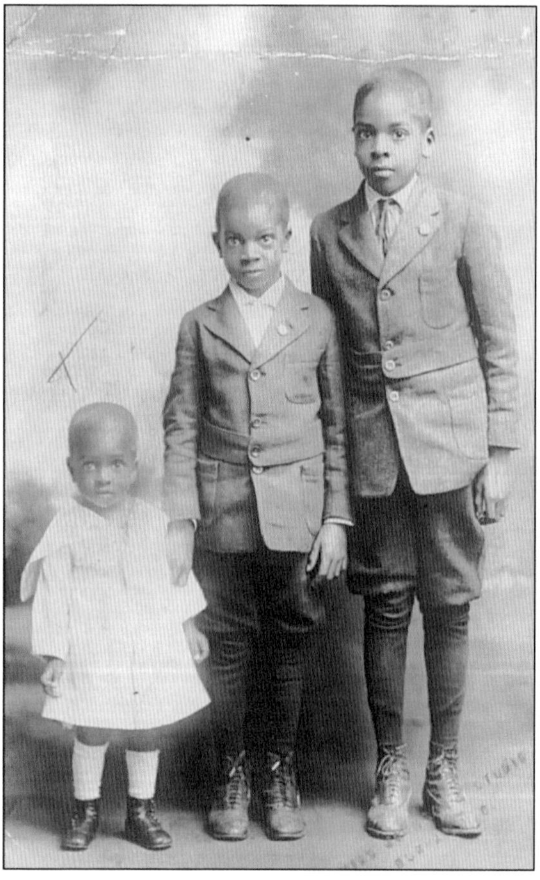

This is an early 1918 photograph of the children of North Carolina Mutual executive Charles C. Spaulding and Fannie Jones Spaulding. They are, from left to right, as follows: Booker Benjamin, John Aaron (1910–1982), and Charles Clinton Spaulding Jr. (1907–1987)—all of whom worked for North Carolina Mutual Life Insurance Company in various capacities. (Courtesy of Andre D. Vann.)

This is a 1920s photo of Cottie S. Moore (1866–1950), pioneer Hayti religious and civic leader and humanitarian. Moore was the widow of Dr. Aaron M. Moore and lived at 606 Fayetteville Street. Educated in the public schools of Tarboro and attending college at St. Augustines in Raleigh, she journeyed to Durham during the 1890s after uniting in marriage to Dr. Moore in 1889. She was the mother of Matte L. McDougald and was a member of the Stanford L. Warren Library, North Carolina Federation of Negro Women's Clubs, and the Daughters of Dorcas Club. Moore also served for decades at the White Rock Baptist Church in various capacities. (Courtesy of Andre D. Vann.)

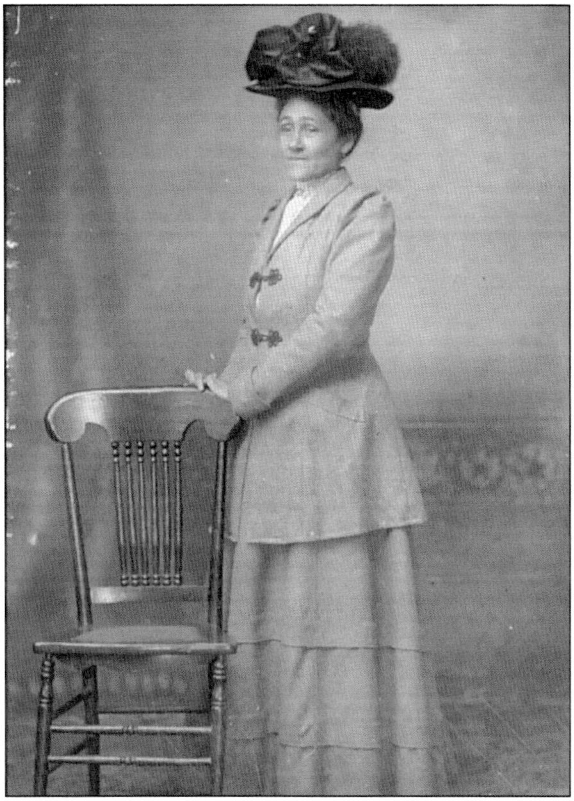

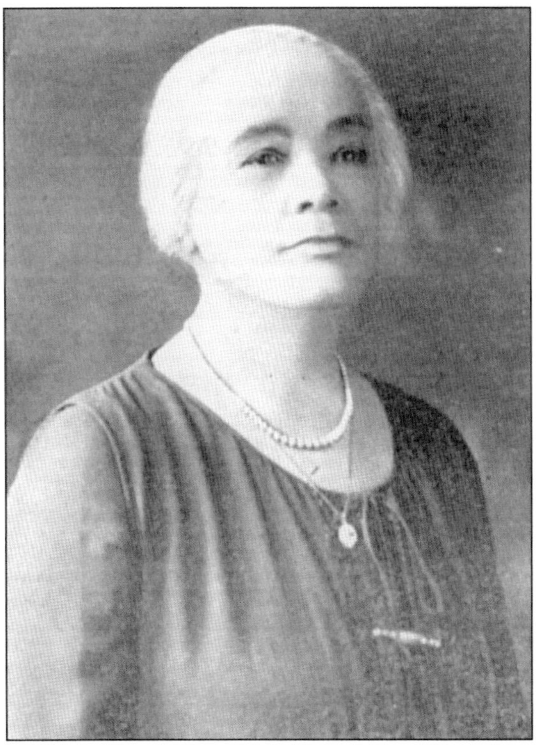

This is a 1930s photograph of Mrs. Martha Hunter Merrick (1860–1939), formerly of Raleigh. In 1880, Martha Hunter was married to John Merrick, the founder of North Carolina Mutual, and from this union five children were born: Geneva B., Mable V., Martha C., Edward R., and John T. Mrs. Merrick died on May 6, 1939, and is interred in the Beechwood Cemetery beside the remains of her husband and children. (Courtesy of Andre D. Vann.)

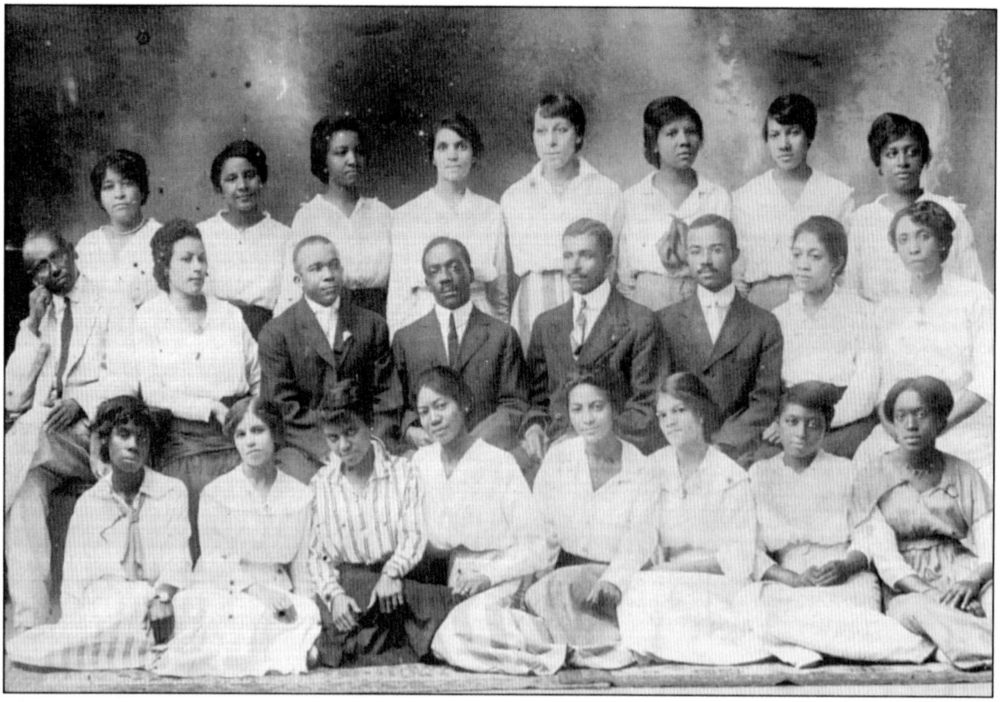

This is a 1921 photograph of the early clerks and managers of the North Carolina Mutual Life Insurance Company. (Courtesy of Andre D. Vann.)

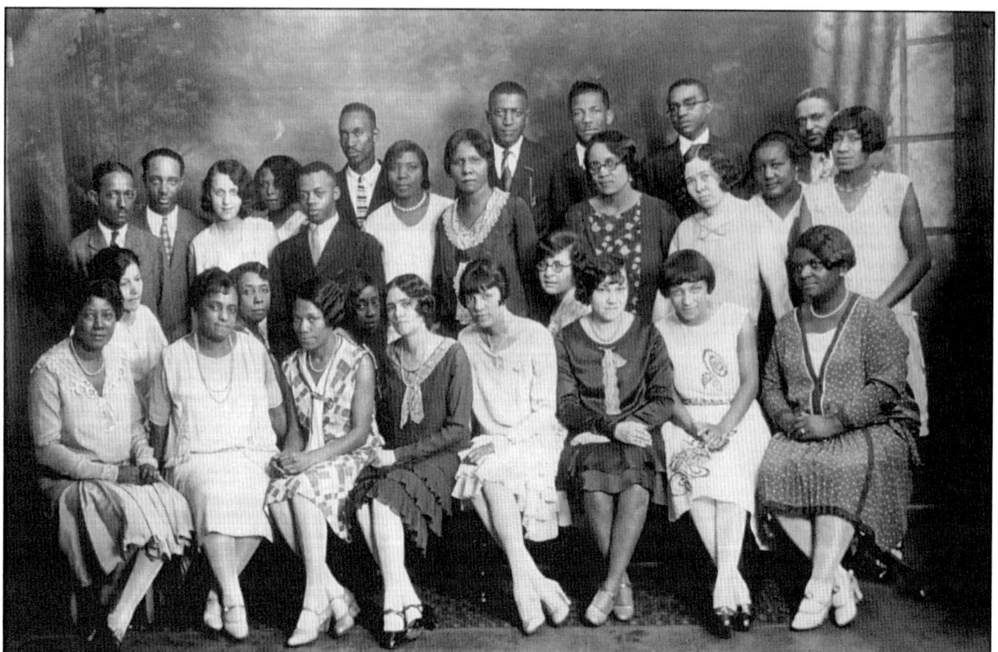

This is a 1929 photograph of the North Carolina Mutual Glee Club. (Courtesy of Maggie P. Bryant.)

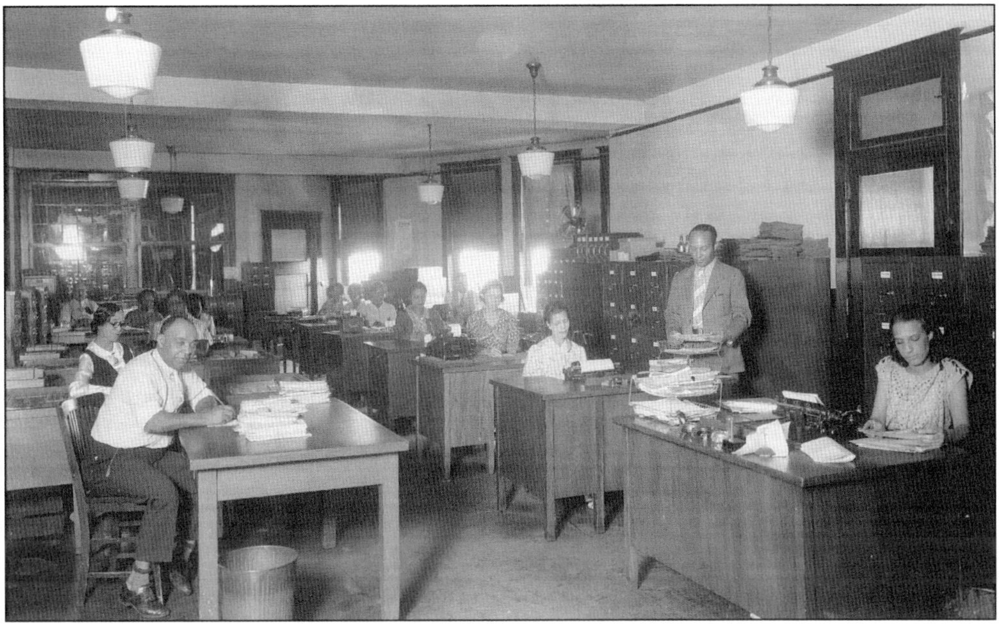

Durham's North Carolina Mutual Life Insurance Company, formed in 1898, became the largest black-owned business in the United States and was a major employer of black professionals. This photograph of clerical workers in the company's "industrial department" was made about 1930. Joseph W. Goodloe, to the extreme right, would go on to become the president in 1967. (Courtesy of Andre D. Vann.)

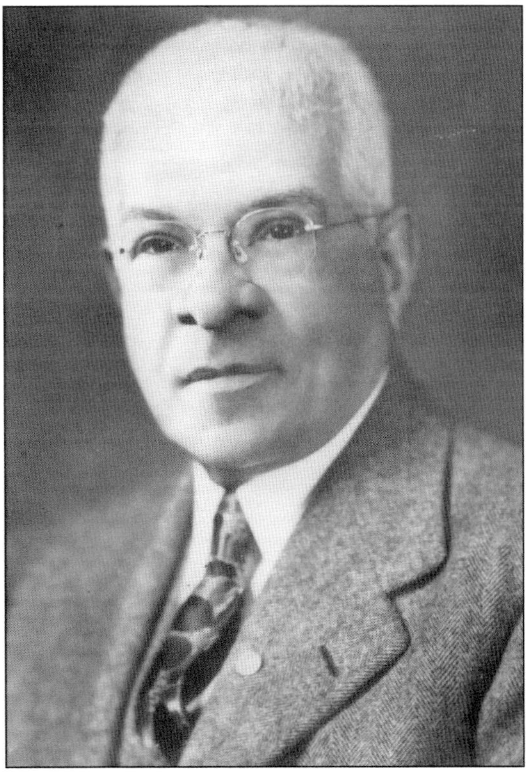

Charles Clinton Spaulding Sr. (1874–1952) was born in Columbus County, North Carolina, and came to Durham to assist his uncle, Dr. Aaron M. Moore. In 1899 he became associated with the North Carolina Mutual and Provident Association as a part-time agent, and on July 1, 1900, he was appointed general manager on a full-time basis. He also was elected a member of the board of directors, and then, in 1919, he was elected secretary treasurer. On April 29, 1923, Spaulding became the president and served until his death in 1952. He also served as the president of the Mechanics and Farmers Bank and Mutual Savings and Loan Association. He was a devoted member of White Rock Baptist Church and served as a deacon and the chairman of the trustee board. He is interred in the Beechwood Cemetery, and C.C. Spaulding Elementary School and Spaulding Street are memorials to his dedication and his life. (Courtesy of Andre D. Vann.)

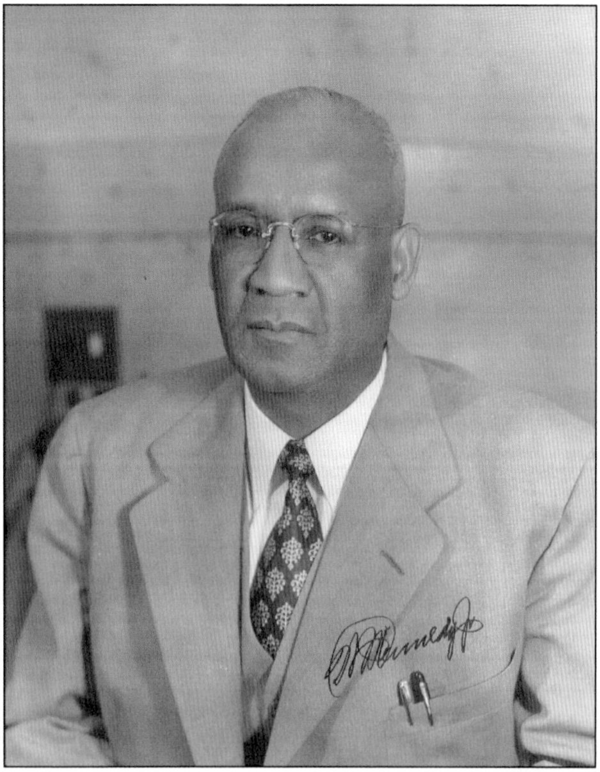

William Jesse Kennedy Jr. (1889–1985) served as the fourth president of North Carolina Mutual Life Insurance Company, from 1952 to 1958. Kennedy was transferred to the home office in 1919 and served as office manager, assistant secretary manager, and vice president secretary. He was a member of the board of directors from 1920 until his death in 1985. He authored the *North Carolina Mutual Story* in 1970. (Courtesy of Andre D. Vann.)

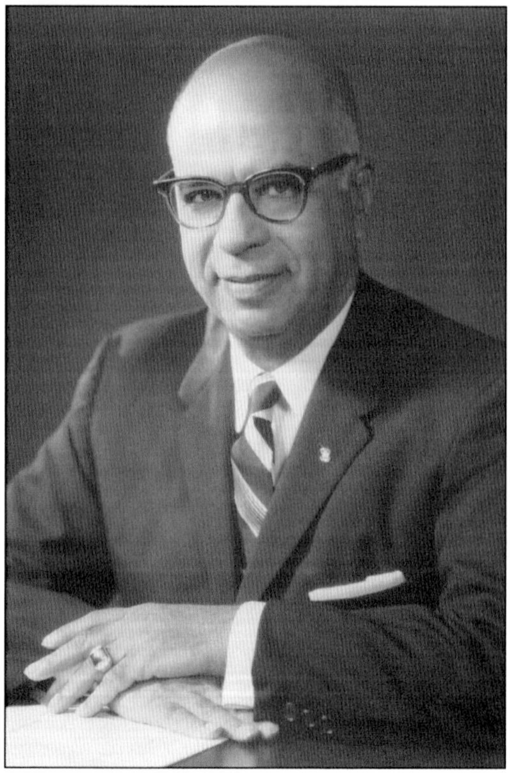

Asa Timothy Spaulding Sr. (1902–1990) was the president of North Carolina Mutual, the nation's largest black-owned company. Under Spaulding's presidency, from 1959 to 1967, North Carolina Mutual was one of Durham's major employers of black professionals. During his presidency, he was appointed to the board of directors of W.T. Grant Company, thus becoming the first black to serve on the board of a major corporation in the United States. He also served on the boards of the Mechanics and Farmers Bank, Mutual Saving and Loan Association, the National Urban League, and was a past national president of the National Negro Insurance Association. In 1946, he received a Presidential Citation from Harry S. Truman for his contributions to the welfare of the nation. He was a member of the 1956 U.S. delegation to the UNESCO General Conference in India. He was married to Elna Bridgeforth and was the father of four children. (Courtesy of Andre D. Vann.)

Born in Durham, Joseph Waverly Goodloe (1906–1990) graduated from Hampton Institute and began his professional career in 1926 at North Carolina Mutual. He held many official positions in the company and served as president from 1967 until 1972. From 1975 to 1978, he was the chairman of the board of directors. (Courtesy of Andre D. Vann.)

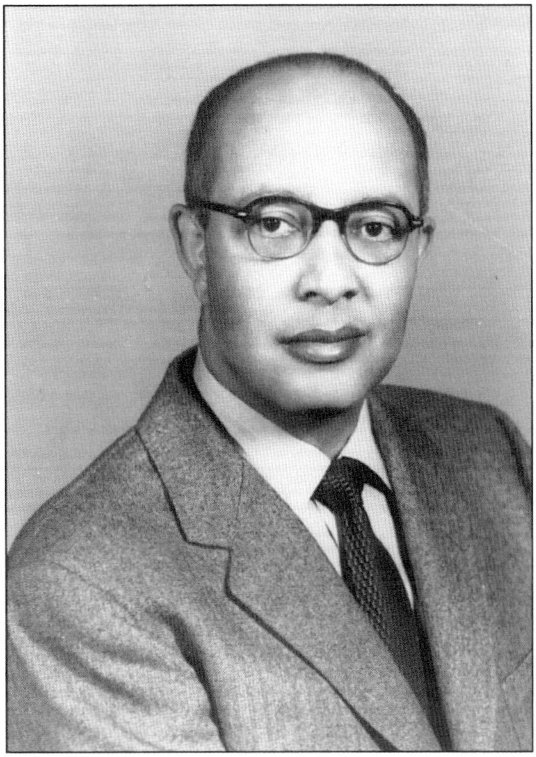

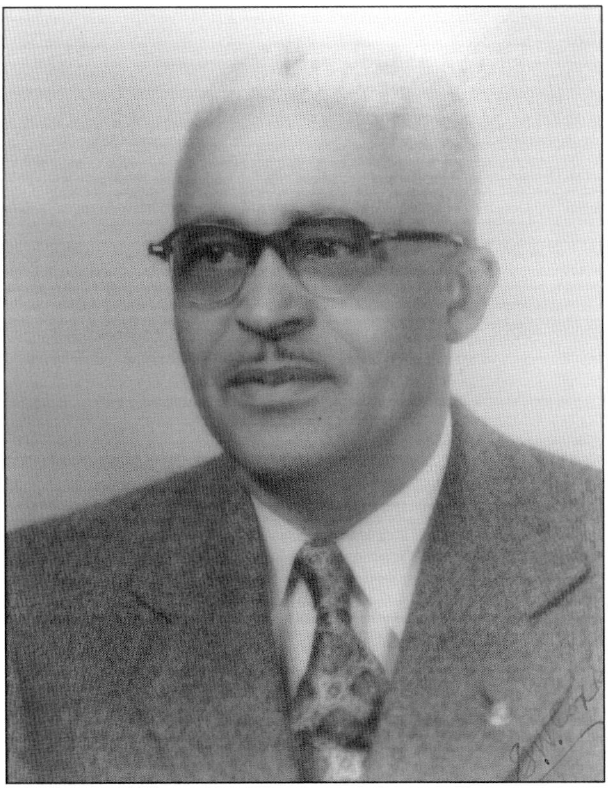

George Wayne Cox Sr. (1890–1956), born at Indianola, Mississippi, was educated at Gardner Seminary of Indianola and received, in 1910, a B.S. degree from Alcorn A&M College in Mississippi. Cox joined North Carolina Mutual in 1919 as an organizer of the company's Southern region and was assigned to the home office in 1923. Cox was elected to the board of directors in 1932 and was elected vice-president in 1934. He was also a founder and past president of the National Negro Insurance Association. He served as vice-president and director for the Mechanics and Farmers Bank and was a member of the Omega Psi Phi Fraternity and the John Avery's Boys Club. (Courtesy of Andre D. Vann.)

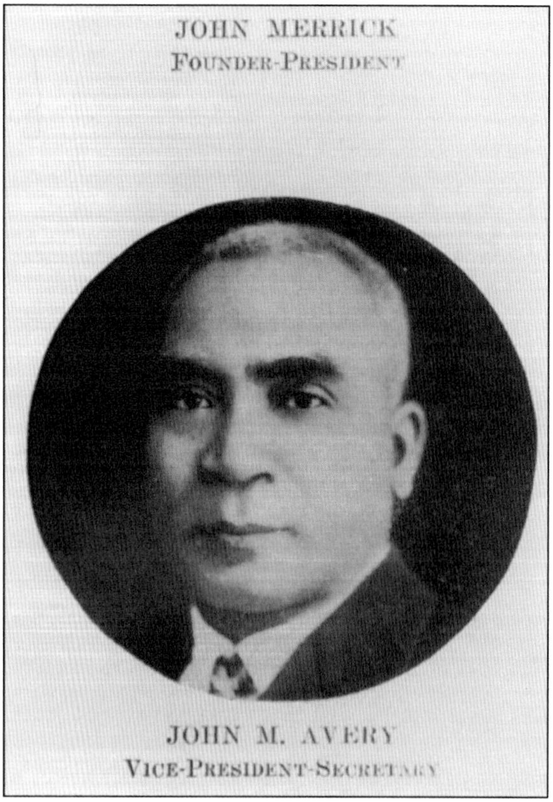

John Moses Avery (1876–1931) was a native of Morganton, North Carolina, and a 1900 graduate of Kittrell College. He came to Durham in 1909 to be the assistant to the general manager in the home office. Avery was elected to the board of directors in 1911, appointed auditor in 1915, assistant manager in 1917, and eventually was elected vice-president, secretary to the board of directors. In 1920 he helped to organize the Bankers Fire Insurance and was a trust officer at Mechanics an Farmers Bank. A member of the Elks and Kappa Alpha Psi Fraternity, Avery was a noted laymen in the A.M.E Church and served on the board of Kittrell College and Lincoln Hospital. The John Avery's Boy's Club is named in his honor. He is interred in Beechwood Cemetery. (Courtesy of Andre D. Vann.)

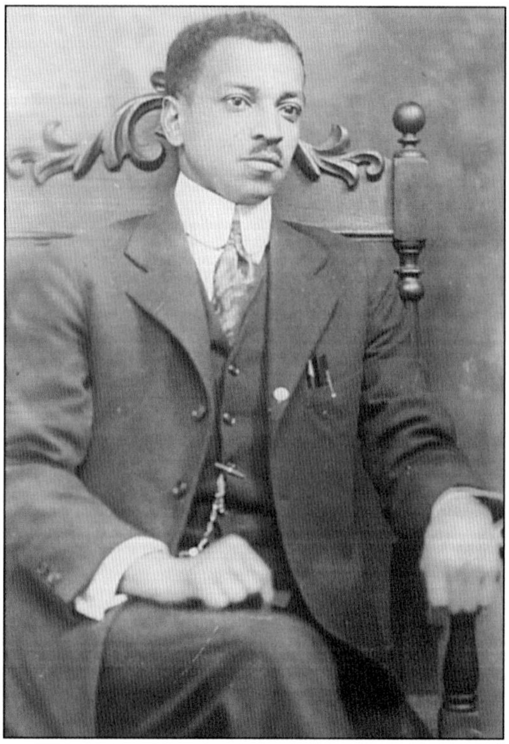

This is an early-1900s photograph of Israel Royal Spaulding (1886–1973), who began his career with the North Carolina Mutual Life Insurance Company around 1908. He was a field supervisor and a district manager in Savannah, Georgia, and then moved to Durham, where he worked in the printing department of North Carolina Mutual. He retired in 1956. He was married to Ruth Whitted Spaulding and was the father of Royal A. Spaulding and Mrs. Ruth S. Boyd. The Spaulding family resides at 1003 Fayetteville Street and were members of the White Rock Baptist Church. (Courtesy of Andre D. Vann.)

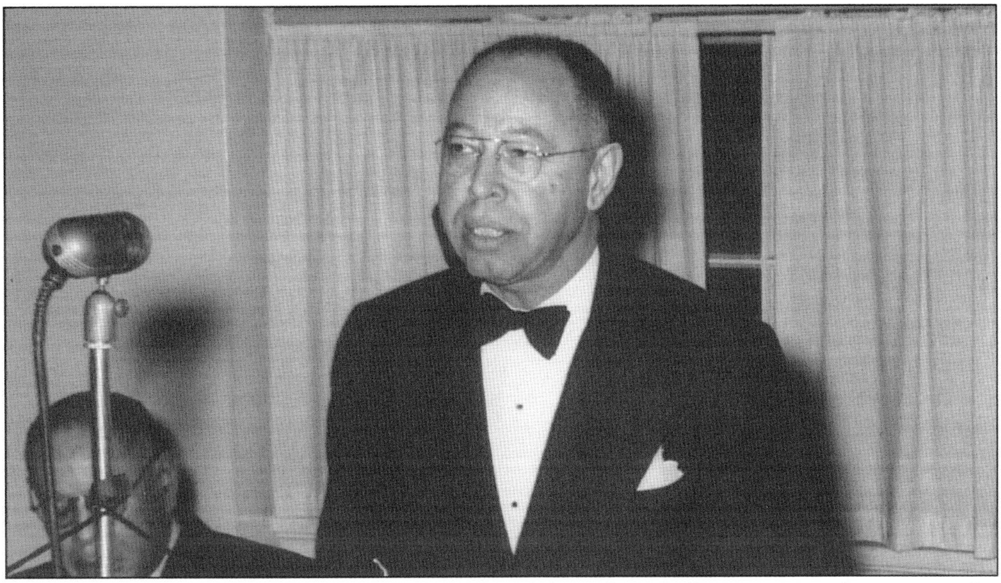

On April 1,1949, North Carolina Mutual Life celebrated its 50th anniversary banquet in the main dining room of North Carolina College. Over 500 invited guests were received and made welcome to the elaborate affair. Shown speaking here was guest speaker W. Ellis Stewart, president of the National Negro Insurance Company of Chicago. Stewart was the first black to hold a college degree in insurance at the University of Illinois. The event was broadcasted live on WDNC radio station. (Courtesy of Andre D. Vann.)

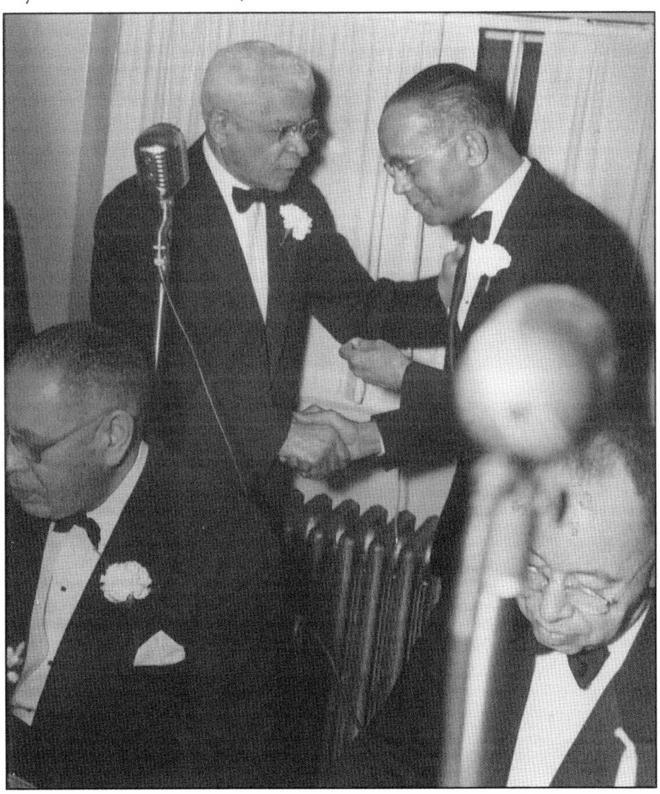

In a scene from North Carolina Mutual's 50th anniversary, President C.C. Spaulding extends congratulations to Edward R. Merrick, treasurer of the Mutual and son of the founder. In the foreground are Dr. Clyde Donnell and W. Ellis Stewart. (Courtesy of Andre D. Vann.)

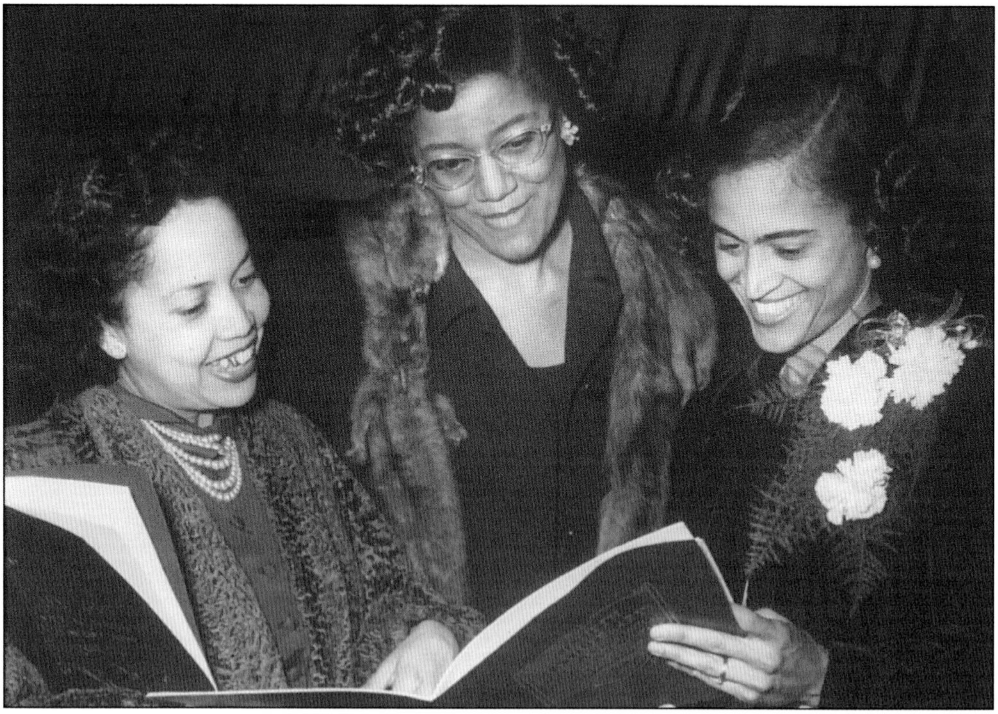

Here, the descendants of the founders examine the first quarter 1949 issue of the *Whetstone*, which served as the golden anniversary brochure that was created by Dr. Charles A. Ray with the assistance of photographer Alex M. Rivera. Shown here is Hazel Bruce Scott, Martha Williams Wheeler, and Vivian Merrick Sansom, all granddaughters of founders Merrick and Moore. (Courtesy of Andre D. Vann.)

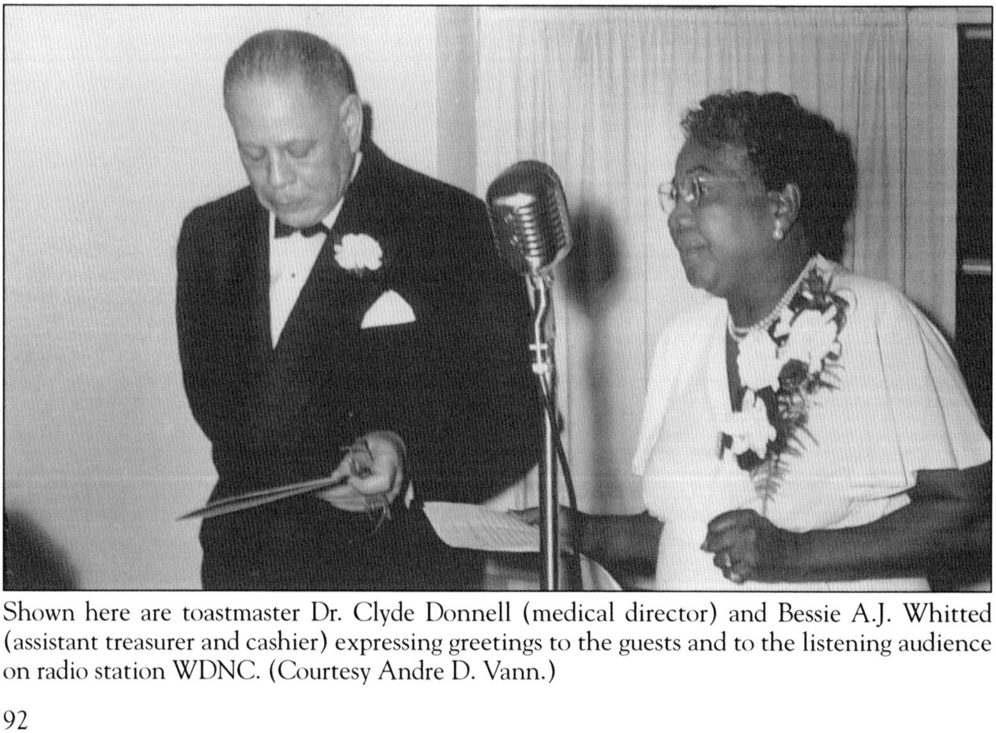

Shown here are toastmaster Dr. Clyde Donnell (medical director) and Bessie A.J. Whitted (assistant treasurer and cashier) expressing greetings to the guests and to the listening audience on radio station WDNC. (Courtesy Andre D. Vann.)

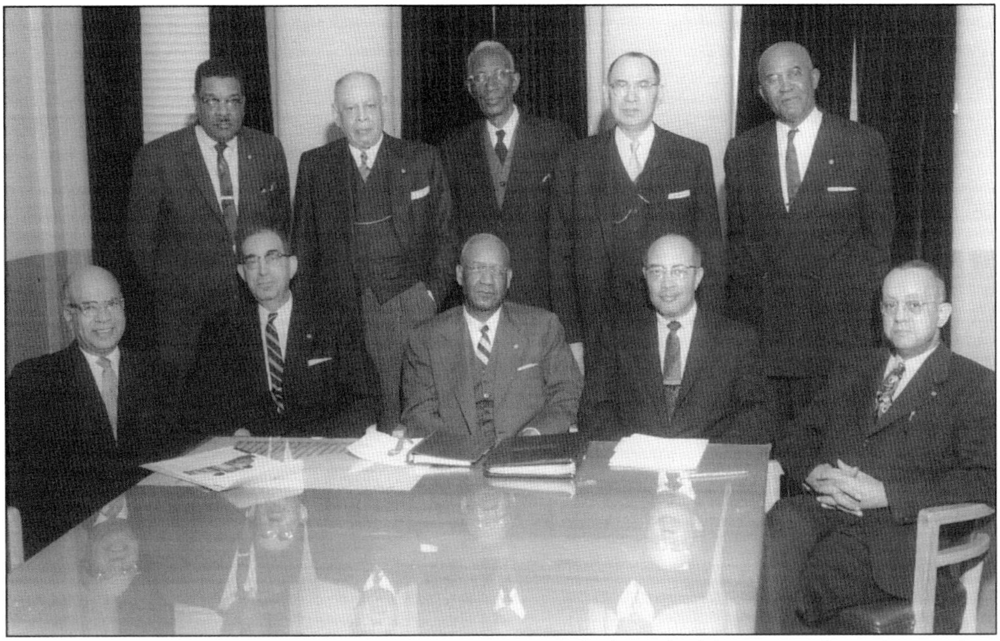

This group photo captures a 1950s board meeting of the board of directors of North Carolina Mutual Life Insurance Company. They are, from left to right, as follows: (first row) Asa T. Spaulding, David C. Crocket Jr., William J. Kennedy Jr. (president), Joseph W. Goodloe, and Edward R. Merrick; (back row) Charles C. Spaulding Jr., Dr. Clyde Donnell, William Harvey, William Rich, and Arthur Spears. (Courtesy of Andre D. Vann.)

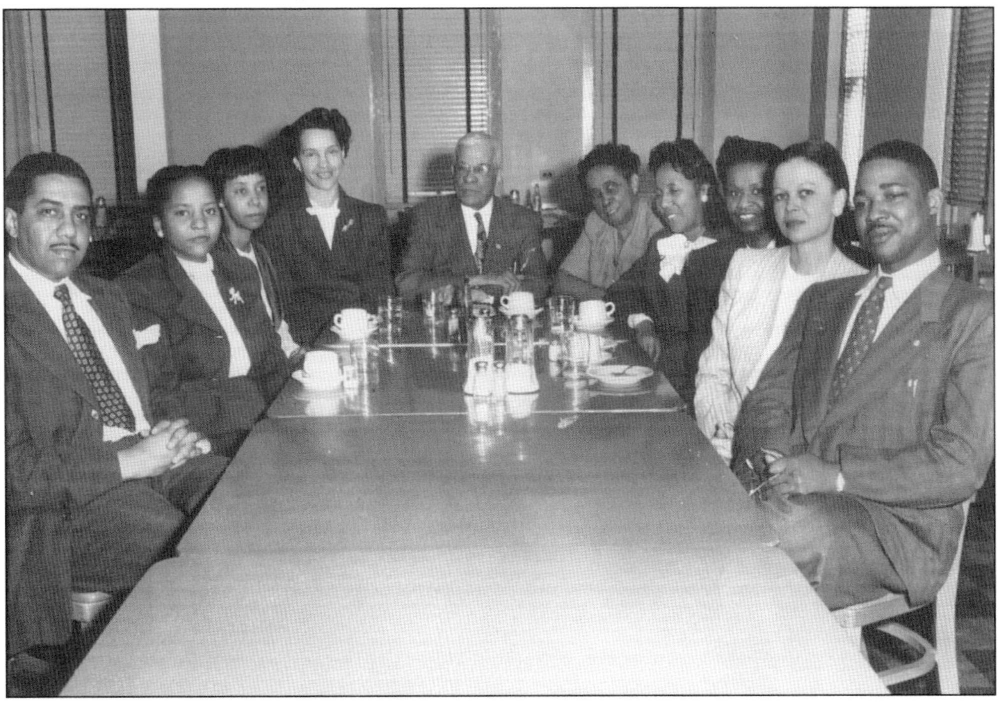

Dr. Charles C. Spaulding, center of photograph, is seen with employees at the weekly luncheon at the Mutual. (Courtesy of Andre D. Vann.)

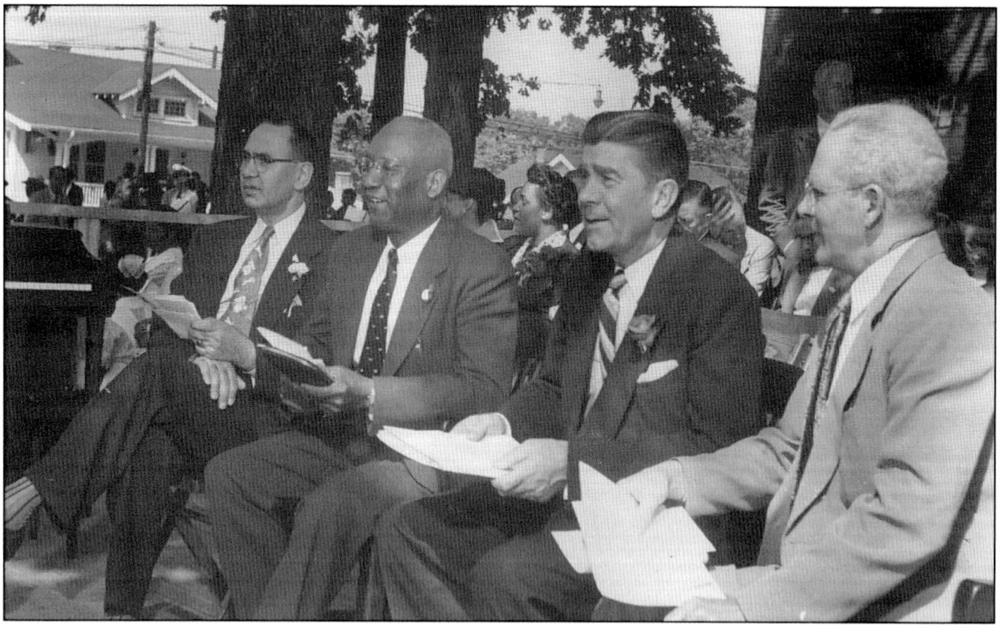

Principals during the 1953 dedication of the new wing to Lincoln Hospital are, from left to right, as follows: William M. Rich, director; William J. Kennedy Jr., chairman of the Building Committee and fourth president of North Carolina Mutual Life Insurance Company; Dr. A. Hollis Edens, president of Duke University and dedication speaker; and Dr. Alfonso Elder, president of North Carolina College, who introduced the speaker. (Courtesy of Andre D. Vann.)

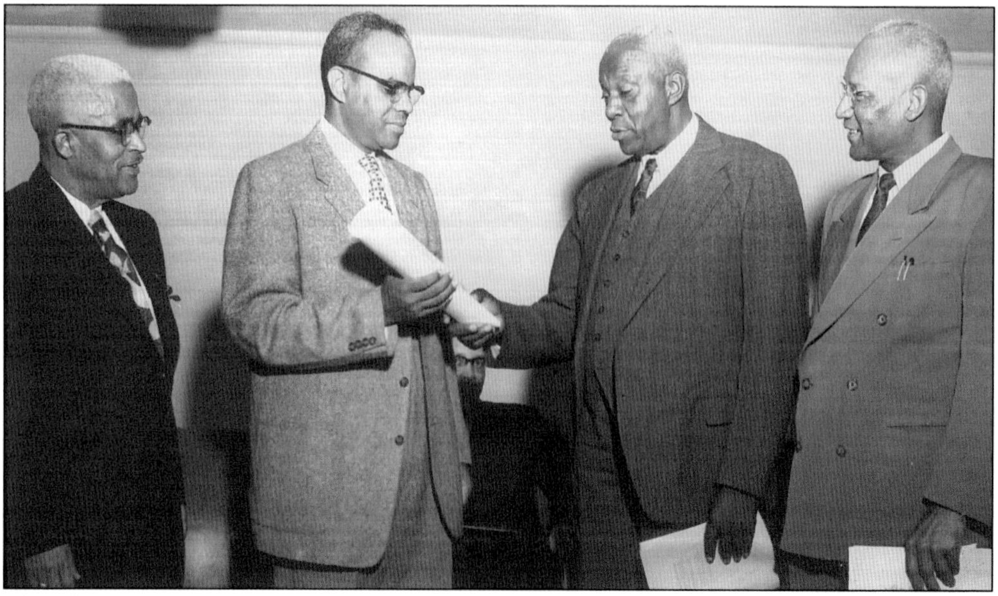

This photograph captures the presentation in 1953 of the Chartered Life Underwriter (CLU) by the College of Life Underwriters to William A. Clement by his father, Arthur J. Clement Sr., a board member of North Carolina Mutual. The following are identified, from left to right: George W. Cox, William Clement, Arthur Clement, and William J. Kennedy Jr., president of Mutual. (Courtesy of Andre D. Vann.)

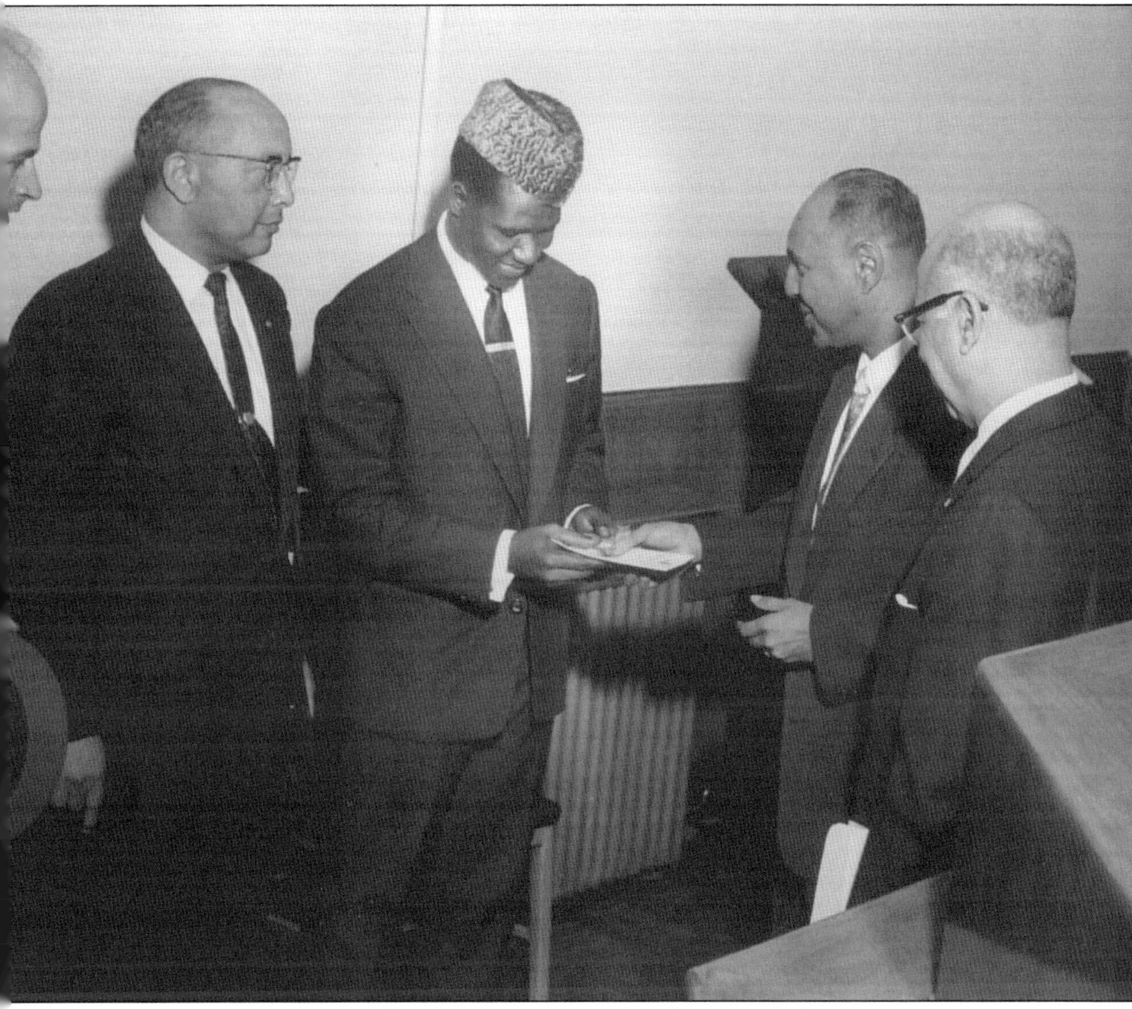

On October 29, 1959, his Excellency Sekou Toure, Mrs. Toure, and their entourage visited the North Carolina Mutual Life Insurance Home Office as guests of Asa and Elna Spaulding, who escorted them on a tour of the office. They are, from left to right, as follows: unidentified; Joseph W. Goodloe, vice-president and secretary, who led the group; Sekou Toure, president of Republic of Guinea; John S. Stewart, city councilman and banker making a presentation; and President Asa T. Spaulding Sr. (Courtesy of Andre D. Vann.)

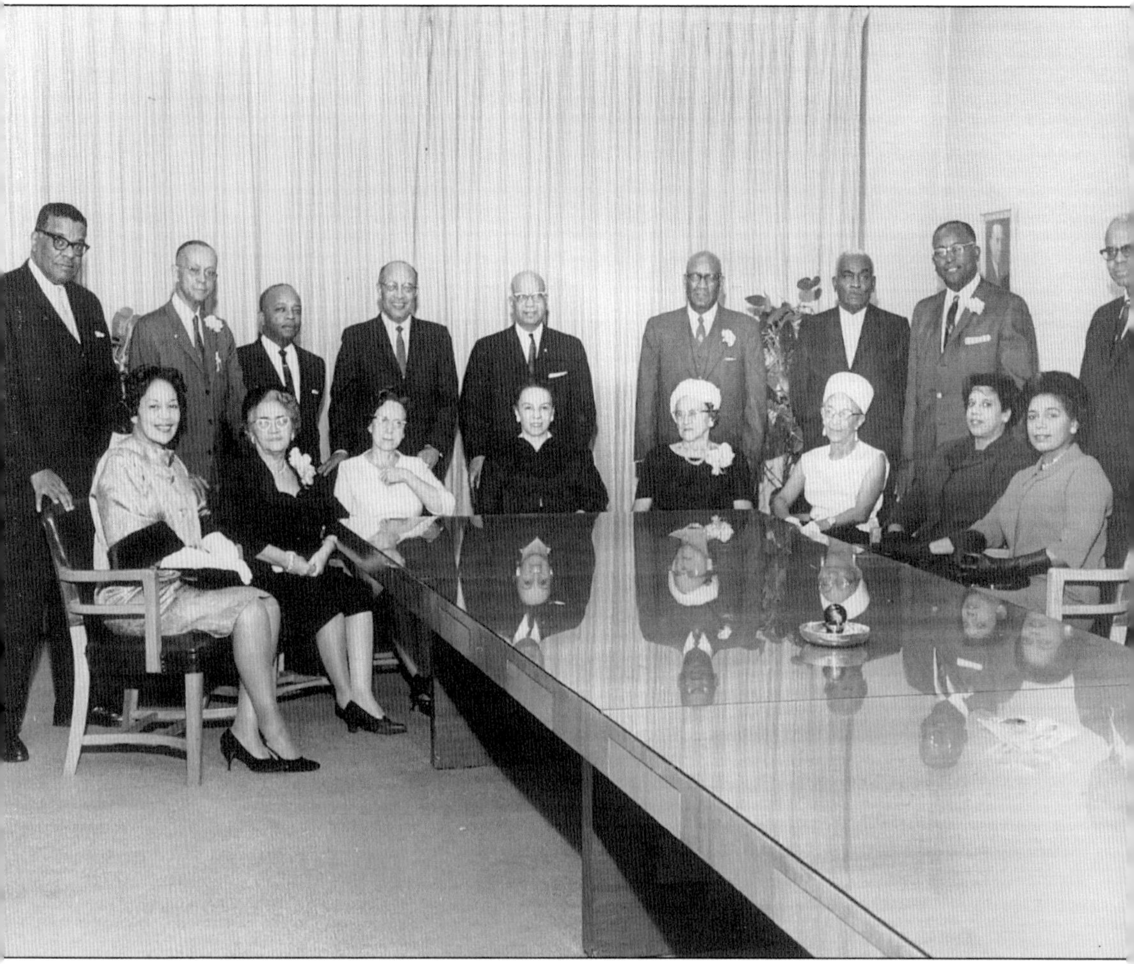

North Carolina Mutual Board of Directors and spouses are assembled for this January 1964 dinner at the Mutual. (Courtesy of Andre D. Vann.)

Nine

North Carolina College

Remember you are Eagles. And the Eagle is no common barnyard fowl.

—Dr. James E. Shepard, founder and president
of North Carolina College for Negroes (1910–1947),
always concluded the speeches he delivered at weekly pep talks in this manner.

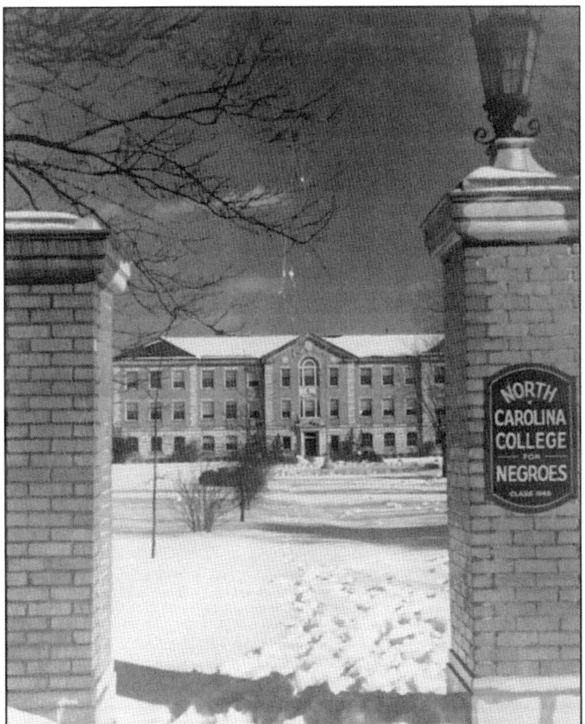

This is a 1940s winter scene of the main entrance looking toward the Clyde R. Hoey Administration Building. The building was built in 1929, dedicated in 1939, and served as the heart of North Carolina College for Negroes, now North Carolina Central University. (Courtesy of Carlton Graham / Andre D. Vann.)

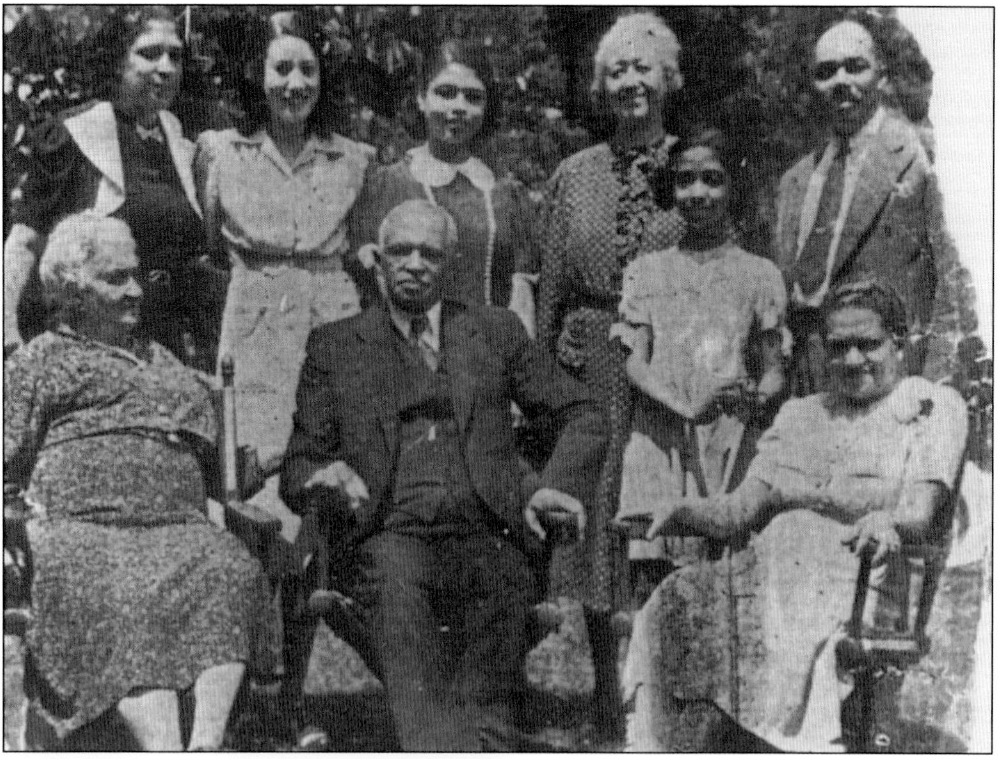

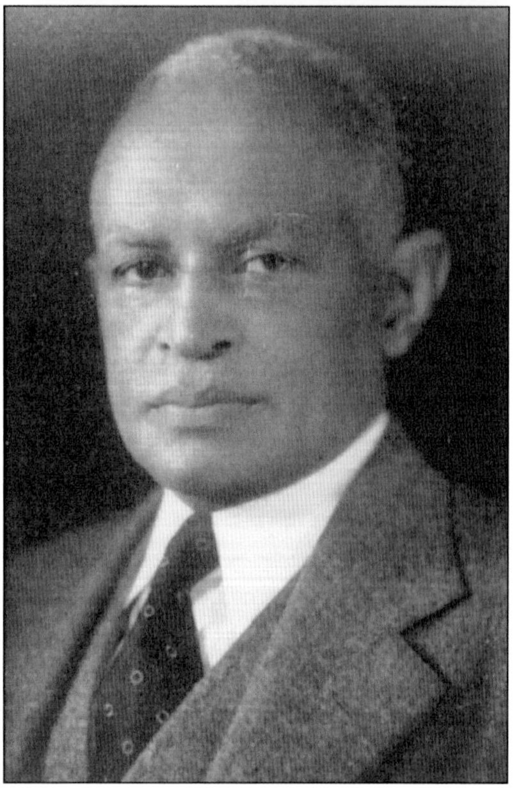

This is a 1941 photograph of Dr. James E. Shepard surrounded by family on the grounds of North Carolina College for Negroes; they are, from left to right, as follows: (front row) his wife, Annie Day Shepard; J.E. Shepard; and daughter Marjorie; (standing) daughter Annie Day Smith; niece Virginia S. Morgan; granddaughter Annie D. Smith; niece Annie Day Fields; granddaughter Carolyn Smith; and Archie J Morgan. (Courtesy of Carolyn S. Green / Andre D. Vann.)

Dr. James E. Shepard served as the president and founder of North Carolina College for Negroes from 1910 until his death in 1947. (Courtesy of Andre D. Vann.)

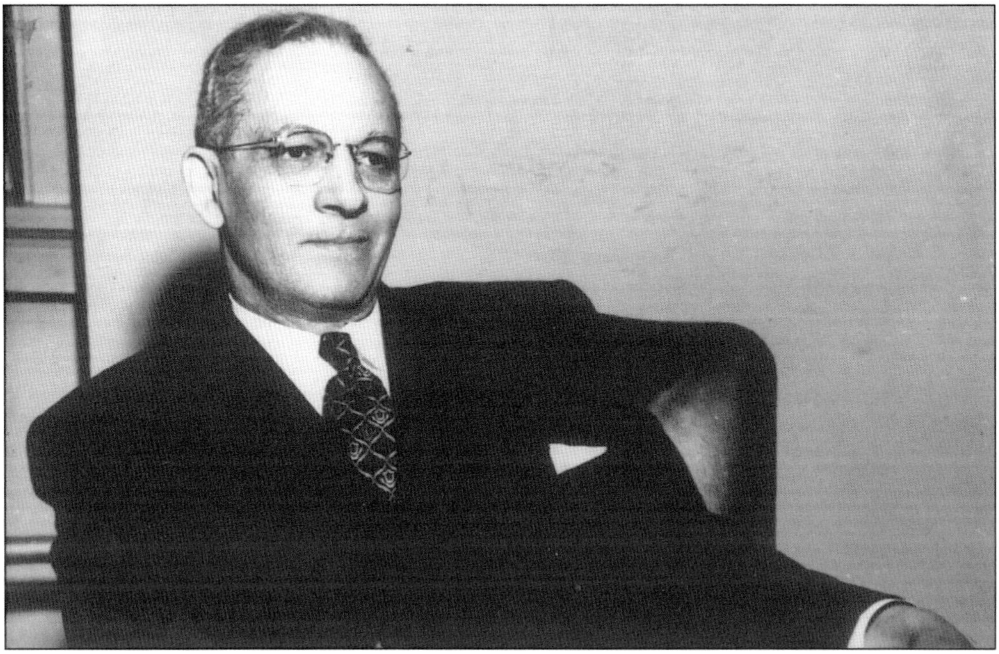

This is a 1948 photograph of Dr. Alfonso Elder (1898–1974), who assumed the presidency of North Carolina College after Dr. James E. Shepard's death in 1947. Born in Sandersville, Georgia, the son of Thomas J. and Lillian Elder, Dr. Elder completed elementary and high school at the Thomas Jefferson Elder School in Sandersville and attended Atlanta University, where he received his A.B. degree in 1921. He later received the M.A. and Ed.D. degrees from Columbia University and completed post-graduate work at Chicago University and the University of Cambridge (England). In 1931, Dr. Elder married Louise Holmes of Atlanta, Georgia. Dr. Elder served as the president of the university from 1948 until 1963. He was a trustee of Lincoln Hospital and a member of Alpha Phi Alpha Fraternity. (Courtesy of Andre D. Vann.)

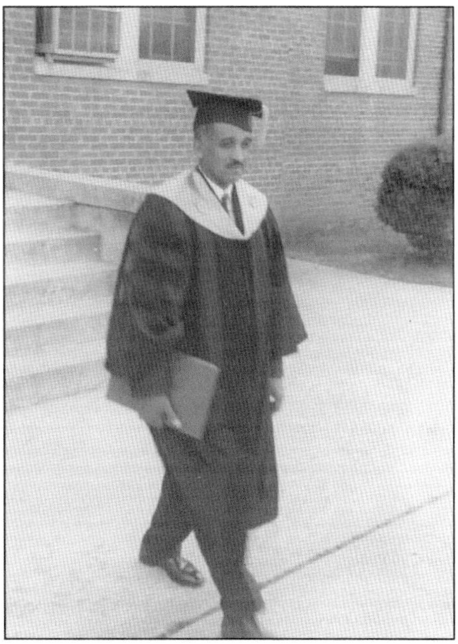

Dr. Samuel Proctor Massie, the third president of North Carolina College, served from 1964 until 1966. (Courtesy of Andre D. Vann.)

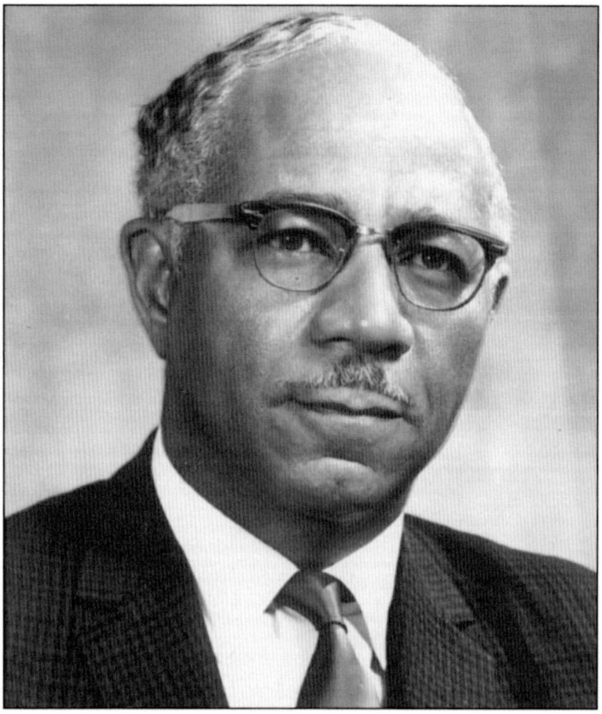

Dr. Albert Whiting served as the president of North Carolina College from 1967 until 1972 and was the first chancellor serving from 1972 until 1983. The Whiting Criminal Justice Building of the NCCU campus is named in his honor. (Courtesy of Andre D. Vann.)

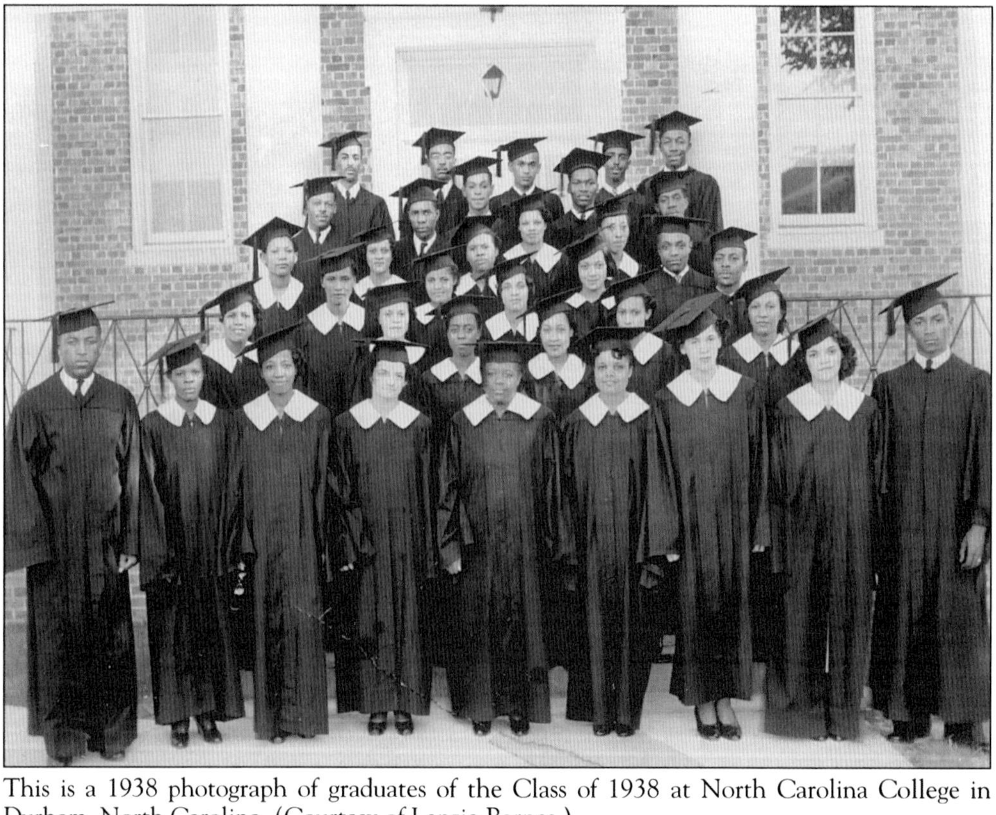

This is a 1938 photograph of graduates of the Class of 1938 at North Carolina College in Durham, North Carolina. (Courtesy of Lenzie Barnes.)

This is a 1958 photograph of Dean Ruth Gwendolyn Rush (1893–1967), who served as the dean of women, teacher of education, and director of student teaching. She was a 1914 graduate of Clark College in Atlanta, and in 1927, she received the Masters degree in education from Harvard University. For over 38 years, beginning in 1915, she served the university. Rush served on the Interim Committee, which administered the university's affairs from 1947 to 1948, following the death of Dr. James E. Shepard. She was a member of the Volkamenia Literary Club and the Daughters of Dorcas Club. From 1946 to 1952, she served as the president of the Association of Deans of Women and Advisers to Girls in Negro Schools. (Courtesy of Andre D. Vann)

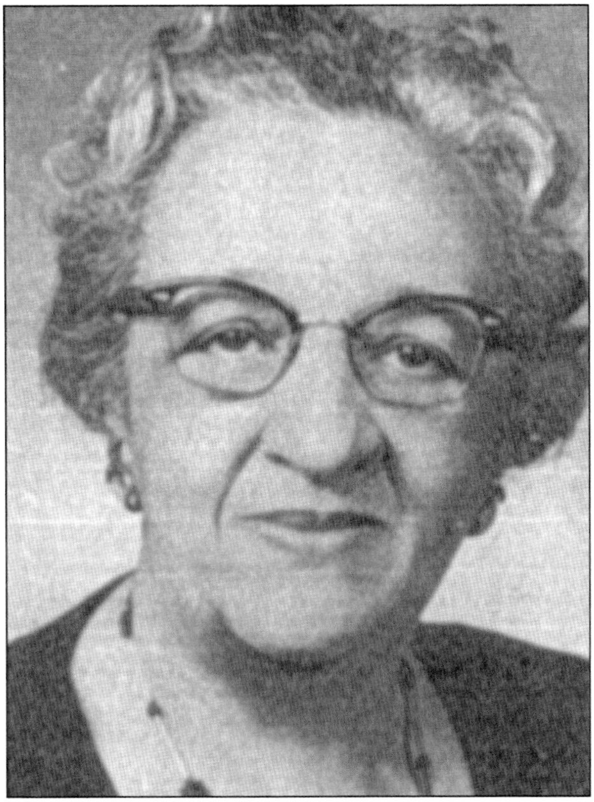

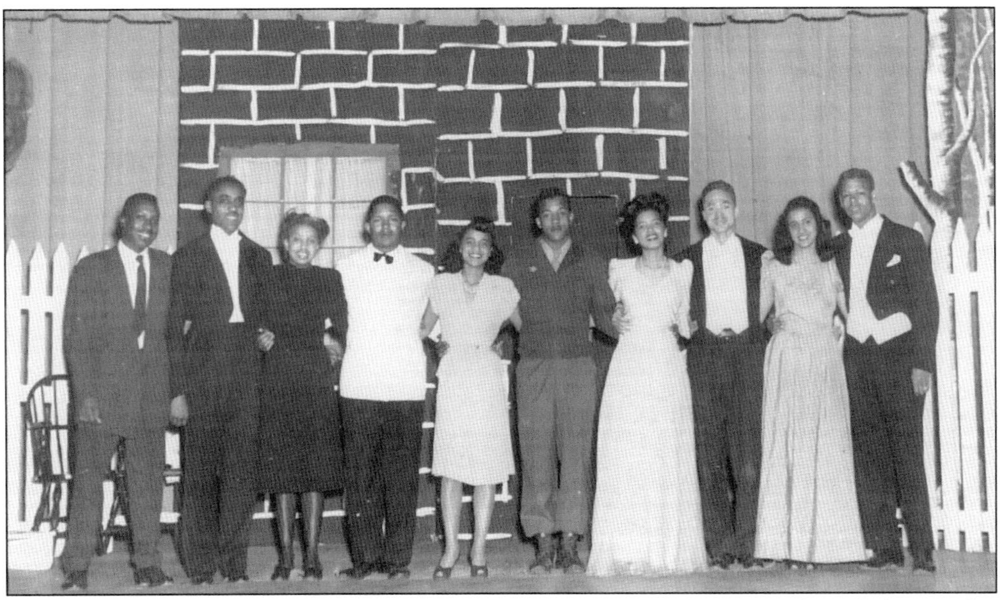

In this view of the college's dramatic arts program are the following, from left to right: Edward Thorpe, Joseph Sheehy, Mary Coles, Milton Reynolds, Pauline Marsh, Sherwood Enloe, Vivian Austin, John Turner, Allayne C. Turner, and Charles Dickerson. (Courtesy of Andre D. Vann.)

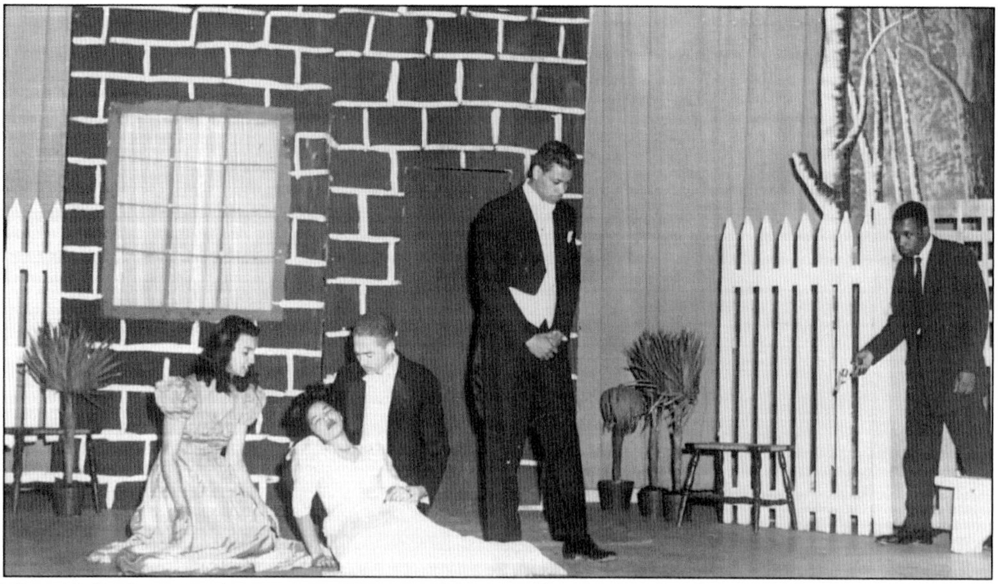

This 1947 photograph captures a scene of the North Carolina College Players and production of *Smilin Through*, under the direction of Dr. Helen G. Edmonds, director of dramatic arts.

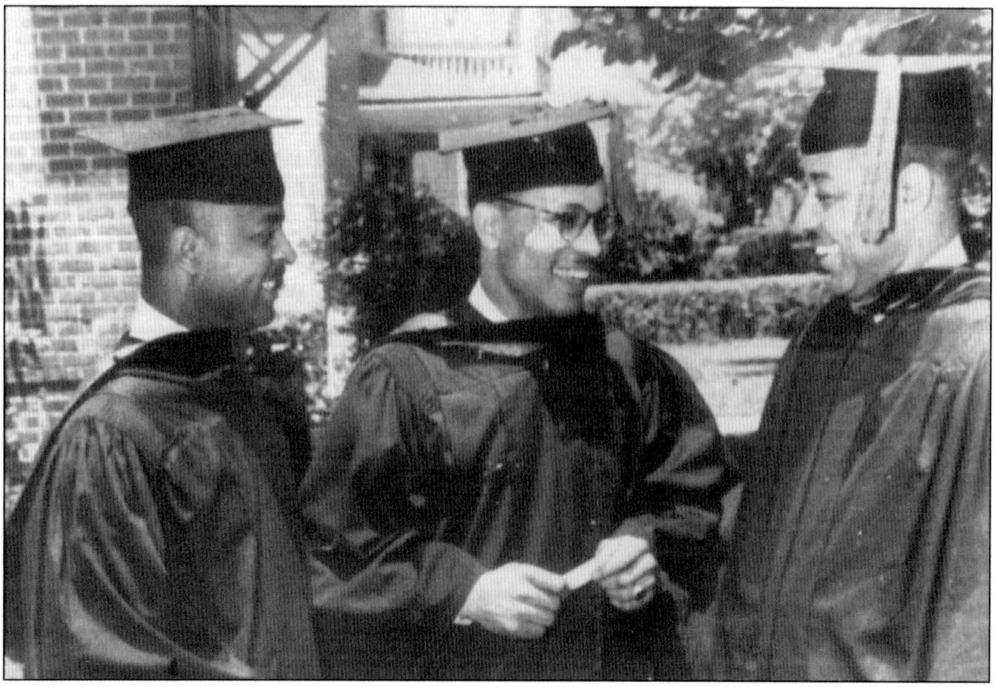

These students comprise the Class of 1947 of the North Carolina College Law School, which was founded in 1939 and opened on September 14, 1940, with seven students as North Carolina's second black law school. They are, from left to right, as follows: John Hamlin Rennick, Frank Brower, and Milton Johnson. Attorney's Brower and Johnson opened practice in the city of Durham and had adjoining offices in the Logan Building. (Courtesy of Gladys H. Rennick / Andre D. Vann.)

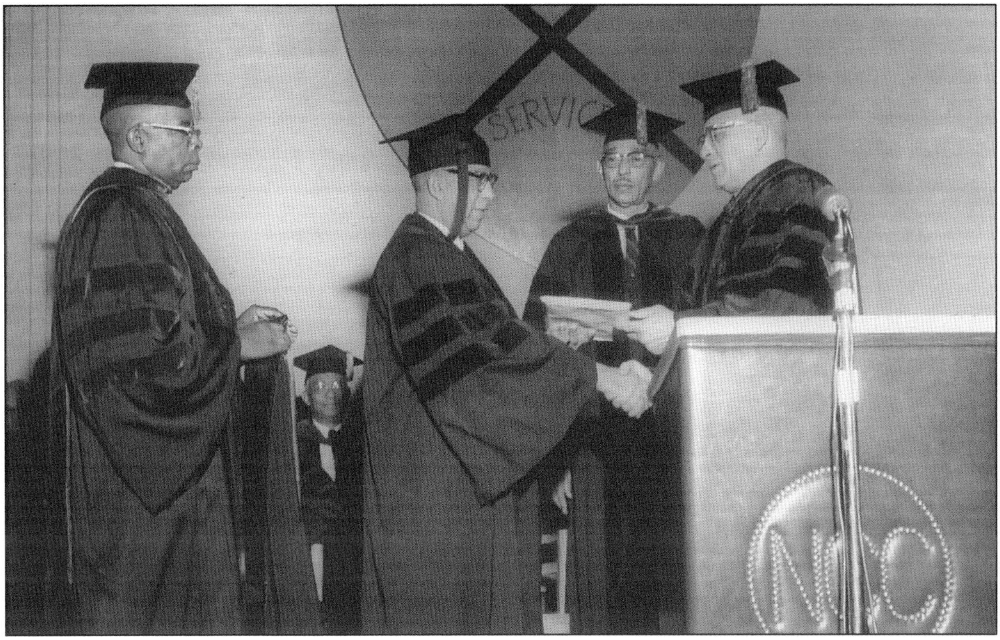

Asa Timothy Spaulding, president of the North Carolina Mutual Life Insurance Company, was presented an honorary doctor of laws degree from Dr. Alfonso Elder of North Carolina College. Pictured, from left to right, are as follows: Dr. Joseph H. Taylor, Dr. Asa T. Spaulding, Dr. William H. Brown, and Dr. Alfonso Elder. (Courtesy of Andre D. Vann.)

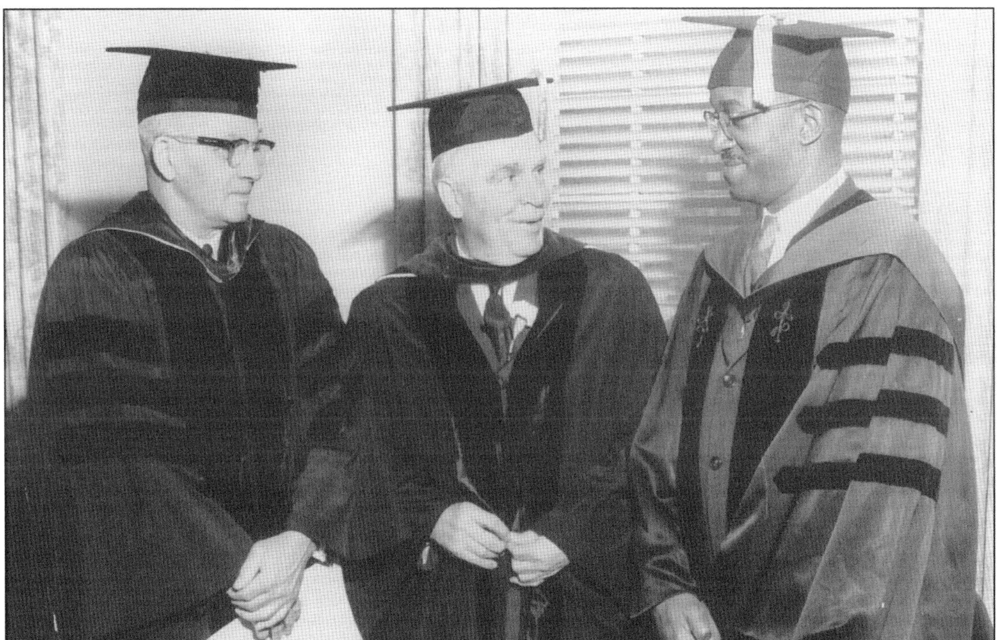

This is a 1960 photograph of principals at the 50th celebration of the founding of North Carolina College. They are, from left to right, as follows: Dr. Aflonso Elder, president of the college; North Carolina Governor Luther Hodges; and famed historian and scholar Dr. John Hope Franklin, who delivered the main address. (Courtesy of Andre D. Vann.)

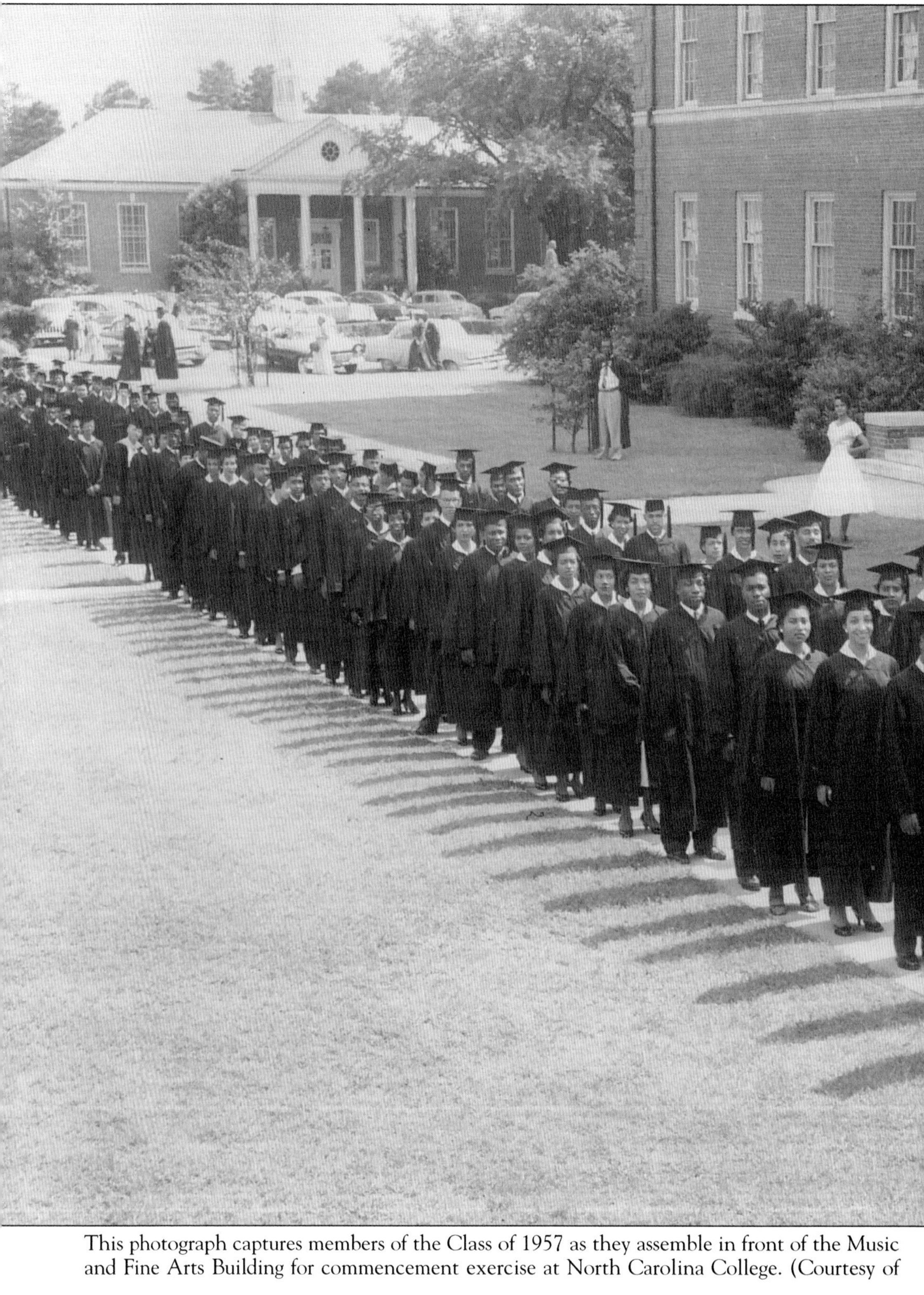

This photograph captures members of the Class of 1957 as they assemble in front of the Music and Fine Arts Building for commencement exercise at North Carolina College. (Courtesy of

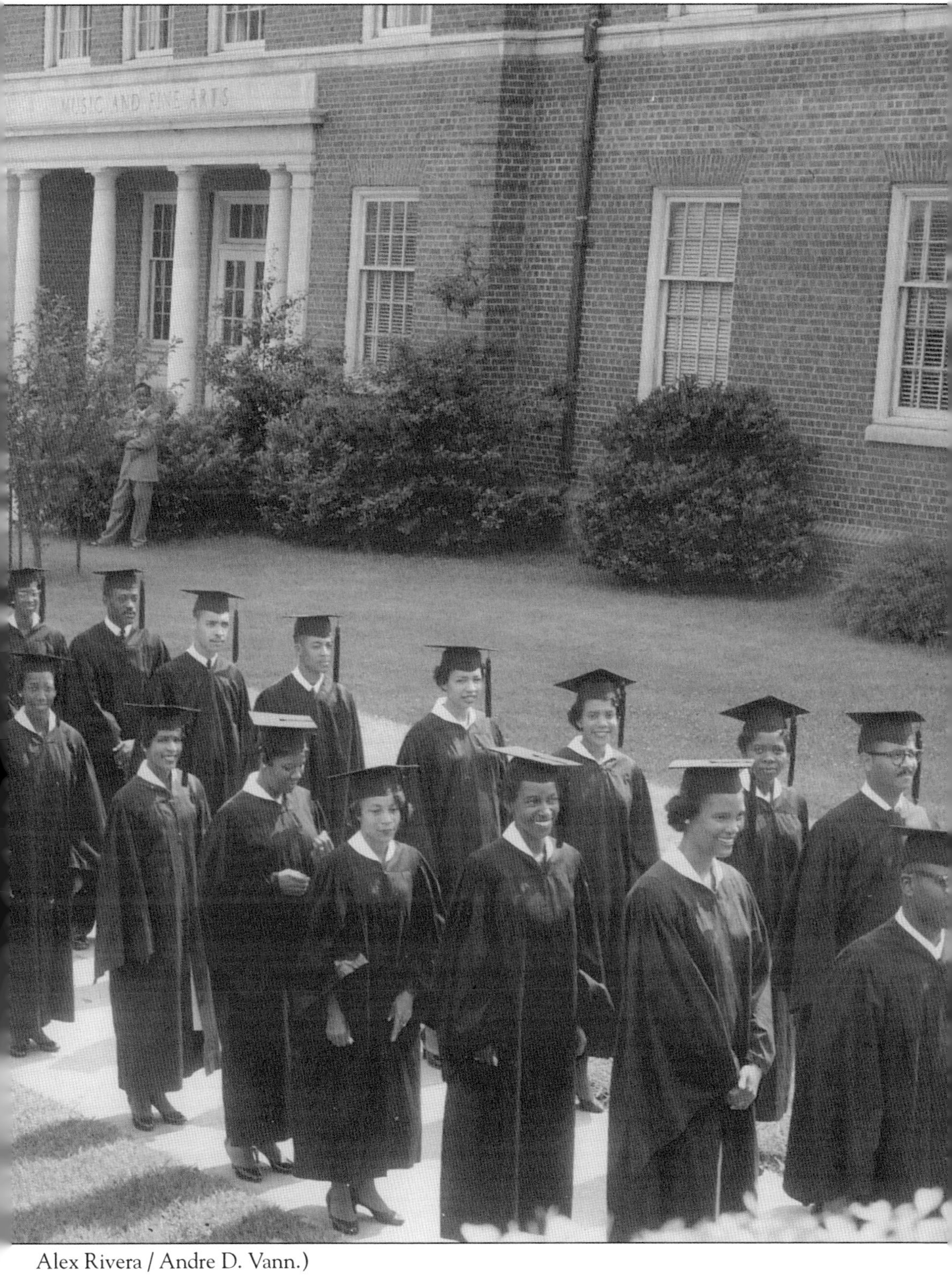

Alex Rivera / Andre D. Vann.)

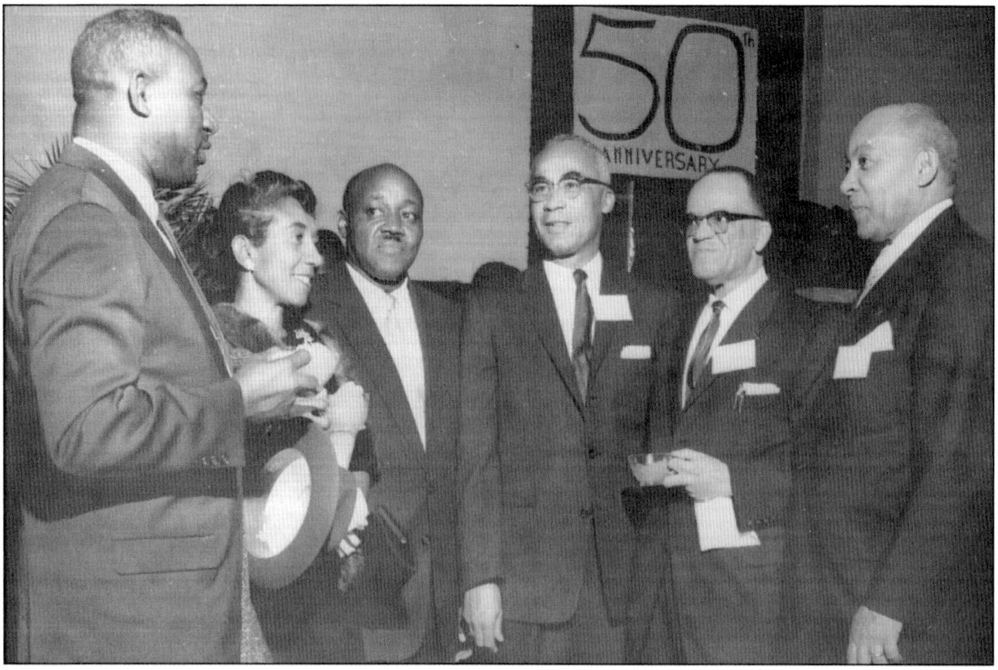

Dr. Ezra Totton, professor of chemistry at North Carolina College (NCC) and pictured third from left, entertains college presidents in attendance at a 50th anniversary of NCC. (Courtesy of Andre D. Vann.)

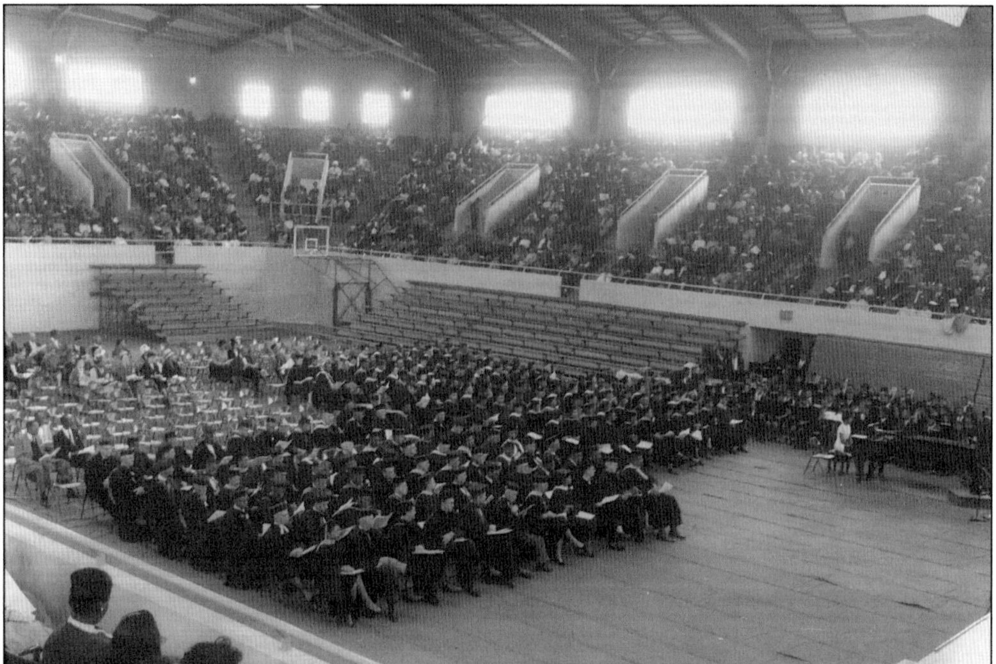

This is a scene from the 50th anniversary celebration of North Carolina College at Durham, which was held on November 9–12, 1960. The photo was taken in the McDougald Gymnasium with thousands in attendance. (Courtesy of Andre D. Vann.)

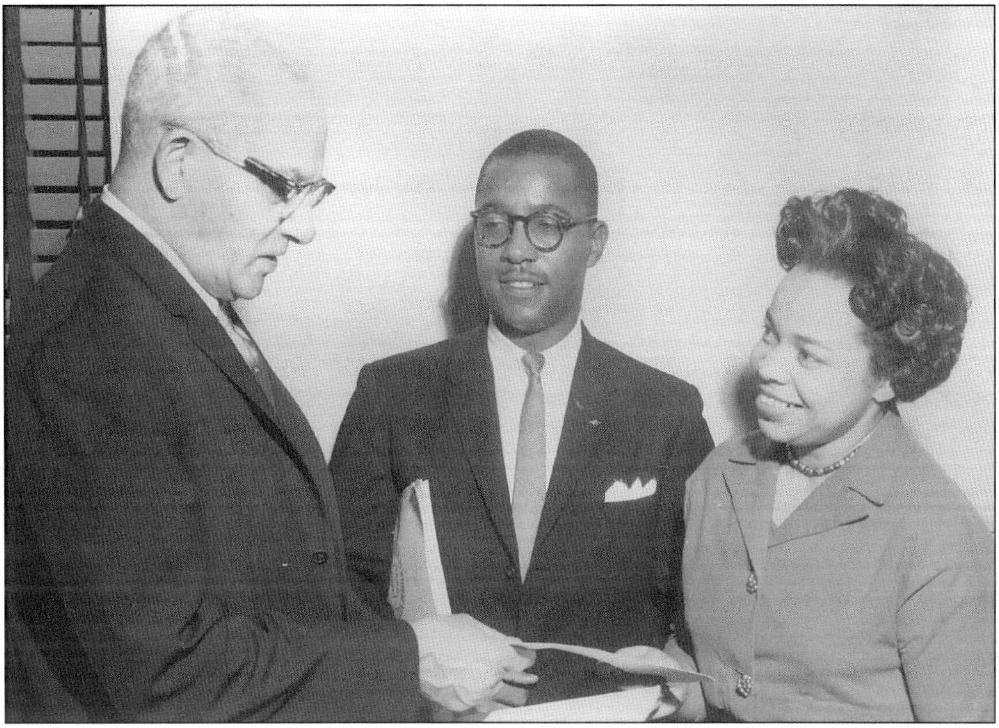

At center, attorney William A. Marsh, president of North Carolina College National Alumni Association, and an unidentified person make a donation to the college as Dr. Alfonso Elder accepts the gift. (Courtesy of Andre D. Vann.)

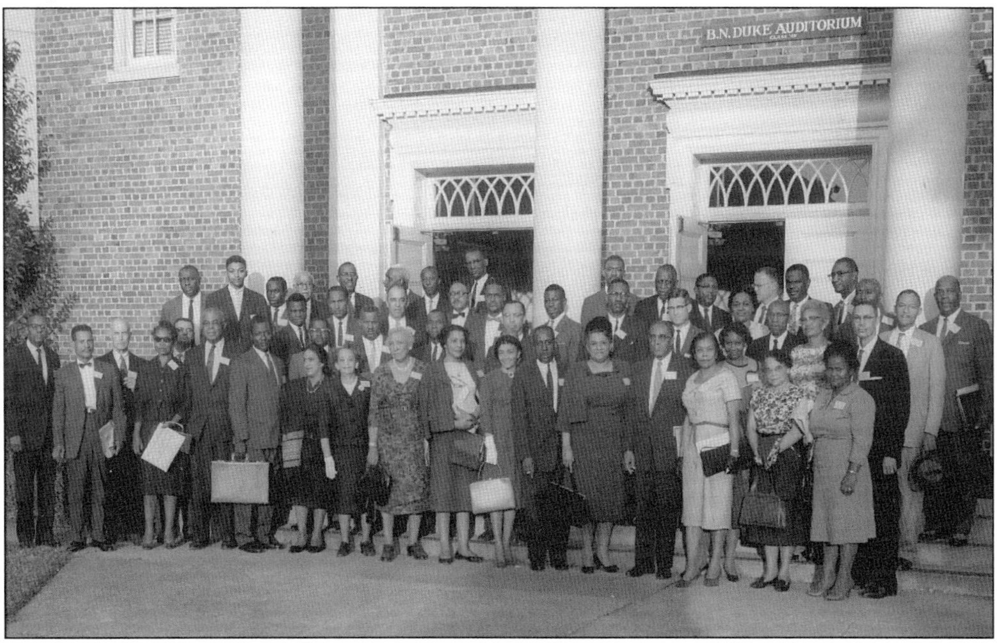

This is a 1961 photograph of members of the Association for the Study of Negro Life and History meeting at North Carolina College. The picture shows the group on the steps of the Benjamin Newton Duke Auditorium. (Courtesy of Andre D. Vann.)

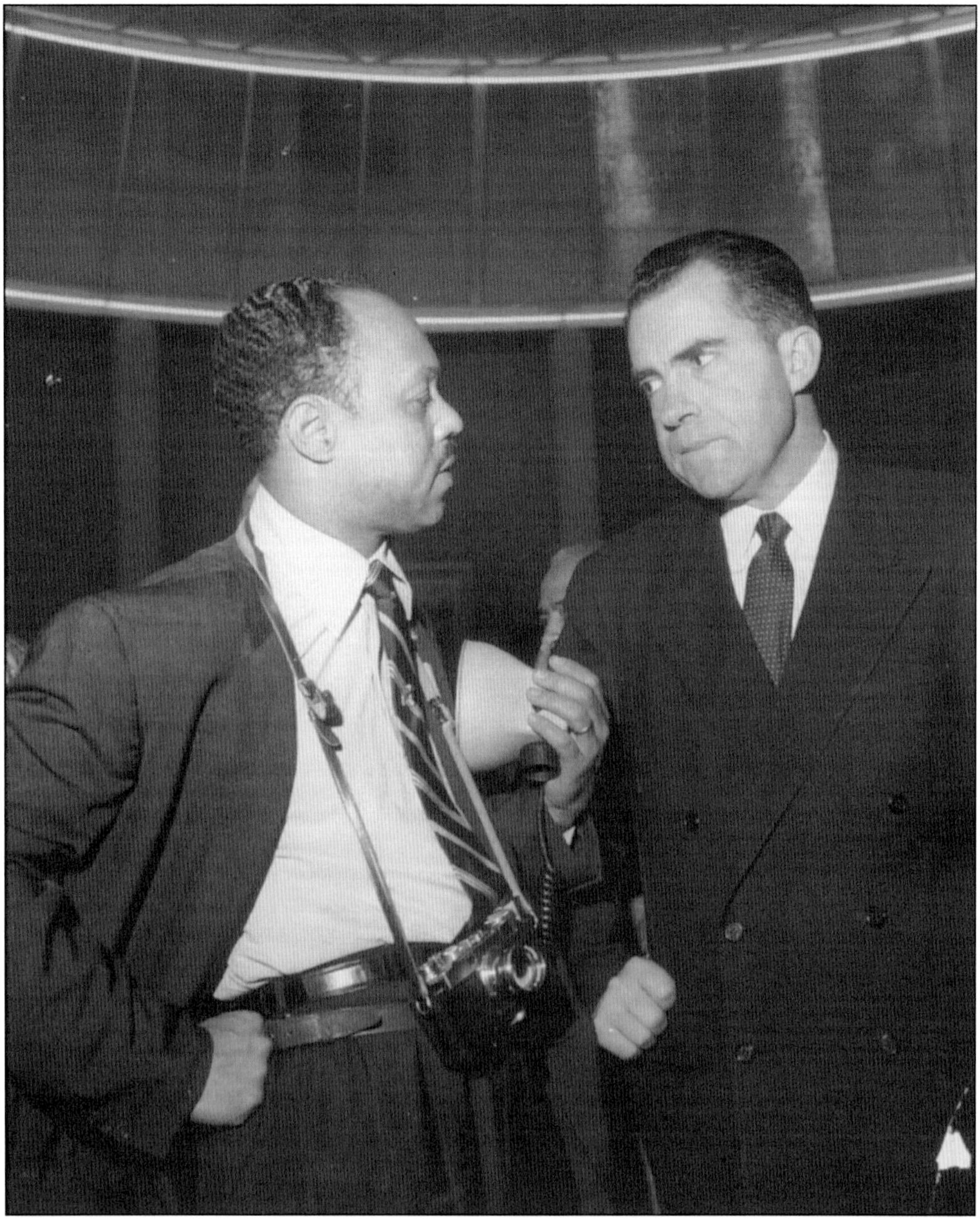

Photojournalist Alexander M. Rivera Jr. grew up in Greensboro, where his father practiced dentistry. Rivera, a student at Howard University in Washington, D.C., and already employed with the *Washington Tribune*, came to Durham in 1939 at the request of Dr. James E. Shepard and became North Carolina College's first paid publicity director and the founder of the institution's News Bureau. His professional career spanned from work with the *Norfolk Journal* and *Guide to the Pittsburg Courier*, where he continued many cases and trials during the early 1950s. He is seen here talking with Vice-President Richard Nixon on a tour of Africa, in which Rivera was selected to journey to Africa as a member of the presidential team. (Courtesy of Alex Rivera / Andre D. Vann.)

Dr. Charles A. Ray, English professor at North Carolina College, was widely recognized as a scholar and intellectual. (Courtesy of Andre D. Vann.)

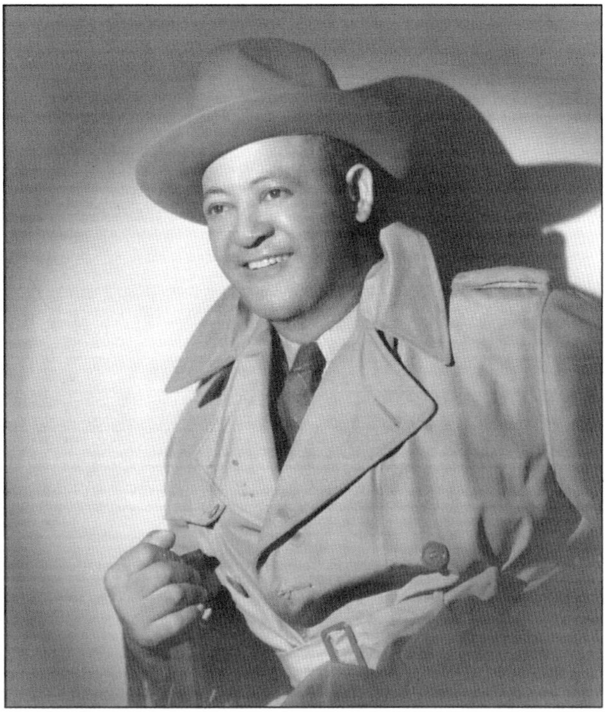

Dr. Helen G. Edmonds, center of photograph, chats with Vice-President Richard M. Nixon as Dr. Marjorie Lee Browne looks on. Dr. Browne, who taught at North Carolina College from 1949 to 1979 in the mathematics department, was one of the first two black women to earn a doctorate in mathematics. (Courtesy of Andre D. Vann.)

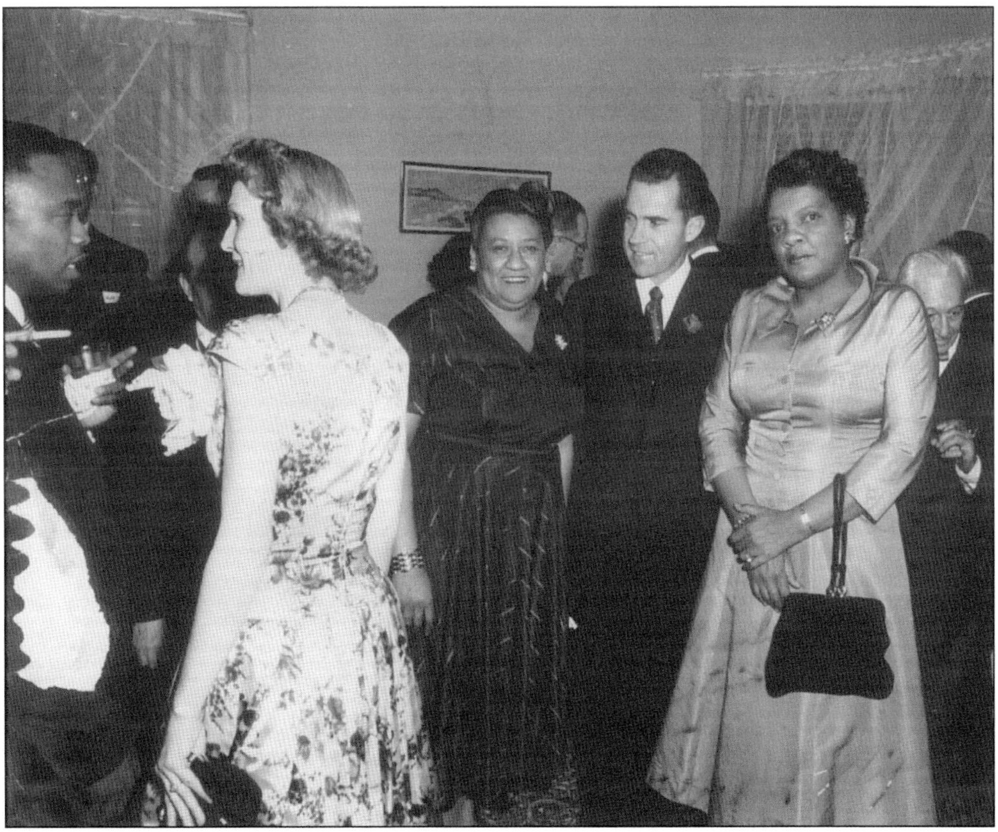

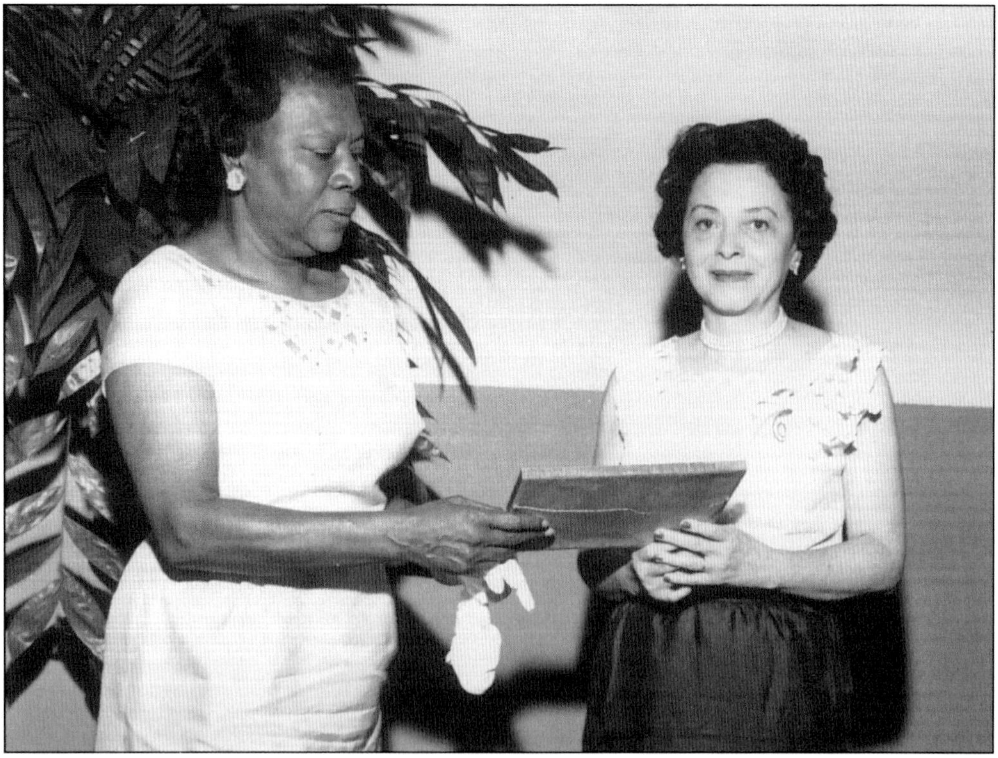

Dr. Rose Butler Brown, left, is shown presenting an award to Louise Holmes Elder, first lady of North Carolina College and wife of Dr. Alfonso Elder. (Courtesy of Andre D. Vann.)

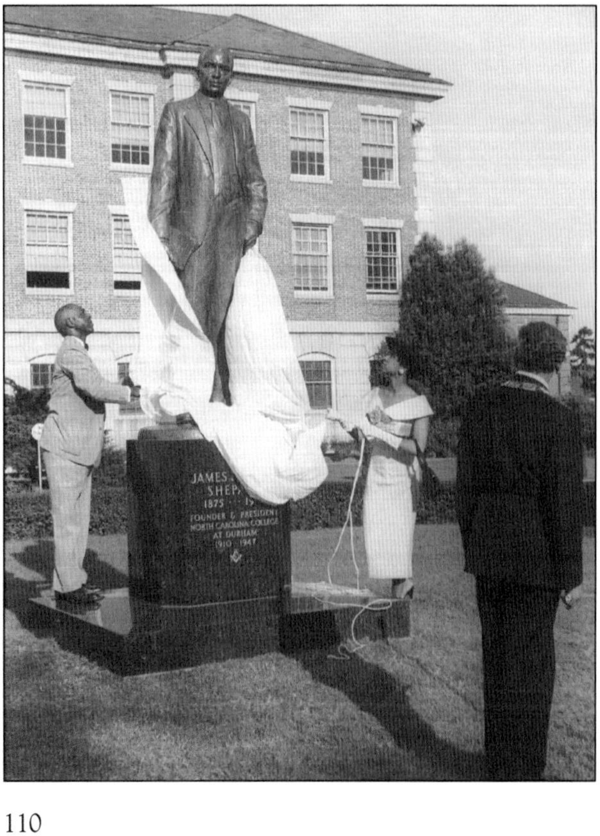

This is a 1957 photograph of the unveiling of the James E. Shepard Statue, which was commissioned by the James E. Shepard Memorial Foundation. William Zorach created the life-size statue as a memorial to the founder of North Carolina College. Dr. James T. Taylor, friend and confidant of Dr. Shepard, and Carolyn Smith Green, granddaughter of Dr. Shepard, unveiled the statue in 1957. (Courtesy of Alex Rivera / Andre D. Vann.)

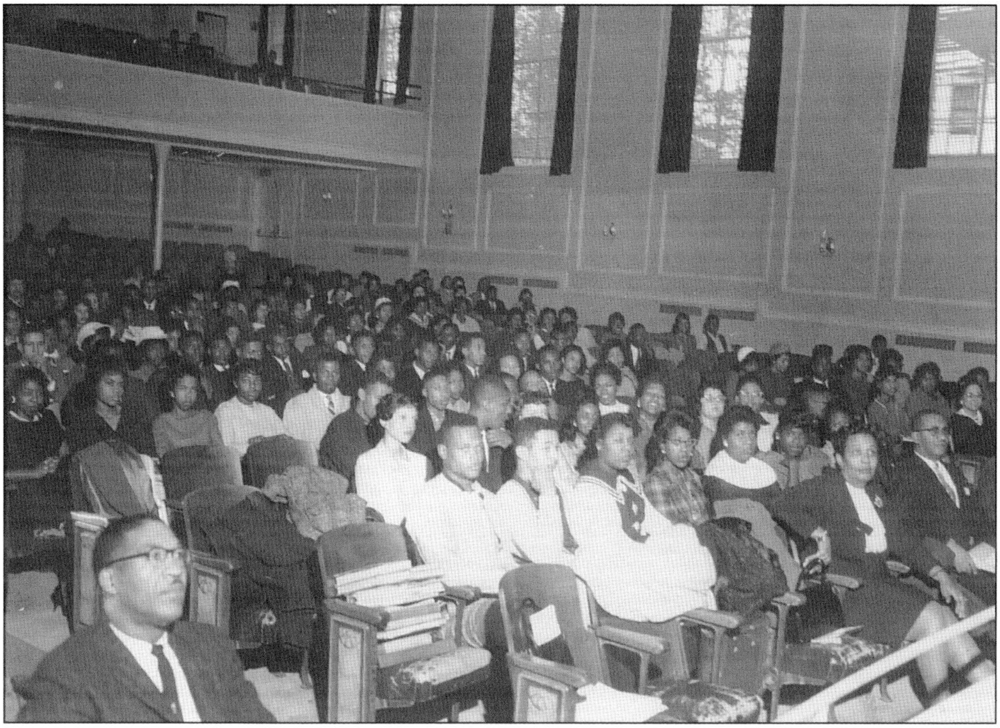

Dr. I. Gregory Newton (1917–1965), professor at North Carolina College (left front of photo), listens along with the student body to one of the many guest speakers brought to the college to lecture in the Benjamin Newton Duke Auditorium. (Courtesy of Andre D. Vann.)

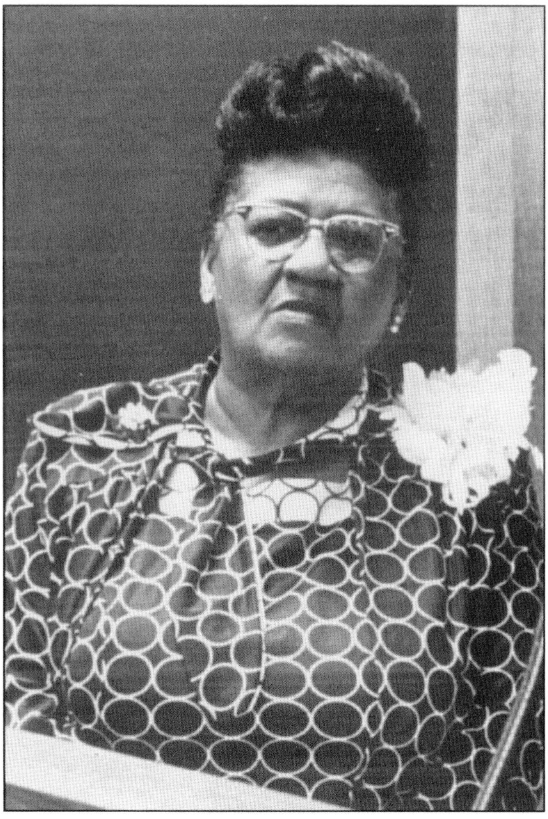

Dr. Helen Gray Edmonds (1911–1995) was actively involved in local, national, and international affairs. A graduate of Saint Paul's Junior College and Morgan State, she went on to receive in 1946 the Doctor of Philosophy from Ohio State University. She became the first black to receive a doctorate from Ohio State and only the third in the United States to receive a doctorate in history. Edmonds served as a faculty member on the NCC campus from 1941 until 1977. In 1946 she seconded the nomination of Dwight D. Eisenhower, a successful candidate for the presidency of the United States. (Courtesy of Andre D. Vann.)

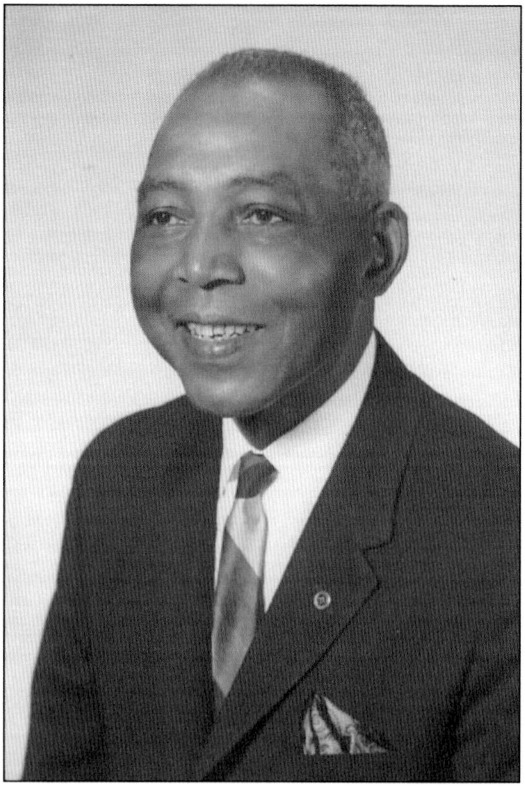

James T. Taylor (1893–1970), a 1921 graduate of the National Training School and a graduate of Ohio State University, served as a professor, athletic director, and dean of men (1926–1943) at North Carolina College. Taylor became a key figure in the Central Intercollegiate Athletic Association, the American Tennis Association, the Good Neighbor Council, and Alpha Phi Alpha Fraternity, Inc. and was a founder of the Durham Committee on Negro Affairs. As president of the North Carolina Teachers Association (1946–1948), he led the fight for the equalization of salaries between African-American and Caucasian teachers in the state. The Taylor Education Building on the campus of NCCU is named in his honor. (Courtesy of Andre D. Vann.)

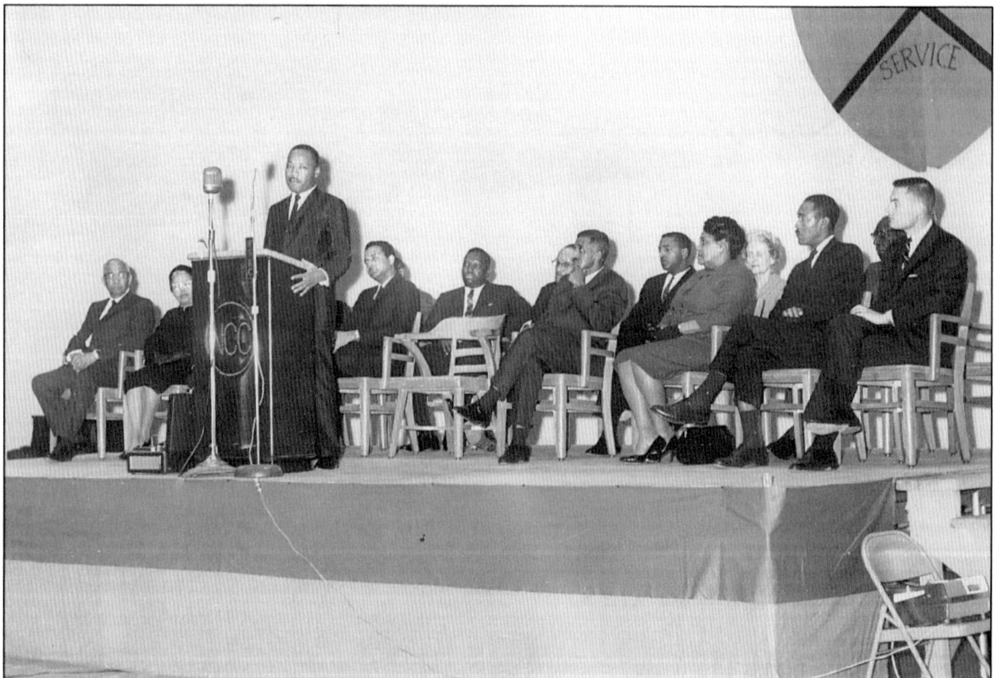

This is a 1966 photograph of Dr. Martin Luther King Jr. speaking in the McDougald Auditorium on the campus of North Carolina College. (Courtesy of Andre D. Vann.)

Ten

THE STANFORD L. WARREN LIBRARY

Stanford L. Warren Branch Library has been more than a library of books. It has served the cultural, educational, civic, and social needs of the citizens of Durham for more than three-quarters of a century. It has been a forum to discuss contemporary issues and recently published books, a meeting place for community and civic organizations, and an enrichment and cultural center for children.

—Dr. Beverly Washington Jones in her book, *Stanford L. Warren Branch Library: 77 Years of Public Service—A Phoenix in the Durham Community*.

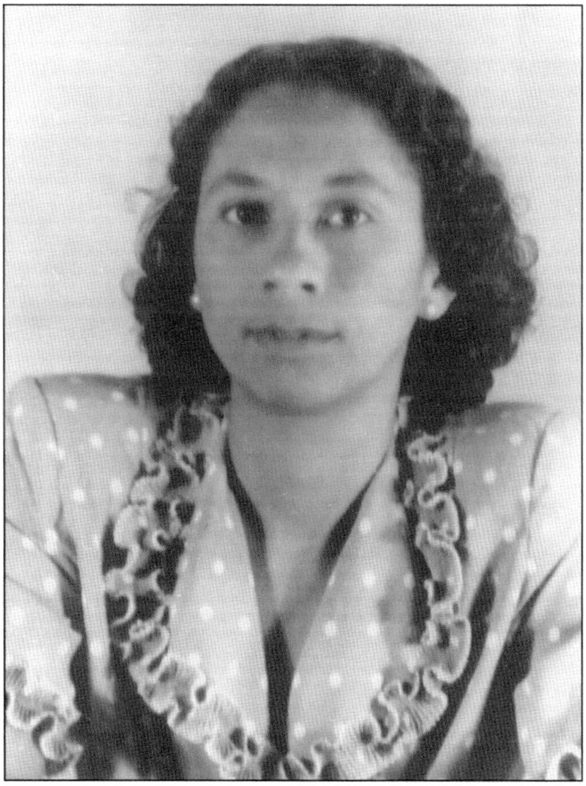

This is a 1945 photograph of Selena Warren Wheeler, who served as the second library director at the Stanford L. Warren Branch Library from 1932 until 1945. Born in Durham to Dr. Stanford L. Warren and Julia M. Warren, she was a Howard University and Hampton Institute graduate. Wheeler succeeded Mrs. Hattie B. Wooten in 1932, when the library was located at the corner of Fayetteville and Pettigrew Streets. Under her leadership, many local services were achieved: the Bookmobile, hospital and school services, an increase of 11,000 catalogued volumes, and an establishment of a modern building. She was married to John H. Wheeler and was the mother of Julia and Warren Wheeler. The Selena Warren Wheeler Collection of Black Books is named in her honor. (Courtesy of Selena W. Wheeler / Andre D. Vann.)

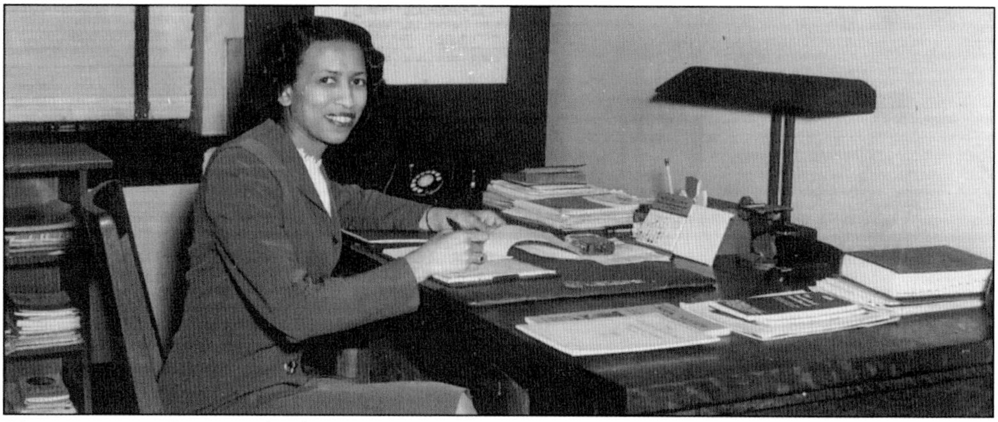

This is a 1946 photograph of Mrs. Onnie Ray Nichols Moore (1914–1975), library director of Stanford L. Warren Public Library. A 1933 graduate of Spelman College and a 1945 graduate of the School Library Science at North Carolina College, she was the director of the Durham City-County Public Library from 1966 to 1975. (Courtesy of Stanford L. Warren Branch Library.)

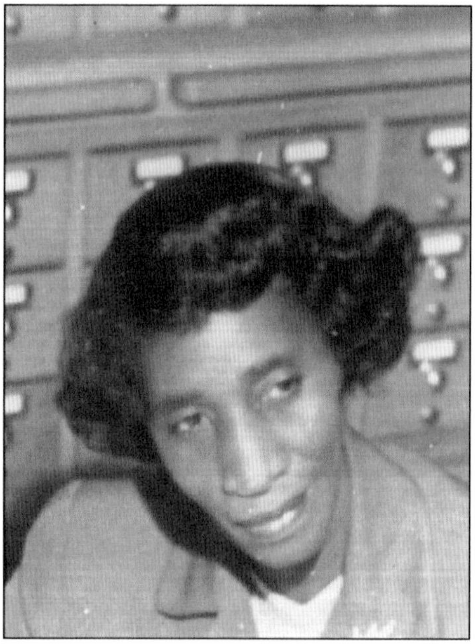

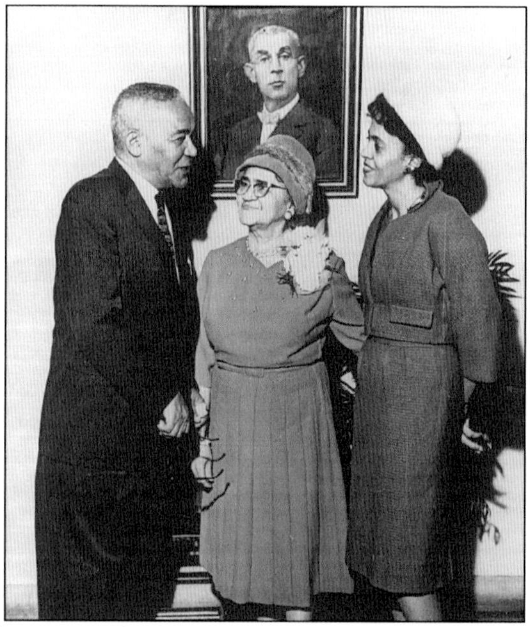

Left: Annie Mae Tucker, a Durham native and a 1933 graduate from North Carolina College, was hired in 1942 as circulation librarian. She worked in several capacities, and eventually, after the merger in 1966, she became branch librarian of Stanford L. Warren Branch Library, a position she held until her retirement in 1976. (Courtesy of Stanford L. Warren Branch Library.)
Right: This is a 1936 photograph of Dr. Horace Mann Bond, Atlanta University author and educator, as he delivered the 50th anniversary founders address of the Stanford L. Warren Library. The picture was taken at the White Rock Baptist Church. Mrs. Lyda Moore Merrick and her daughter, Mrs. Constance Merrick Watts, are standing under the portrait of Dr. Moore, who founded the library in 1913 in the basement of Durham's White Rock Baptist Church with a small collection of donated books and without financial appropriations from any source. (Courtesy Stanford L. Warren Branch Library.)

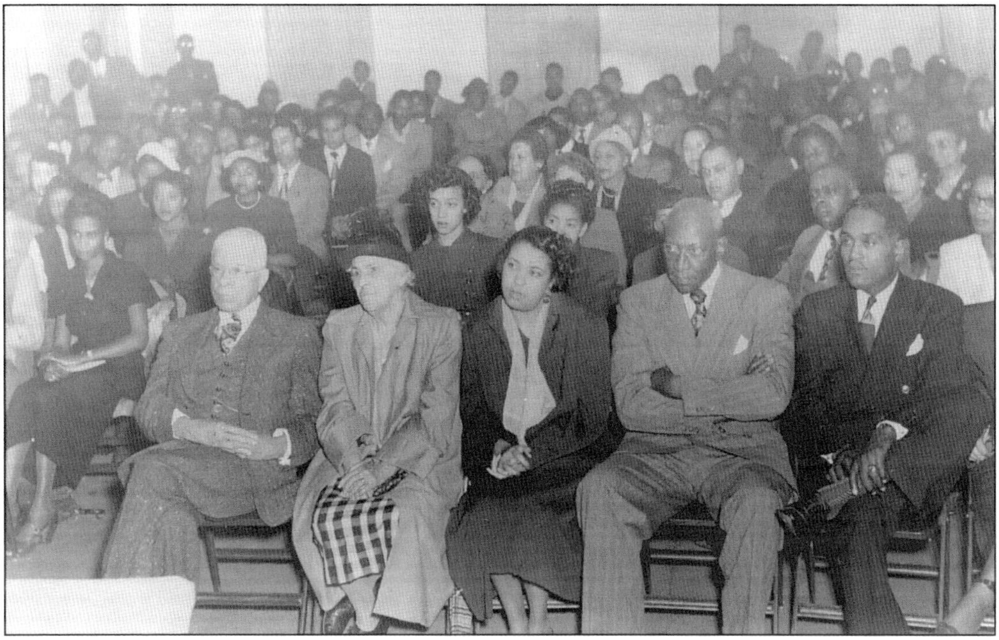

This 1946 photo shows the members of the Book Review group at the Stanford L. Warren Library. The Book Review Forum is a series of one-hour programs that sought to stimulate interest in books. The program was begun in 1945 and was meant to encourage adults to become patrons of the library. (Courtesy of Stanford L. Warren Branch Library.)

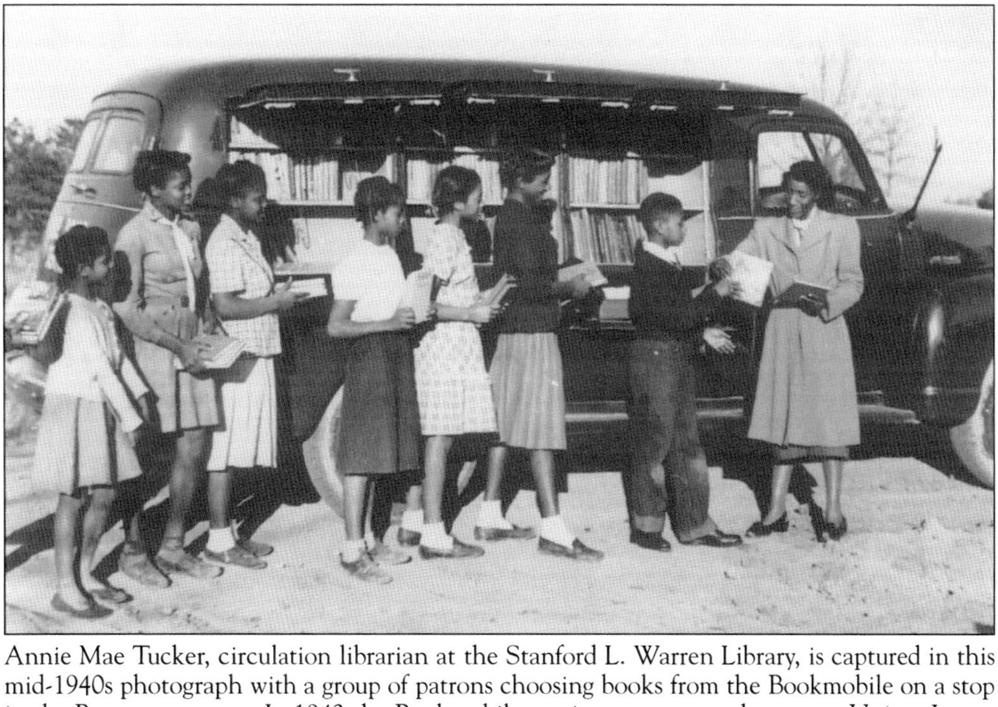

Annie Mae Tucker, circulation librarian at the Stanford L. Warren Library, is captured in this mid-1940s photograph with a group of patrons choosing books from the Bookmobile on a stop in the Rougemont area. In 1942 the Bookmobile services went to such areas as Union, Lower Fayetteville Road, Hickstown, Rocky Knoll, Bragtown, Rougemont, South Lowell, and Barbee's Chapel. (Courtesy of Dr. Beverly W. Jones.)

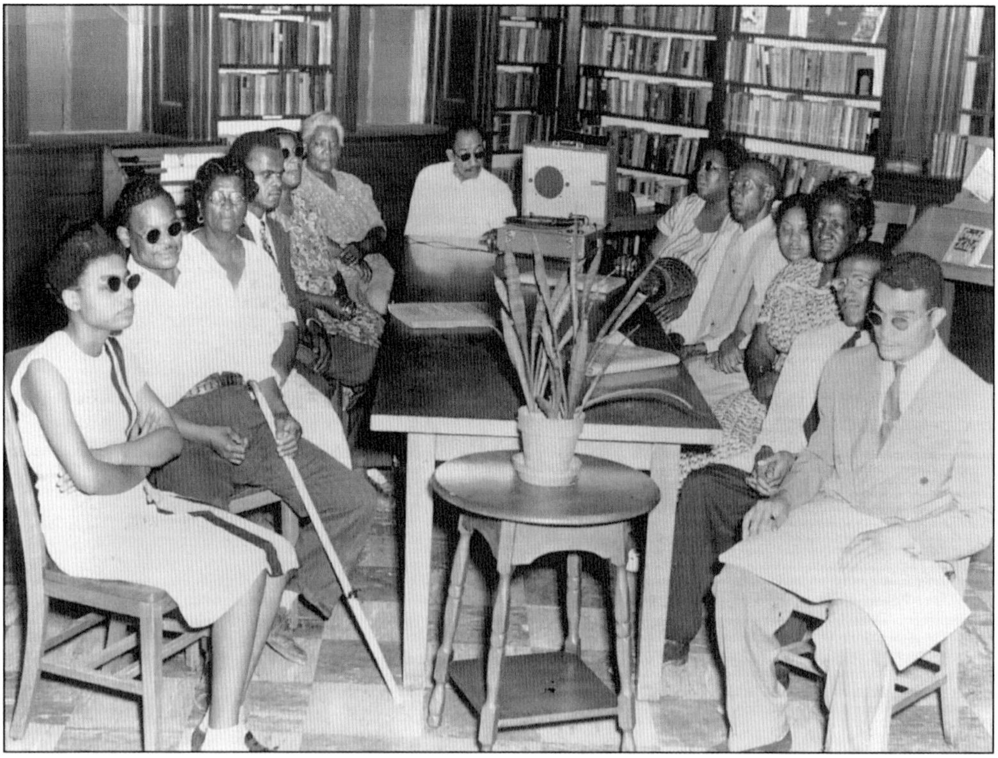

This 1940s photo shows a groups of blind patrons listening to a talking book in the Library Corner for the Blind at the S.L. Warren Library. John C. Washington, Lyda Moore Merrick, and librarian Ray N. Moore established the Library Corner for the Blind. (Courtesy of Dr. Beverly W. Jones.)

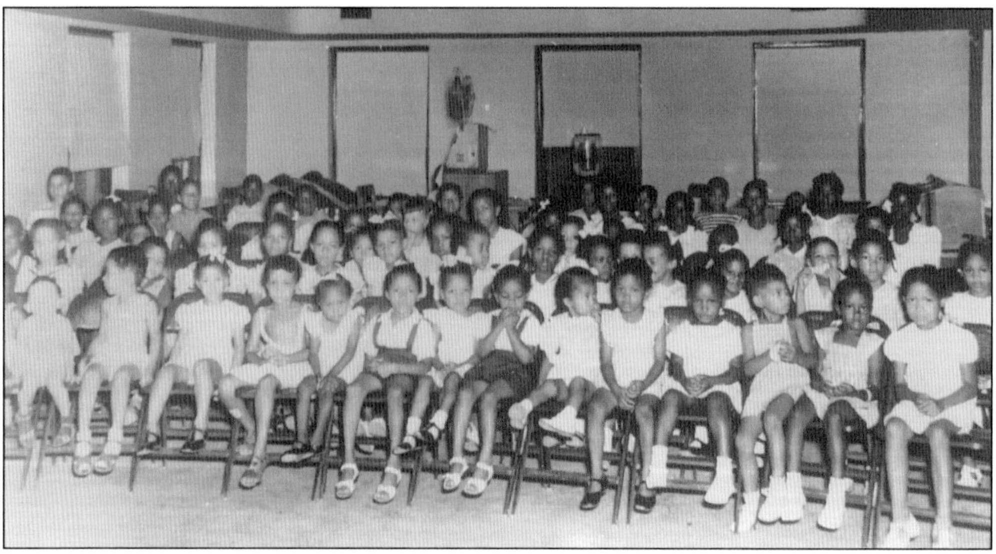

This 1940s photograph captures children enjoying the movie shown at the Saturday Morning Movie Hour at the Stanford L. Warren Library. For many housewives and mothers, the Movie Hour afforded them a productive way to spend their leisure time. (Courtesy of Stanford L. Warren Branch Library.)

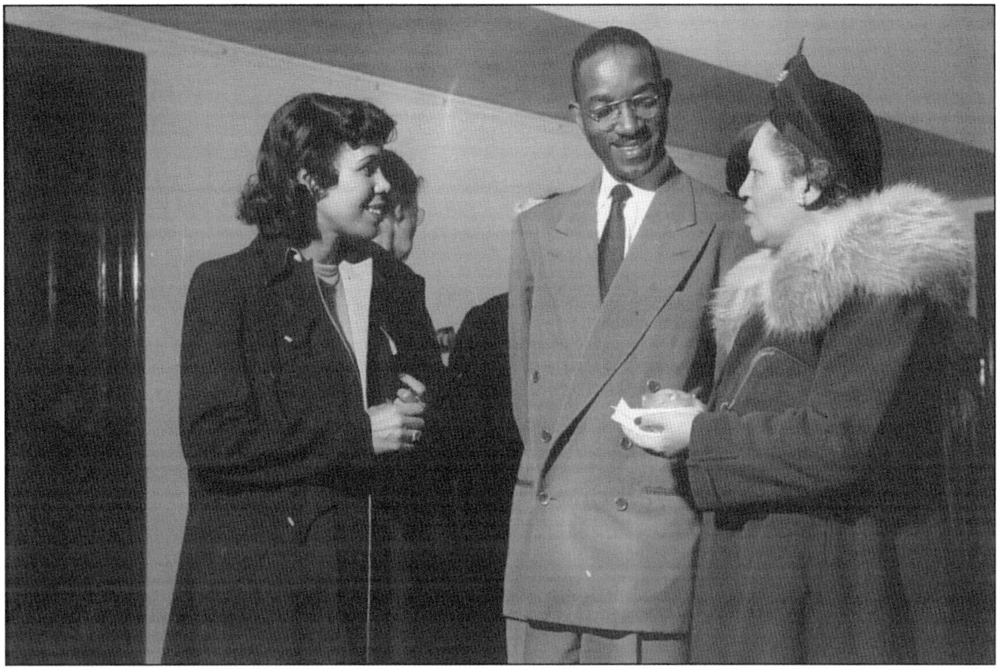

Stanford L. Warren librarian Sadie Hughley entertains Dr. John Hope Franklin, a faculty member at North Carolina College and Book Review guest speaker, and Evelyn Pope. (Courtesy of Beverly Washington Jones.)

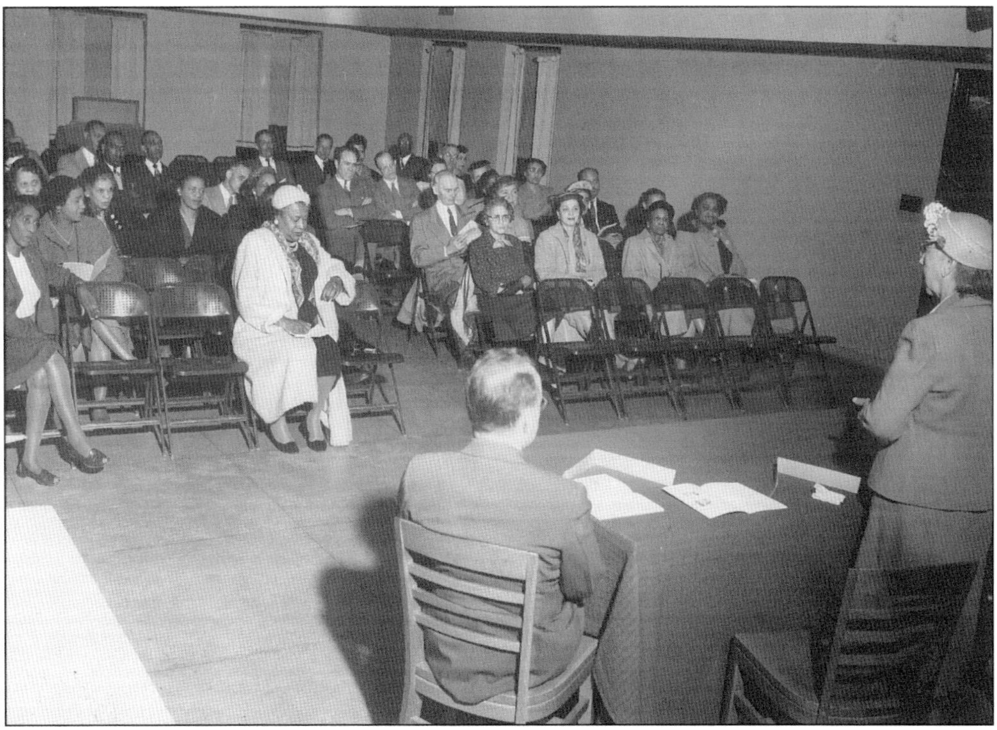

Ella Earls Cotton is seen discussing her book, *Queen of Persia*, at the Warren Library. (Courtesy of Beverly W. Jones.)

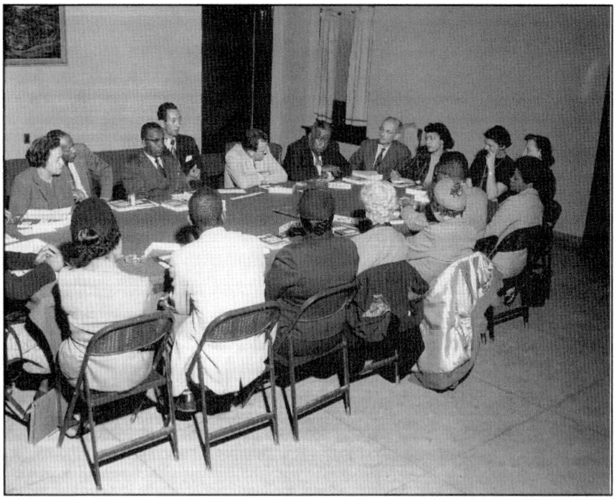

A roundtable discussion is the focus of the American Heritage Series at the Stanford L Warren Library. (Courtesy of Beverly Washington Jones.)

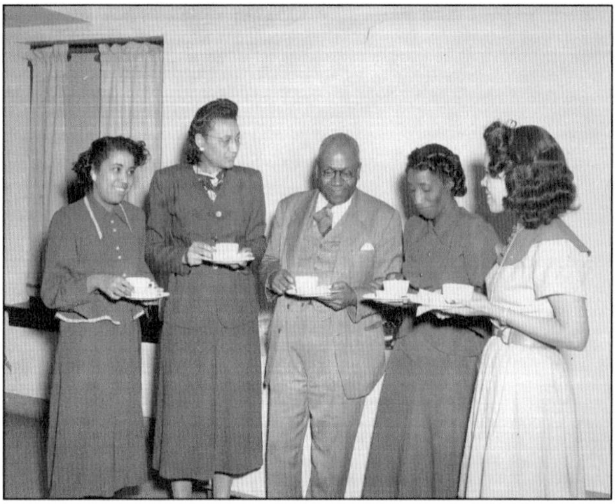

The S.L. Warren Library hosted a reception and book signing for voted author Henry Lee Moon, in the center. They are, from left to right, as follows: Margaret Whisenton, Gladys W. Hawkins, Henry Lee Moon, Annie M. Tucker, and Sadie S. Hughley. (Courtesy of S.L. Warren Branch Library.)

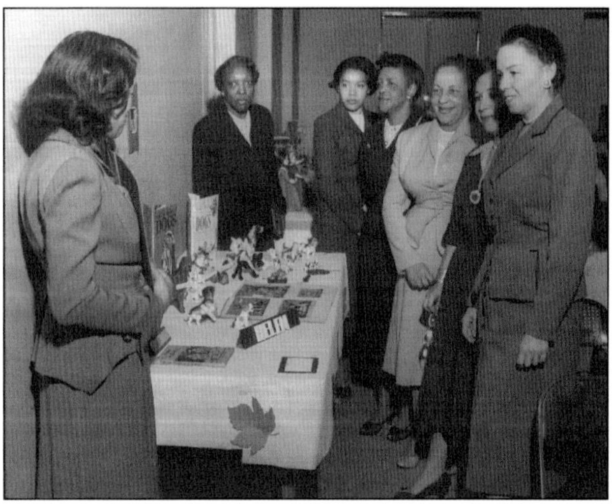

Sadie Hughley, librarian, leads a book discussion with visiting guests. To the extreme right of the photo is Elna B. Spaulding, prominent civic, social, and religious leader. (Courtesy of Dr. Beverly W. Jones.)

Eleven

Hayti's Homes and Buildings

Hayti . . . was the cultural center of Durham's colored community. Along Fayetteville Street, its main thoroughfare, were the library, the two fashionable churches—White Rock Baptist and Saint Joseph A.M.E.—the Negro college, numerous colored-owned business enterprises, Lincoln Hospital, and the spacious homes of many of the leading colored families—Moores, Spauldings, Whitteds, Merricks, Pearsons, Scarboroghs, Shepards, and others. We had no lack of role models for successful business and professional careers.

—Pauli Murray, black activist, feminist, priest, and poet, who offered her earliest impressions of Hayti during the early twentieth century in her work *Song in a Weary Throat: An American Pilgrimage.*

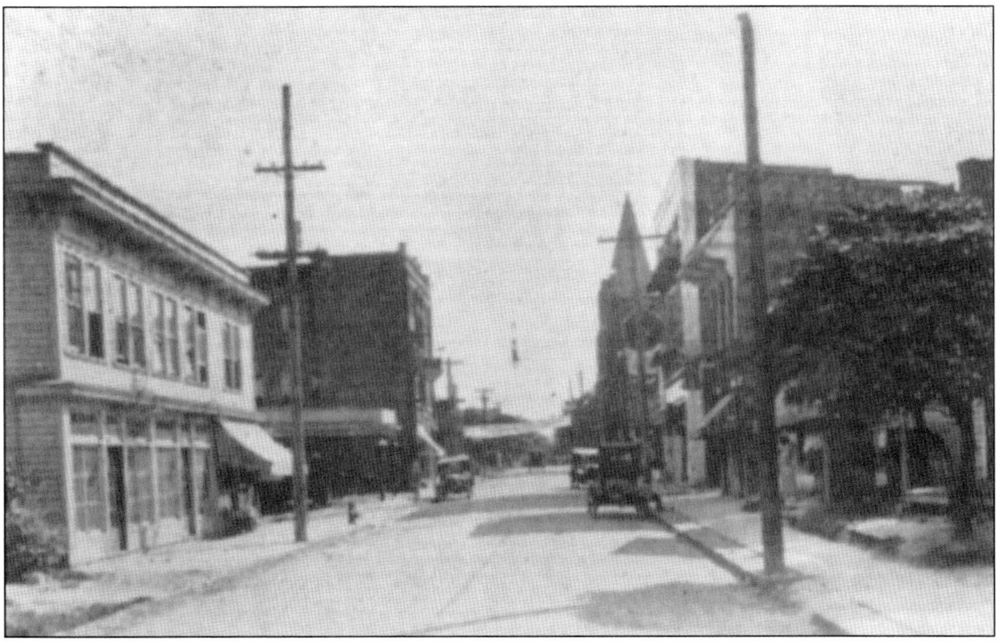

This early-1900s photograph shows a view of the Fayetteville Street business section. Several commercial building are shown along Fayetteville Street including the spire of St. Joseph's A.M.E Church on the right. (Courtesy of Durham County Public Library.)

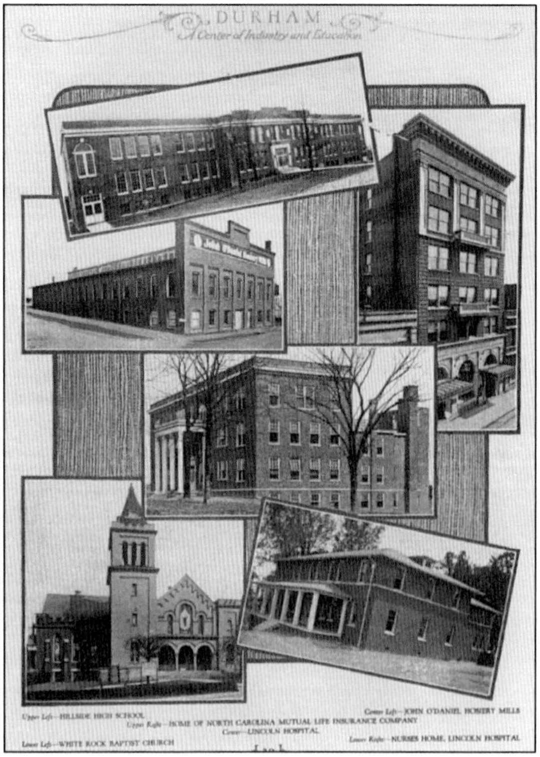

This is a 1928 postcard of six black institutions, which was published by the Durham Real Estate Board. (Courtesy of Durham County Public Library.)

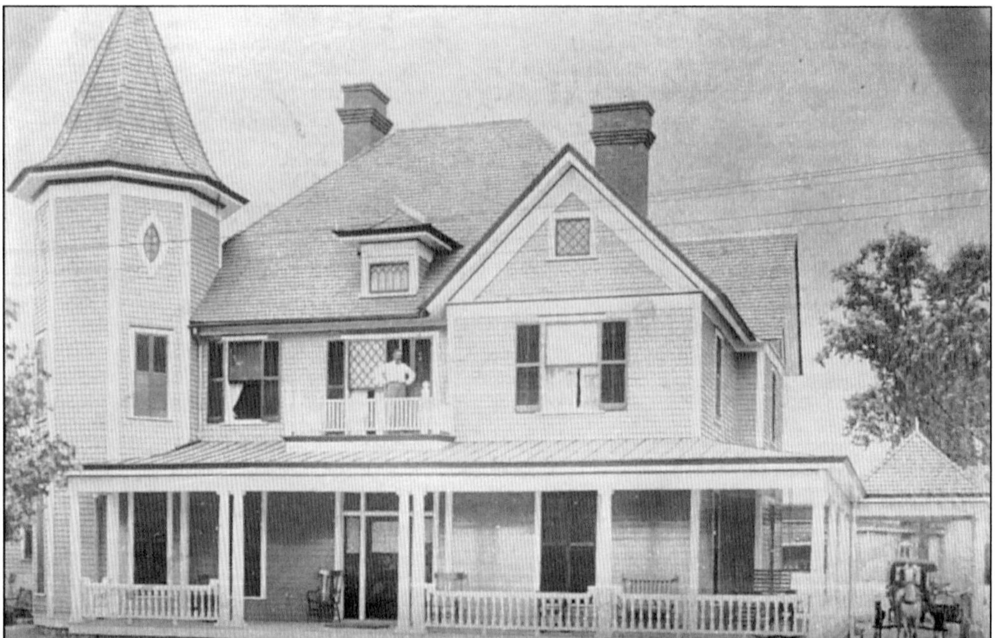

This 1910 photograph captures John Merrick (1859–1919), founder of North Carolina Mutual Life Insurance Company, on the balcony of his spacious Victorian home at 506 Fayetteville Street. There is a street named in his honor in the old Hayti community. (Courtesy of the Durham County Public Library.)

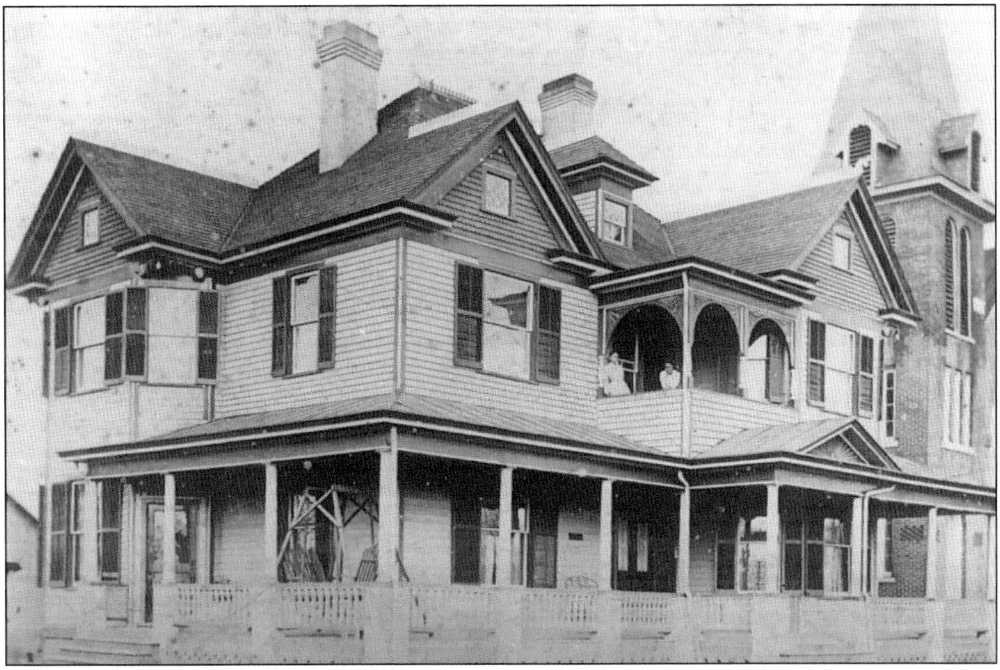

This 1900s photograph captures the home of Dr. Aaron M Moore, Durham's first black doctor and founder of North Carolina Mutual Life Insurance Company. The home was located at 606 Fayetteville Street. (Courtesy Ruth S. Boyd / Andre D. Vann.)

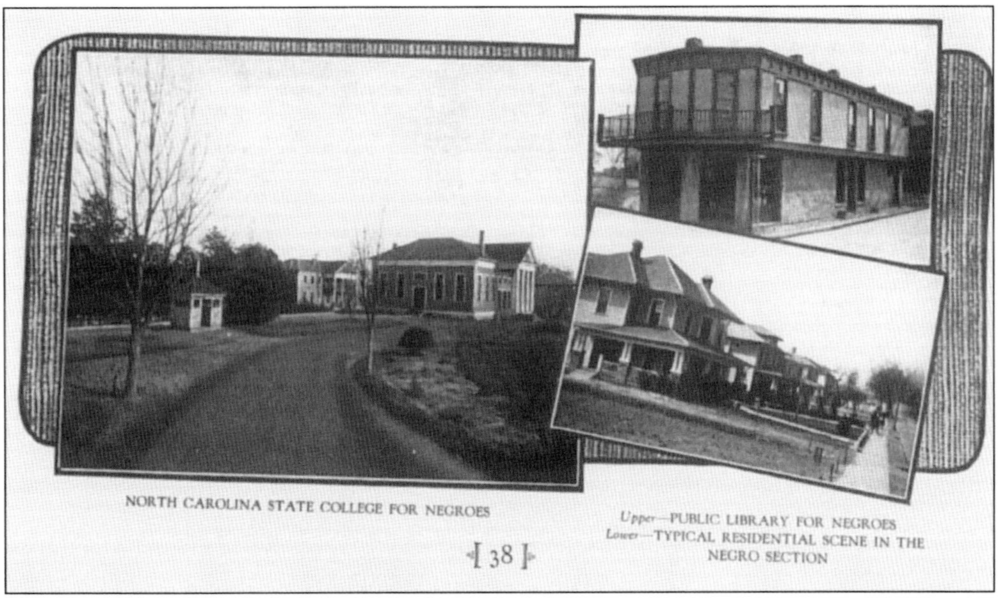

This 1928 photograph shows the buildings and grounds of the North Carolina State College for Negroes (now North Carolina Central University), Durham Colored Library (now Stanford L. Warren Library), and a section of a residential street in Hayti. (Courtesy of Durham Country Public Library.)

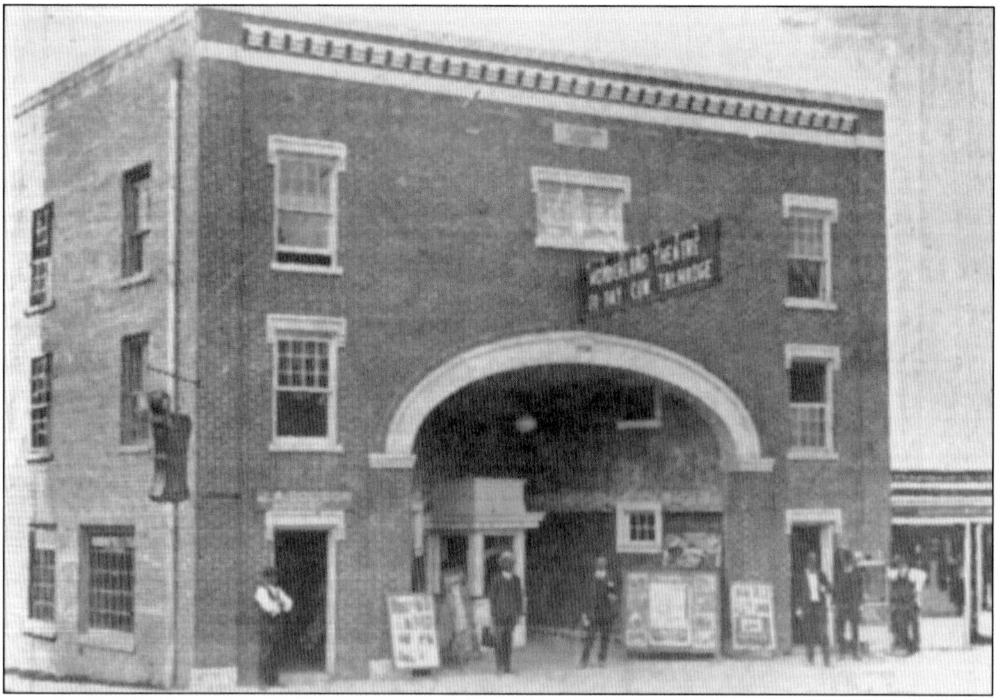

This early-1920s photograph captures Frederick K. Watkins, "The Movie King," in front of his second picture theater in Hayti, which was erected in 1920. Watkins started his career by shooting his own movies and then toting them to public schools, where he would charge each student 5¢ per screening. He managed a chain of 16 theaters in North Carolina, South Carolina, and Virginia, before retiring in 1929 to enter the real state business. In 1935, Mr. Watkins was elected a justice of the peace and became the first black in the South to be elected on the Democratic ticket. He developed property on Pettigrew Street and built several stores and a theater. (Courtesy of Durham County Public Library.)

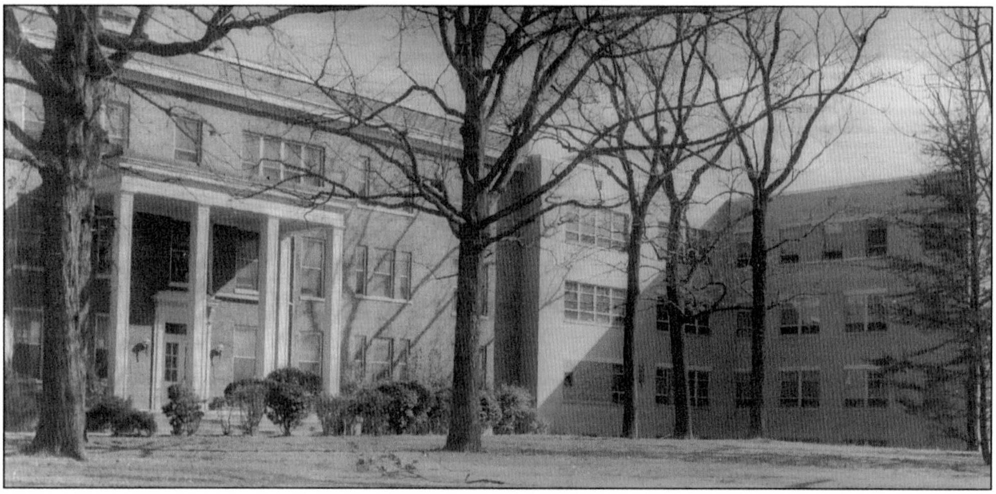

This is a 1940s view of the front of Durham's Lincoln Hospital, which served the black population in Hayti and other surrounding areas. Lincoln was begun in 1901, largely through the efforts of Washington Duke and his sons, and was founded by John Merrick, Dr. Aaron Moore, and Dr. Stanford L. Warren. (Courtesy of Andre D. Vann.)

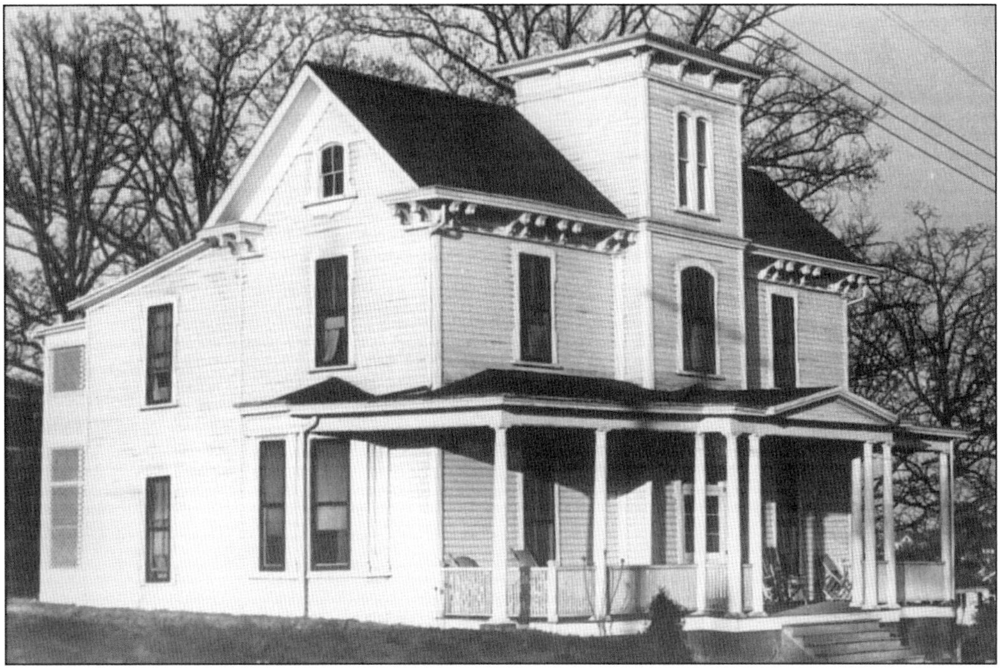

This is a 1920s photograph of the Lincoln Hospital Stokes Nurses Home Annex. (Courtesy of Durham County Public Library.)

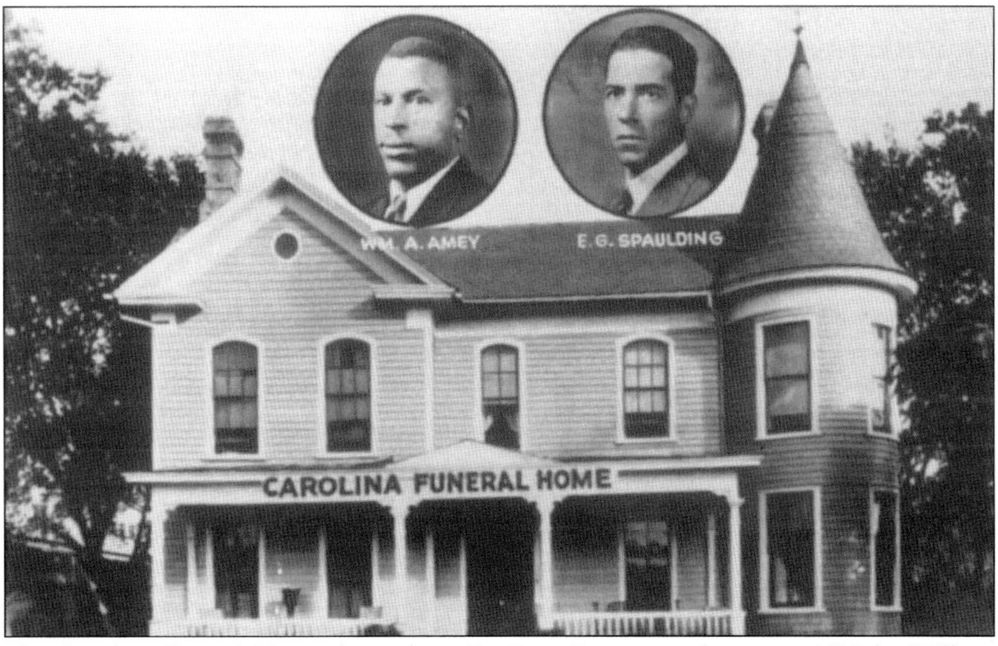

The Carolina Funeral Home, located at 401 Pine Street, was begun in 1933 by William Anderson Amey (1900–1981) and Emanuel G. Spaulding (1886–1969) with the assistance of Amey's wife, Essie Amey, who operated the Amey's Florist at the same address. William A. Amey assisted his father at the funeral home. After E.G. Spaulding moved to Brooklyn, New York, the business became know as Amey's Funeral Home. (Courtesy of Durham County Public Library.)

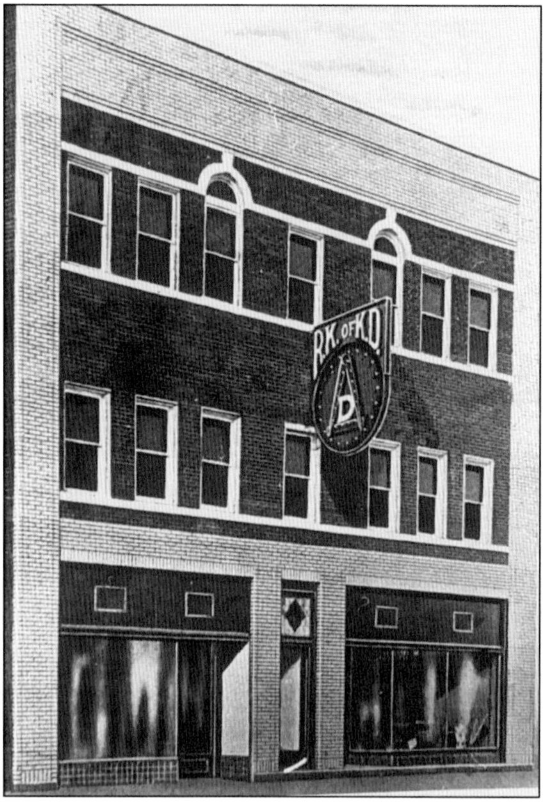

This is a 1920 photograph of the Royal Knights of King David Hall. The Royal Knights of King David was a fraternal insurance society that was purchased in 1883 by John Merrick, John Wright, W.A. Day, J.D. Morgan, and, T.J. Jones. The three-story press brick home office contained offices for the Supreme Grand Lodge, store rooms, and a banking house. (Courtesy of Durham County Public Library.)

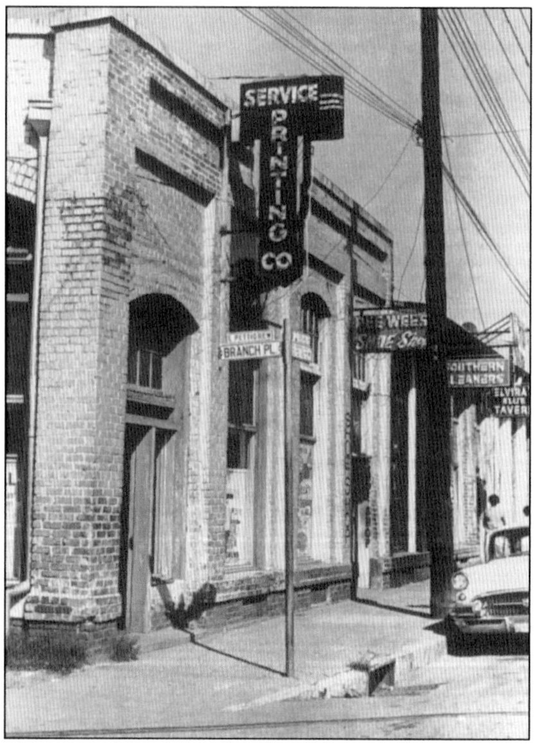

The Service Printing Company was originally organized in 1934 by the T.D. Parham family and in 1941 was purchased by Day F. Reed, Walter G. Swann, George D. White Jr., and Nathaniel B. White. The building, which was located at 504 E. Pettigrew Street, served the black population in Hayti as the main printer, and the company employed nine people. (Courtesy of the Durham County Public Library.)

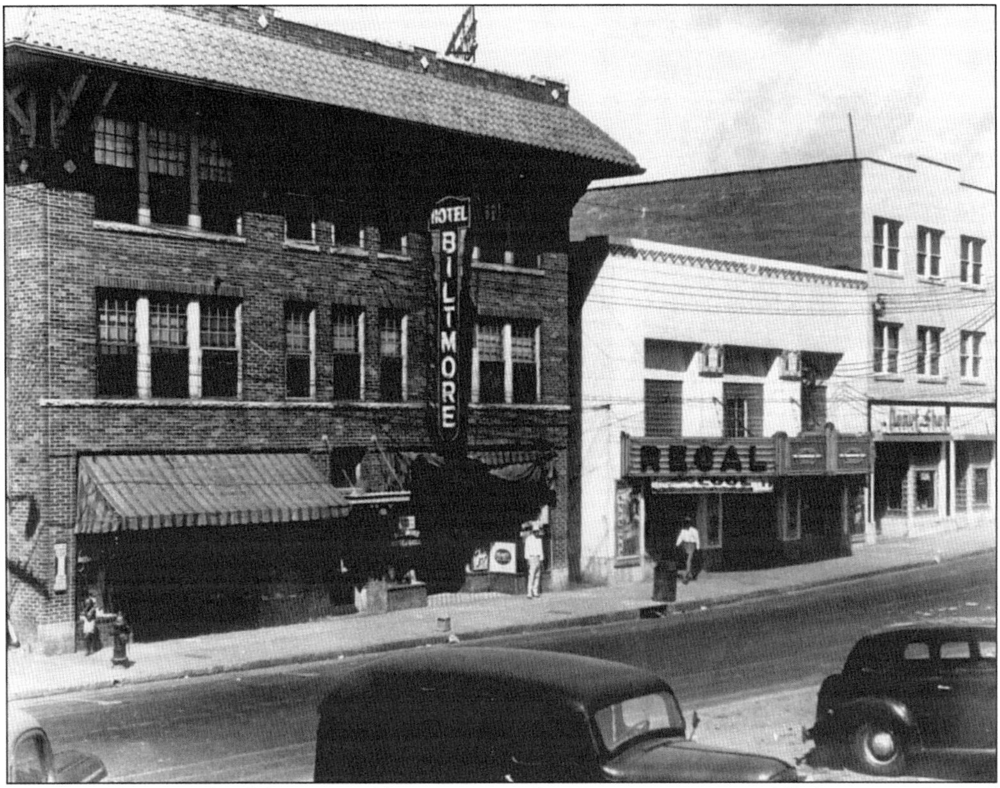

This is a photograph of three noted businesses in the Hayti community. All three were located on Pettigrew Street and are, from left to right, as follows: the Biltmore Hotel, the Regal Theatre, and the Donut Shop. (Courtesy of Durham County Public Library.)

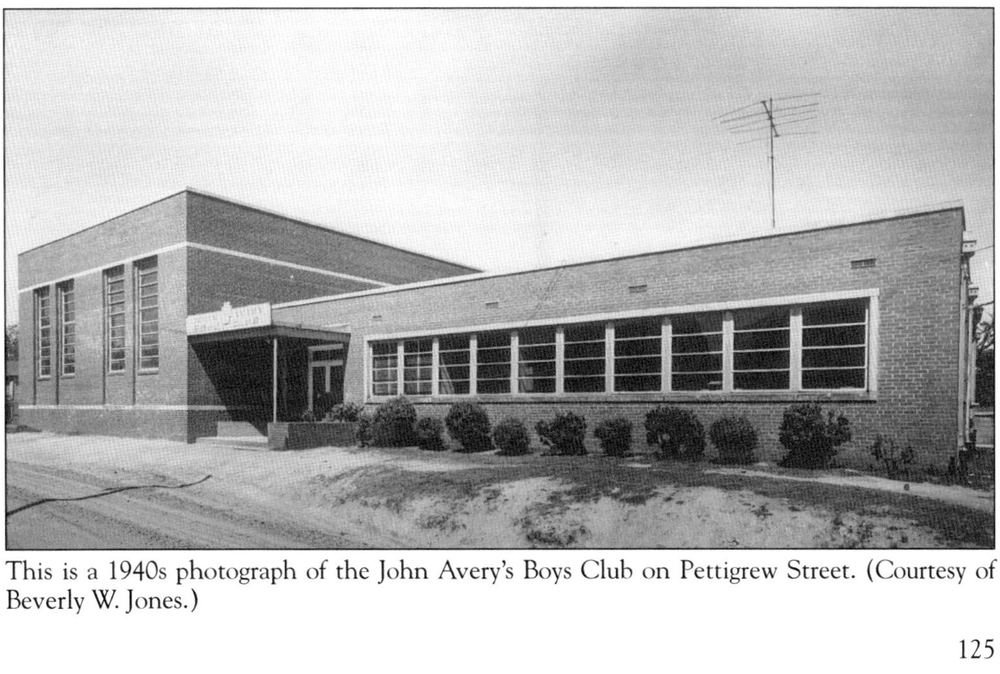

This is a 1940s photograph of the John Avery's Boys Club on Pettigrew Street. (Courtesy of Beverly W. Jones.)

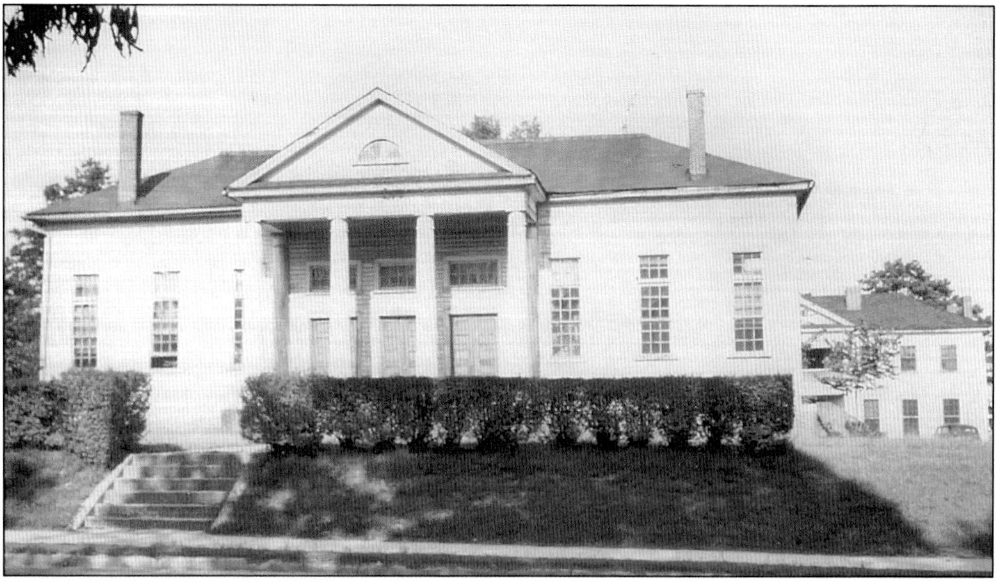

This is a 1948 photograph of Avery Auditorium on the campus of North Carolina College. Avery Auditorium, on the site of the present James S. Lee Biology Building, was succeeded by B.N. Duke Auditorium. (Courtesy of Andre D. Vann.)

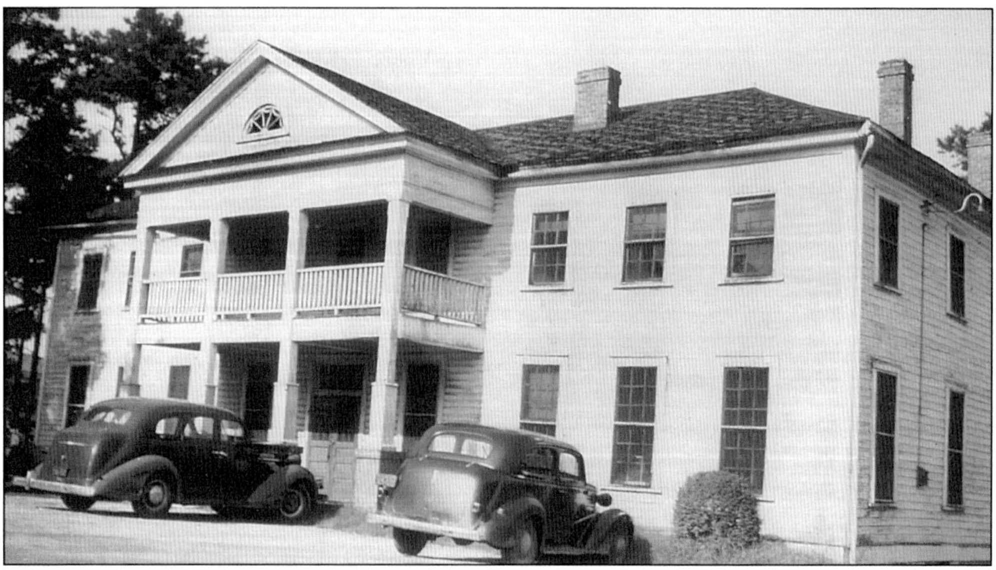

This photograph is a 1948 view of the Old Florence Burroughs Chidley Hall Dormitory, on the site of the present-day James M. Hubbard and Ezra Totten Chemistry Building. (Courtesy of Andre D. Vann.)

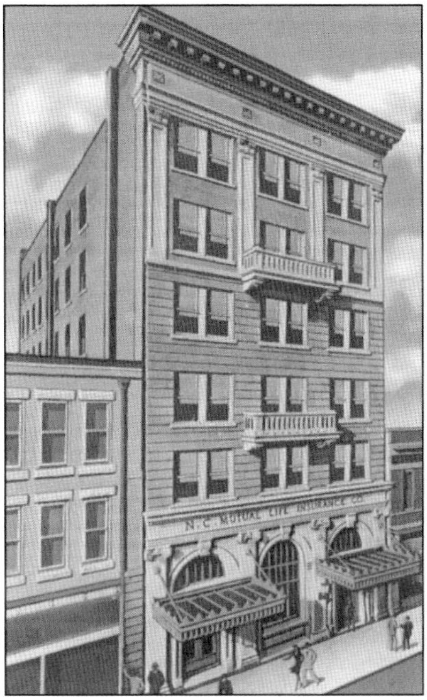

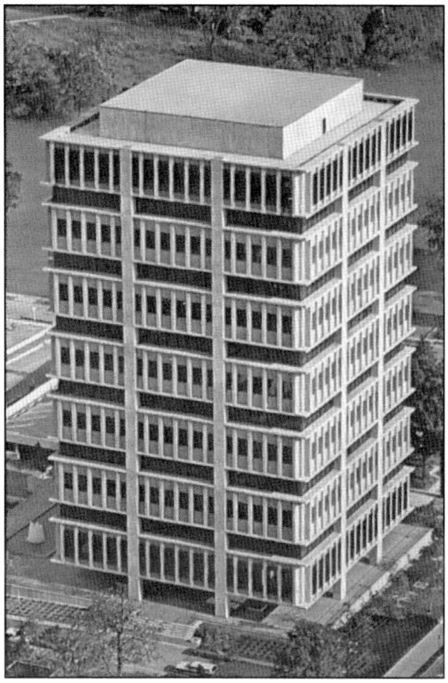

Left: Located at 116 East Parrish Street, the North Carolina Mutual Life Insurance Company's Home Office Building was erected and completed in October 1921. The Mechanics and Farmers Bank presently operates the building, which is listed as a National Historic Landmark. This institution and building were largely responsible for Parrish Street being called the "Black Wall Street of America." The building later was renamed the Mechanics and Farmers Bank Building. (Courtesy of North Carolina Mutual Life Insurance Company.)
Right: North Carolina Mutual Life Insurance Company, located at Mutual Plaza (Duke and West Chapel Hill Streets), stands on land that once belonged to Benjamin N. Duke's estate, Four Acres. The 10-story building was listed by *Fortune Magazine* as one of the ten outstanding buildings appearing in the United States in 1966. Vice-President Hubert H. Humphrey delivered the dedication address at the Home Office Building on April 2, 1966. (Courtesy of North Carolina Mutual Life Insurance Company.)

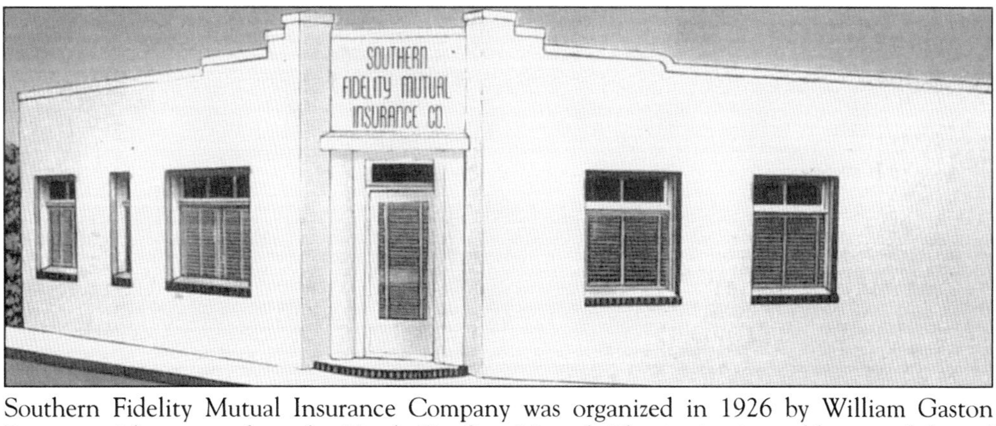

Southern Fidelity Mutual Insurance Company was organized in 1926 by William Gaston Pearson, with support from the North Carolina Mutual. The institution sold automobile and health insurance, refinanced mortgages, granted long-term loans, and dealt in stocks and bonds. On March 1, 1963, Southern Fidelity Mutual Insurance Company merged with the Banker's Fire and Casualty Insurance Company of Durham. (Courtesy of Andre D. Vann.)

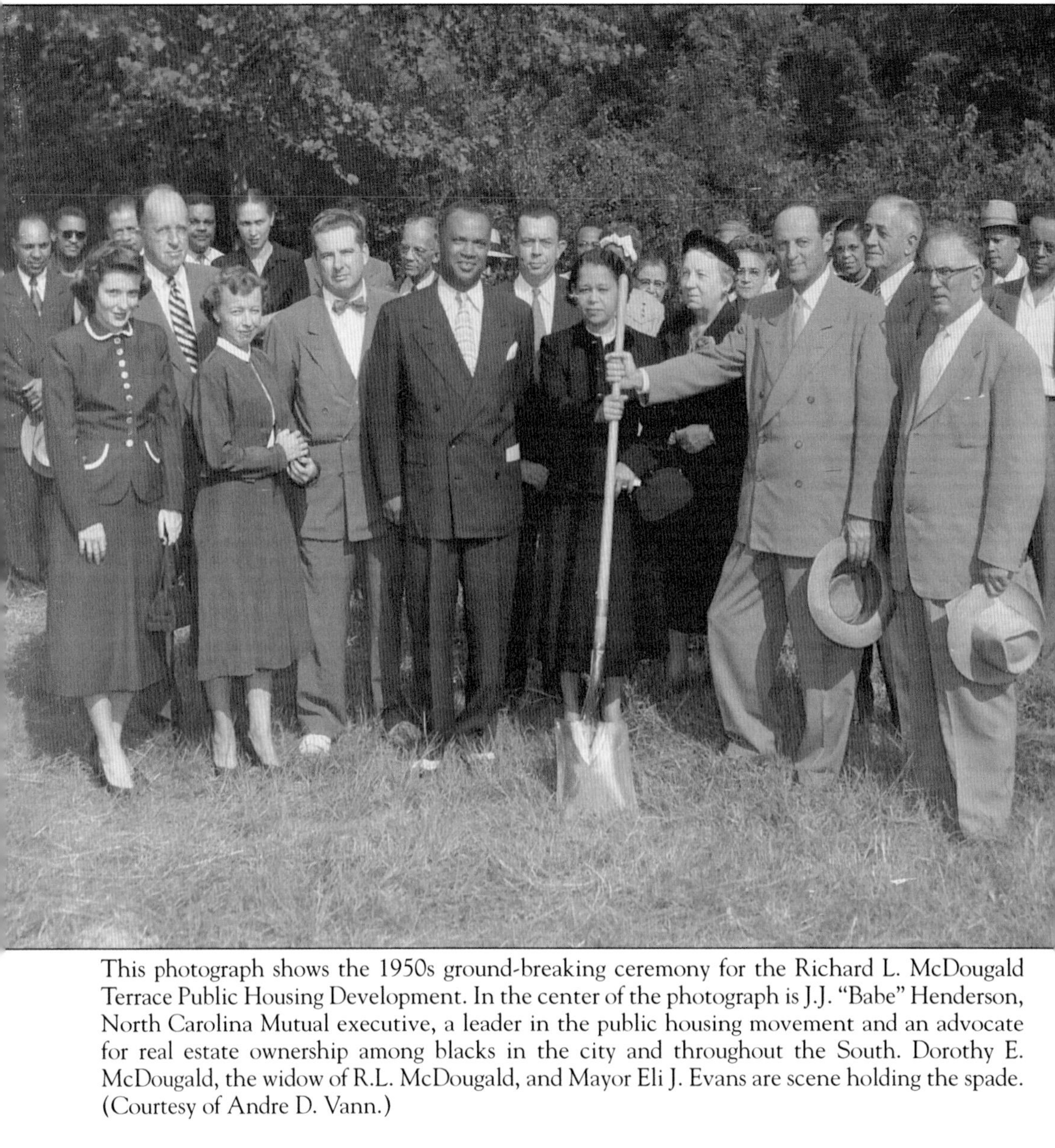

This photograph shows the 1950s ground-breaking ceremony for the Richard L. McDougald Terrace Public Housing Development. In the center of the photograph is J.J. "Babe" Henderson, North Carolina Mutual executive, a leader in the public housing movement and an advocate for real estate ownership among blacks in the city and throughout the South. Dorothy E. McDougald, the widow of R.L. McDougald, and Mayor Eli J. Evans are scene holding the spade. (Courtesy of Andre D. Vann.)